THE THEOLOGY OF
MARRIAGE
&CELIBACY

THE THEOLOGY OF
MARRIAGE
&CELIBACY

Catechesis on Marriage and Celibacy in the Light of the Resurrection of the Body

JOHN PAUL II

**Preface by
Most Reverend
Donald W. Wuerl, D.D.**

ST. PAUL EDITIONS

Reprinted with permission of *L'Osservatore Romano*, English Edition.

ISBN 0-8198-7333-0c
0-8198-7334-9p

Printed in the U.S.A., by the Daughters of St. Paul
50 St. Paul's Ave., Boston, MA 02130

The Daughters of St. Paul are an international congregation of women religious serving the Church with the communications media.

CONTENTS

Preface

Nothing, perhaps, more clearly points out the prophetic nature of the Gospel message and its counter cultural force than matters of human sexuality. The radical, primordial nature of human sexuality brings with it atavistic responses. The urges and drives that sexuality evoke are capable of sanctified human union as well as violent dehumanizing degradation. What separates the two responses in either pole and the vast range of area in between is our understanding of what is the nature of the human body. For the believer this necessarily takes into account as normative, God's revelation.

What our Holy Father has done in this series of talks is to address the subject of human sexuality from a deep, theological perspective that brings us face to face with God's ultimate plan, revelation's articulation of that plan, and the Church's perennial proclamation of it. Given the strong secular view of sex for "fun and profit" it should not be surprising that the only major media coverage of these talks was confined to a narrow, distorted presentation that at times stooped to ridicule. In part this was due to a lack of understanding of the wider context of Catholic theology as expressed in these talks, or to a direct rejection of the validity of Catholic teaching. Hence, the importance of this volume. It provides the reader with the entire series of talks and thus the whole scope of the theological context of the Holy Father's presentation of the Church's position which is reductively the teaching of Christ.

This book begins with a perspective—shared also by the documents of the Second Vatican

Council—that the Church is the home of all those things that tell us about the meaning of this life as it prepares for the life to come in Christ. When Christ returned to His Father, He did not leave us orphans in a foreign land but adopted children in a Church that already had within it the seeds of His eternal kingdom. This Church, the visible presence of the coming kingdom of God, this Church on pilgrimage, is then, among other things, a sign. It is a holy sign, a sacrament, of the life that is ours for all eternity—the life of the resurrection. The Second Vatican Council tells us that the Church is a sacrament precisely because she makes the great mystery of God's love and activity in the world seen and felt. The visible Church is the kingdom of Christ now present in mystery (cf. *Lumen gentium,* 3).

But this kingdom of God, as the U.S. Bishops noted in their first collective pastoral letter *The Church in Our Day,* "does not hover formlessly over the cities or exist unseen among the nations of the world. The People of God, the Body of Christ, the Temple of the Spirit, His Church is organized, structured, visible" (part 2). This presence of Christ is incarnational, sacramental. It finds expression in the way we live and move and have our being.

Thus our lives lived in the mystery of Christ's incarnation, the Church's extension of it and our participation in it make visible to the eyes of the world what is otherwise invisible. For through our participation in the mystery of the Church we can see toward the fullness of God's kingdom in eternity. Our faith tells us this. The Gospels proclaim it. The ancient Church, the Fathers, the saints, the heroes of our religion bear witness to the fact: life is not of this world alone. We are meant for another land, a greater home. We are citizens of another and greater kingdom.

At the same time Christian life is not a life turned solely toward another world. We are part of this creation. Our roots are here. Our love, our dedication to Christ must somehow overflow to reach all people here and now—or at least begin now—to be completed perfectly in the Father. The Gospel, in describing God's eternal, divine, immense love, saw it as one that "loved the world...unto the death of His only Son." So, too, the believer, married or celibate, must somehow turn outward to the world to make it see in our own manifestation of Christ's love the Love that is God.

Here we touch one of our tasks regarding the Christian community and the world of the believer. Within the Church, which is itself a sign, the believer is a sign. St. Paul speaks at length about the sign value of both married love and celibate love. Both are expressions of a greater love, the love of Christ for His Church which is but another way of saying God's love for each of us. The sacrament of marriage is both a deep expression of mutual human love and a sign of divine love. Celibacy is not only a living dedication to love in Christ but a witness to its transcendence.

It is in the light of our long, slow stumbling march to another more perfect home that the Christian life makes sense. We are a pilgrim people...on the way to a perfect kingdom. But now we are both the signs of what the kingdom will be like, and the means by which it is realized. As a witness to the kingdom of God, the believer is a visible marker on a rough road to an invisible kingdom. By our visible, dedicated appreciation of our own human destiny and the place our sexuality has in this reality we can show to all that God has already begun His final work on earth and that this divine labor will be glorified in the life to come.

Human sexuality is one area most visible and most contested in the present struggle to make present the Word of God. It is no secret that the Gospel value of enduring human love, self-giving love and other-serving love is out of step with the brand of love that sells on TV, whether during the program or the commercial break. Part of the conflict is that there are definitely two or more views about the purpose of sex. To some extent the physical dimension of sex has so dominated the scene that even minimal interpersonal and spiritual aspects of this basic human reality are so clouded over as to be lost.

What the present volume offers is a coherent, deeply spiritual appreciation of the Gospel vision of love, human and divine, physical and spiritual. It is so welcome because it provides sound Catholic principles in the context of a penetrating theological analysis. It can only help in the discussion today that occupies so much of the time and energy of believer and nonbeliever alike. In a time when it is increasingly difficult to have access to complete and faithful presentations of the teachings of the Holy Father, a collection of talks such as this is most well received. Certainly we owe a debt to the Daughters of St. Paul for making available this work so rich in profound insight.

✠Most Reverend Donald W. Wuerl
Auxiliary Bishop of Seattle
Easter Sunday, 1986

Marriage and Celibacy in the Light of the Resurrection of the Body

General audience of November 11, 1981.

1. After a rather long pause, today we will resume the meditations which have been going on for some time now and which we have called reflections on the theology of the body.

In continuing, it is opportune at this time to go back to the words of the Gospel in which Christ refers to the resurrection: words which are of fundamental importance for understanding marriage in the Christian sense and also the "renunciation" of conjugal life "for the kingdom of heaven."

The complex casuistry of the Old Testament in the field of marriage not only drove the Pharisees to go to Christ to pose to Him the problem of the indissolubility of marriage (cf. Mt. 19:3-9; Mk. 10:2-12), but also, another time, drove the Sadducees to question Him about the law of the so-called levirate.[1] This conversation is harmoniously reported by the synoptic Gospels (cf. Mt. 22:24-30; Mk. 12:18-27; Lk. 20:27-40). Although all three accounts are almost identical, yet we note some differences, slight, but at the same time significant. Since the conversation is reported in three versions, those of Matthew, Mark and Luke, a deeper analysis is necessary, since it contains elements which have an essential significance for the theology of the body.

Alongside the other two important conversations—namely, the one in which Christ refers to the "beginning" (cf. Mt. 19:3-9; Mk. 10:2-12), and the other in which an appeal is made to man's inner self (to the "heart"), indicating desire and the lust of the flesh as a source of sin (cf. Mt. 5:27-32)—the conversation which we now propose to analyze constitutes, I would say, the third element of the triptych of the enunciations of Christ Himself: a triptych of words that are essential and constitutive for the theology of the body. In this conversation Jesus refers to the resurrection, thus revealing a completely new dimension of the mystery of man.

CHRIST REFUTES THE BELIEF OF THE SADDUCEES

2. The revelation of this dimension of the body, stupendous in its content—and yet con-

nected with the Gospel reread as a whole and in depth—emerges in the conversation with the Sadducees, "who say that there is no resurrection" (Mt. 22:23).[2] They have come to Christ to set before Him an argument which—in their judgment—confirms the soundness of their position. This argument was to contradict "the hypothesis of the resurrection." The Sadducees' argument is the following: "Teacher, Moses wrote for us that if a man's brother dies and leaves a wife, but leaves no child, the man must take the wife, and raise up children for his brother" (Mk. 12:19). The Sadducees are referring here to the so-called law of the levirate (cf. Dt. 25:5-10), and drawing upon the prescription of this ancient law, they present the following "case": "There were seven brothers; the first took a wife, and when he died left no children; and the second took her, and died, leaving no children; and the third likewise; and the seven left no children. Last of all the woman also died. In the resurrection whose wife will she be? For the seven had her as wife" (Mk. 12:20-23).[3]

THE WISDOM AND POWER OF GOD HIMSELF

3. Christ's answer is one of the answer-keys of the Gospel, in which there is revealed—

precisely starting from purely human argu-
ments and in contrast with them—another
dimension of the question, that is, the one that
corresponds to the wisdom and power of God
Himself. Similarly, for example, the case had
arisen of the tax coin with Caesar's image and
of the correct relationship between what is
divine and what is human (Caesar's) in the
sphere of authority (cf. Mt. 22:15-22). This
time Jesus replies as follows: "Is not this why
you are wrong, that you know neither the
scriptures nor the power of God? For when
they rise from the dead, they neither marry nor
are given in marriage, but are like angels
in heaven" (Mk. 12:24-25). This is the fundamental reply to the "case," that is, to the
problem it contains. Christ, knowing the thoughts
of the Sadducees, and realizing their real
intentions, subsequently takes up again the
problem of the possibility of resurrection,
denied by the Sadducees themselves: "And as
for the dead being raised, have you not read
in the book of Moses, in the passage about the
bush, how God said to him, 'I am the God of
Abraham, and the God of Isaac, and the God
of Jacob'? He is not a God of the dead, but
of the living" (Mk. 12:26-27). As we can
see, Christ quotes the same Moses to whom
the Sadducees had referred, and ends with
the affirmation: "You are quite wrong"
(Mk. 12:27).

ANOTHER AFFIRMATION

4. Christ repeats this conclusive affirmation even a second time. In fact, He spoke it the first time at the beginning of His explanation. Then He said: "You are wrong, because you know neither the scriptures nor the power of God": so we read in Matthew (22:29). And in Mark: "Is not this why you are wrong, that you know neither the scriptures nor the power of God?" (12:24) In Luke's version (20:27-36), on the contrary, Christ's same answer is without polemical tones, without that "you are quite wrong." On the other hand, He proclaims the same thing since in His answer He introduces some elements which are not found either in Matthew or in Mark. Here is the text: "Jesus said to them, 'The sons of this age marry and are given in marriage; but those who are accounted worthy to attain to that age and to the resurrection from the dead neither marry nor are given in marriage, for they cannot die any more, because they are equal to angels and are sons of God, being sons of the resurrection'" (Lk. 20:34-36). With regard to the very possibility of resurrection, Luke—like the other two synoptics—refers to Moses, that is, to the passage in the book of Exodus 3:2-6, in which it is narrated, in fact, that the great legislator of the old covenant had heard from the bush, which "was burning, yet it was not consumed,"

the following words: "I am the God of your father, the God of Abraham, the God of Isaac, and the God of Jacob" (Ex. 3:6). In the same place, when Moses had asked God's name, he had heard the answer: "I am who am" (Ex. 3:14).

In this way, therefore, speaking of the future resurrection of the body, Christ refers to the very power of the living God.

NOTES

1. This law, contained in Deuteronomy 25:7-10, concerns brothers who lived under the same roof. If one of them died without leaving children, the dead man's brother had to marry his brother's widow. The child born of this marriage was recognized as the son of the deceased, so that his stock would not be extinguished and the inheritance would be kept in the family (cf. 3:9—4:12).

2. In the time of Christ, the Sadducees formed, within Judaism, a sect bound to the circle of the priestly aristocracy. In opposition to the oral tradition and theology elaborated by the Pharisees, they proposed the literal interpretation of the Pentateuch, which they considered the main source of the jahwist religion. Since there was no mention of life after death in the most ancient books of the Bible, the Sadducees rejected the eschatology proclaimed by the Pharisees, affirming that "souls die together with the body" (cf. Joseph, *Antiquitates Judaicae*, XVII 1.4. 16).

The conceptions of the Sadducees are not directly known to us, however, since all their writings were lost after the destruction of Jerusalem in the year 70, when the sect itself disappeared. We get what little information there is about the Sadducees from the writings of their ideological opponents.

3. The Sadducees, turning to Jesus for a purely theoretical "case," at the same time attack the primitive conception of the Pharisees on life after the resurrection of the body; they insinuate, in fact, that faith in the resurrection of the body leads to admitting polyandry, which is contrary to God's law.

The Living God Continually Renews the Very Reality of Life

General audience of November 18, 1981.

1. "You are wrong, because you know neither the Scriptures nor the power of God" (Mt. 22:29), Christ said to the Sadducees, who—rejecting faith in the future resurrection of the body—had proposed to Him the following case: "Now there were seven brothers among us; the first married, and died, and having no children left his wife to his brother" (according to the Mosaic law of the "levirate"). "So too the second and third, down to the seventh. After them all, the woman died. In the resurrection, therefore, to which of the seven will she be wife?" (Mt. 22:25-28)

Christ answers the Sadducees by stating, at the beginning and at the end of His reply, that they are greatly mistaken, not knowing either the Scriptures or the power of God (cf. Mk. 12:24; Mt. 22:29). Since the conversation with the Sadducees is reported by all three synoptic Gospels, let us briefly compare the texts in question.

2. Matthew's version (22:24-30), although it does not refer to the burning bush, agrees almost completely with that of Mark (12:18-25). Both versions contain two essential elements: 1) the enunciation about the future resurrection of the body; 2) the enunciation about the state of the body of risen man.[1] These two elements are also found in Luke (20:27-36).[2] The first element, concerning the future resurrection of the body, combined, especially in Matthew and Mark, with the words addressed to the Sadducees, according to which they "know neither the Scriptures nor the power of God." This statement deserves particular attention, because precisely in it Christ defines the very foundations of faith in the resurrection, to which He had referred in answering the question posed by the Sadducees with the concrete example of the Mosaic law of levirate.

ADMITTING THE REALITY OF LIFE AFTER DEATH

3. Unquestionably, the Sadducees treat the question of resurrection as a type of theory or hypothesis which can be disproved.[3] Jesus first shows them an error of method: they do not know the Scriptures; and then an error of substance: they do not accept what is re-

vealed by the Scriptures—they do not know the power of God, they do not believe in Him who revealed Himself to Moses in the burning bush. It is a very significant and very precise answer. Here Christ encounters men who consider themselves experts and competent interpreters of the Scriptures. To these men—that is, to the Sadducees—Jesus replies that mere literal knowledge of Scripture is not sufficient. The Scriptures, in fact, are above all a means to know the power of the living God who reveals Himself in them, just as He revealed Himself to Moses in the bush. In this revelation He called Himself "the God of Abraham, the God of Isaac and the God of Jacob"[4]—of those, therefore, who had been Moses' ancestors in the faith that springs from the revelation of the living God. They had all been dead for a long time. Christ, however, completes the reference to them with the statement that God "is not God of the dead, but of the living." This statement, in which Christ interprets the words addressed to Moses from the burning bush, can be understood only if one admits the reality of a life which death does not end. Moses' fathers in faith, Abraham, Isaac and Jacob, are living persons for God (cf. Lk. 20:38: "for all live for him"), although according to human criteria, they must be numbered among the dead. To reread the Scriptures correctly, and in particular the aforementioned words of God, means to know and accept with faith the power of the Giver of life, who is not bound by the law of death which rules man's earthly history.

CHRIST'S ANSWER

4. It seems that Christ's answer given to the Sadducees about the possibility of resurrection,[5] according to the version of all three synoptics, is to be interpreted in this way. The moment will come in which Christ will give the answer, on this matter, with His own resurrection. For now, however, He refers to the testimony of the Old Testament, showing how to discover there the truth about immortality and resurrection. It is necessary to do so not by dwelling only on the sound of the words, but by going back also to the power of God which is revealed by those words. The reference to Abraham, Isaac and Jacob in that theophany granted to Moses, of which we read in the book of Exodus (3:2-6), constitutes a testimony that the living God gives to those who live "for him": to those who, thanks to His power, have life, even if, according to the dimensions of history, it would be necessary to include them among those who have been dead for a long time.

5. The full significance of this testimony, to which Jesus refers in His conversation with

the Sadducees, could be grasped (still only in the light of the Old Testament) in the following way: He who is—He who lives and is Life—is the inexhaustible source of existence and of life, as was revealed at the "beginning," in Genesis (cf. Gn. 1:3). Although, due to sin, physical death has become man's lot (cf. Gn. 3:19),[6] and although he has been forbidden (cf. Gn. 3:22) access to the Tree of Life (the great symbol of the book of Genesis), yet the living God, making His covenant with man (Abraham—the patriarchs, Moses, Israel), continually renews, in this covenant, the very reality of life, reveals its perspective again and in a certain sense opens access again to the Tree of Life. Along with the covenant, this life, whose source is God Himself, is communicated to those very men who, as a result of the breaking of the first covenant, had lost access to the Tree of Life, and, in the dimensions of their earthly history, had been subject to death.

POWER AND TESTIMONY OF THE LIVING GOD

6. Christ is God's ultimate word on this subject; in fact the covenant, which with Him and for Him is established between God and mankind, opens an infinite perspective of life: and access to the Tree of Life—according to the original plan of the God of the cove-

nant—is revealed to every man in its definitive fullness. This will be the meaning of the death and resurrection of Christ; this will be the testimony of the Paschal Mystery. However, the conversation with the Sadducees takes place in the pre-paschal phase of Christ's messianic mission. The course of the conversation according to Matthew (22:24-30), Mark (12:18-27), and Luke (20:27-36) manifests that Christ—who had spoken several times, particularly in talks with His disciples, of the future resurrection of the Son of Man (cf., e.g., Mt. 17:9, 23; 20:19 and paral.)—does not refer to this matter in the conversation with the Sadducees. The reasons are obvious and clear. The discussion is with the Sadducees, "who say that there is no resurrection" (as the evangelist stresses), that is, they question its very possibility, and at the same time they consider themselves experts on the Old Testament Scriptures, and qualified interpreters of them. And that is why Jesus refers to the Old Testament and shows, on its basis, that they "do not know the power of God."[7]

7. Regarding the possibility of resurrection, Christ refers precisely to that power which goes hand in hand with the testimony of the living God, who is the God of Abraham, of Isaac, of Jacob—and the God of Moses. God, whom the Sadducees "deprive" of this power,

is no longer the true God of their fathers, but the God of their hypotheses and interpretations. Christ, on the contrary, has come to bear witness to the God of Life in the whole truth of His power which is unfolded upon man's life.

NOTES

1. Although the expression "the resurrection of the body" is not known in the New Testament (it will appear for the first time in St. Clement: 2 Clem. 9:1 and in Justin: Dial 80:5), which uses the expression "resurrection of the dead," intending thereby man in his integrity; it is possible, however, to find in many New Testament texts faith in the immortality of the soul and its existence also outside the body (cf., for example, Lk. 23:43; Phil. 1:23-24; 2 Cor. 5:6-8).

2. Luke's text contains some new elements which are an object of discussion among exegetes.

3. As is known, in the Judaism of that period there was no clearly formulated doctrine concerning the resurrection; there existed only the various theories launched by the individual schools.

The Pharisees, who cultivated theological speculation, greatly developed the doctrine on the resurrection, seeing allusions to it in all the Old Testament books. They understood the future resurrection, however, in an earthly and primitive way, announcing, for example, an enormous increase of crops and of fertility in life after the resurrection.

The Sadducees, on the other hand, polemicized with such a conception, starting from the premise that the Pentateuch does not speak of eschatology. It must also be kept in mind that in the first century the canon of the Old Testament books had not yet been established.

The case presented by the Sadducees directly attacks the Pharisaic concept of the resurrection. In fact, the Sadducees were of the opinion that Christ was one of their followers.

Christ's answer equally corrects the conceptions of the Pharisees and those of the Sadducees.

4. This expression does not mean: "God who was honored by Abraham, Isaac and Jacob," but: "God who took care of the Patriarchs and liberated them."

This formula returns in the book of Exodus: 3:6; 3:15, 16; 4:5, always in the context of the promised liberation of Israel; the name of the God of Abraham, Isaac and Jacob is a token and guarantee of this liberation.

"The God of X is synonymous with help, support and shelter for Israel." A similar sense is found in Genesis 49:24: "God of Jacob—the Shepherd and Rock of Israel, the God of your Fathers who will help you" (cf. Gn. 49:24-25; cf. also: Gn. 24:27; 26:24; 28:13; 32:10; 46:3).

Cf. F. Dreyfus, O.P., *L'argument scripturaire de Jésus en faveur de la résurrection des morts* (Mk. 12:26-27), Revue Biblique 66 (1959) 218.

The formula: "God of Abraham, Isaac and Jacob" in which all three names of the Patriarchs are mentioned, indicated in Judaic exegesis in Jesus' time God's relationship with the People of the Covenant as a community.

Cf. E. Ellis, "Jesus, the Sadducees and Qumran," New Testament Studies 10 (1963-64) 275.

5. In our modern way of understanding this Gospel text, the reasoning of Jesus concerns only immortality; if in fact the Patriarchs still now live after their death, before the eschatological resurrection of the body, then the statement of Jesus concerns the immortality of the soul and does not speak of the resurrection of the body.

But the reasoning of Jesus was addressed to the Sadducees who did not know the dualism of body and soul, accepting only the biblical psycho-physical unity of man who is "the body and the breath of life." Therefore, according to them the soul dies with the body. The affirmation of Jesus, according to which the Patriarchs are alive, could mean for the Sadducees only resurrection with the body.

6. We will not dwell here on the concept of death in the purely Old Testament sense, but take into consideration theological anthropology as a whole.

7. This is the determinant argument that proves the authenticity of the discussion with the Sadducees.

If the passage were "a post-paschal addition of the Christian community" (as R. Bultmann thought, for example), faith in the resurrection of the body would be supported by the fact of the resurrection of Christ, which imposed itself as an irresistible force, as St. Paul, for example, has us understand (cf. 1 Cor. 15:12).

Cf. J. Jeremias, *Neutestamentliche Theologie,* I Teil, Gutersloh 1971 (Mohn); cf. besides I. H. Marshall, "The Gospel of Luke," Exeter 1978, The Paternoster Press, p. 738.

The reference to the Pentateuch—while in the Old Testament there were texts which dealt directly with resurrection (as, for example, Is. 26:19 or Dt. 12:2)— bears witness that the conversation really took place with the Sadducees, who considered the Pentateuch the only decisive authority.

The structure of the controversy shows that this was a rabbinic discussion, according to the classical models in use in the academies of that time.

Cf. J. Le Moyne, OSB, *Les Sadducéens,* Paris 1972 (Gabalda), pp. 124f.: E. Lohmeyer, *Das Evangelium des Markus,* Göttingen 1959, p. 257; D. Daube, "New Testament and Rabbinic Judaism," London 1956, pp. 158-163; J. Radamakers, SJ, *La bonne nouvelle de Jésus silon St. Marc,* Bruxelles 1974, Institut d'Etudes Théologiques, p. 313.

The Resurrection
and Theological Anthropology

General audience of December 2, 1981.

1. "When they rise from the dead, they neither marry nor are given in marriage" (Mk. 12:25). Christ utters these words, which have a key meaning for the theology of the body, after having affirmed, in the conversation with the Sadducees, that the resurrection is in conformity with the power of the living God. All three synoptic Gospels report the same statement, except that Luke's version is different in some details from that of Matthew and Mark. Essential for them all is the fact that, in the future resurrection, human beings, after having reaquired their bodies in the fullness of the perfection characteristic of the image and likeness of God—after having reacquired them in their masculinity and femininity—"neither marry nor are given in marriage." Luke expresses the same idea in chapter 20:34-35, in the following words: "The

sons of this age marry and are given in marriage; but those who are accounted worthy to attain to that age and to the resurrection from the dead neither marry nor are given in marriage."

DEFINITIVE FULFILLMENT OF MANKIND

2. As can be seen from these words, marriage, that union in which, according to the book of Genesis, "a man cleaves to his wife, and they become one flesh" (2:25)—the union characteristic of man right from the "beginning"—belongs exclusively to "this age." Marriage and procreation do not constitute, on the other hand, the eschatological future of man. In the resurrection they lose, so to speak, their *raison d'être*. "That age," of which Luke speaks (20:35), means the definitive fulfillment of mankind, the quantitative closing of that circle of beings, who were created in the image and likeness of God, in order that, multiplying through the conjugal "unity in the body" of men and women, they might subdue the earth. "That age" is not the world of the earth, but the world of God, who, as we know from the first letter of Paul to the Corinthians, will fill it entirely, becoming "everything to everyone" (1 Cor. 15:28).

3. At the same time "that age," which according to revelation is "the kingdom of God," is also the definitive and eternal "homeland" of man (cf. Phil. 3:20); it is the "Father's house" (Jn. 14:2). "That age," as man's new homeland, emerges definitively from the present world, which is temporal—subjected to death, that is, to the destruction of the body (cf. Gen. 3:19: "to dust you shall return")—through the resurrection. The resurrection, according to Christ's words reported by the synoptic Gospels, means not only the recovery of corporeity and the reestablishment of human life in its integrity by means of the union of the body with the soul, but also a completely new state of human life itself.

We find the confirmation of this new state of the body in the resurrection of Christ (cf. Rom. 6:5-11). The words reported by the synoptic Gospels (Mt. 22:30; Mk. 12:25; Lk. 20:34-35) will ring out then (that is, after Christ's resurrection) to those who had heard them—I would say almost with a new probative force—and at the same time they will acquire the character of a convincing promise. For the present, however, we will dwell on these words in their "pre-paschal" phase, referring only to the situation in which they were spoken. There is no doubt that already in the answer given to the Sadducees, Christ reveals the new condition of the human body in the resurrection, and

He does so precisely by proposing a reference and a comparison with the condition in which man had participated since the "beginning."

RENEWED IN RESURRECTION

4. The words: "they neither marry nor are given in marriage" seem to affirm at the same time that human bodies, recovered and at the same time renewed in the resurrection, will keep their masculine or feminine peculiarity and that the sense of being a male or a female in the body will be constituted and understood in "that age" in a different way from what it had been "from the beginning" and then in the whole dimension of earthly existence. The words of Genesis: "A man leaves his father and mother and cleaves to his wife, and they become one flesh" (2:24), constituted right from the beginning that condition and relationship of masculinity and femininity, extended also to the body, which must rightly be defined "conjugal" and at the same time "procreative" and "generative." It is connected, in fact, with the blessing of fertility, pronounced by God (Elohim) when He created man "male and female" (Gn. 1:27). The words spoken by Christ about the resurrection enable us to deduce that the dimension of masculinity and femininity—that is, being male and female in the body—will again be constituted together with the resurrection of the body in "that age."

LIKE THE ANGELS

5. Is it possible to say something more detailed on this subject? Beyond all doubt, Christ's words reported by the synoptic Gospels (especially in the version of Luke 20:27-40) authorize us to do so. We read there, in fact, that "those who are accounted worthy to attain to that age and to the resurrection from the dead...cannot die any more, because they are equal to angels and are sons of God" (Matthew and Mark report only that "they are like angels in heaven"). This statement makes it possible above all to deduce a spiritualization of man according to a different dimension from that of earthly life (and even different from that of the "beginning" itself). It is obvious that it is not a question here of transforming man's nature into that of the angels, that is, a purely spiritual one. The context indicates clearly that man will keep in "that age" his own human psychosomatic nature. If it were otherwise, it would be meaningless to speak of the resurrection.

The resurrection means the restoring to the real life of human corporeity, which was subjected to death in its temporal phase. In the expression of Luke (20:36) just quoted (and in that of Mt. 22:30 and Mk. 12:25), it is certainly a question of human, that is, psychosomatic nature. The comparison with heavenly beings, used in the context, is no novelty in the Bible. Among others, already in a Psalm, exalting man as the work of the Creator, it is said: "you have made him little less than the angels" (Ps. 8:5). It must be supposed that in the resurrection this similarity will become greater: not through a disincarnation of man, but by means of another kind (we could also say another degree) of spiritualization of his somatic nature—that is, by means of another "system of forces" within man. The resurrection means a new submission of the body to the spirit.

PLATO AND ST. THOMAS

6. Before beginning to develop this subject, it should be recalled that the truth about the resurrection had a key meaning for the formation of the whole of theological anthropology, which could be considered simply as "anthropology of the resurrection." As a result of reflection on the resurrection, Thomas Aquinas neglected in his metaphysical (and at the same time theological) anthropology Plato's philosophical conception on the relationship between the soul and the body and drew closer to the conception of Aristotle.[1] The resurrection, in fact, bears witness, at least indirectly, that the body, in the composite being of man as a whole, is not only connected temporarily with the soul (as its earthly "prison," as Plato believed),[2] but that together with the soul

it constitutes the unity and integrity of the human being. Aristotle taught precisely that,[3] unlike Plato. If St. Thomas accepted Aristotle's conception in his anthropology, he did so taking into consideration the truth about the resurrection. The truth about the resurrection clearly affirms, in fact, that the eschatological perfection and happiness of man cannot be understood as a state of the soul alone, separated (according to Plato: liberated) from the body, but it must be understood as the state of man definitively and perfectly "integrated" through such a union of the soul and the body, which qualifies and definitively ensures this perfect integrity.

Let us interrupt at this point our reflection on the words spoken by Christ about the resurrection. The great wealth of contents enclosed in these words induces us to take them up again in further considerations.

NOTES

1. Cf., e.g.: "Habet autem anima alium modum essendi cum unitur corpori, et cum fuerit a corpore separata, manente tamen eadem animae natura; *non ita quod uniri corpori sit ei accidentale, sed per rationem suae naturae corpori unitur...*" (St. Thomas, *Sum. Theol.* Ia, q.89, a. 1).

"Si autem hoc non est ex natura animae, sed per accidens hoc convenit ei ex eo quod *corpori alligatur, sicut Platonici posuerunt...remoto impedimento corporis, rediret anima ad suam naturam....* Sed, secundum hoc, non esset anima corpori unita propter melius animae...;

sed hoc esset solum propter melius corporis: quod est irrationabile, cum materia sit propter formam, et non e converso..." *(Ibid.).*

"Secundum se convenit animae corpori uniri.... Anima humana manet in suo esse cum fuerit a corpore separata, habens aptitudinem et inclinationem naturalem ad corporis unionem" *(Ibid.,* 1a. q. 76, a. 1 ad 6).

2. To men *soma estin hemin sema* (Platone, *Gorgias* 493 A; cf. also *Phaedo* 66B; *Cratylus* 400C).

3. Aristotle, *De anima,* II, 412a, 19-22; cf. also *Metaph.* 1029 b 11; 1030 b 14.

The Resurrection Perfects the Person

General audience of December 9, 1981.

1. "At the resurrection they neither marry nor are given in marriage, but are like angels in heaven" (Mt. 22:30; similarly Mk. 12:25). "They are equal to angels and are sons of God, being sons of the resurrection" (Lk. 20:36).

Let us try to understand these words of Christ about the future resurrection in order to draw a conclusion with regard to the "spiritualization" of man, different from that of earthly life. We could speak here also of a perfect system of forces in mutual relations between what is spiritual in man and what is physical. "Historical" man, as a result of original sin, experiences a multiple imperfection in this system of forces, which is expressed in Saint Paul's well-known words: "I see in my members another law at war with the law of my mind" (Rom. 7:23).

"Eschatological" man will be free from that "opposition." In the resurrection the body will return to perfect unity and harmony with the spirit: man will no longer experience the opposition between what is spiritual and what is physical in him. "Spiritualization" means not only that the spirit will dominate the body, but, I would say, that it will fully permeate the body, and that the forces of the spirit will permeate the energies of the body.

PERFECT REALIZATION IN THE LIFE TO COME

2. In earthly life, the dominion of the spirit over the body—and the simultaneous subordination of the body to the spirit—can, as the result of persevering work on themselves, express a personality that is spiritually mature. However, the fact that the energies of the spirit succeed in dominating the forces of the body does not remove the very possibility of their mutual opposition. The "spiritualization," to which the synoptic Gospels refer (Mt. 22:30; Mk. 12:25; Lk. 20:34-35) in the texts analyzed here, already lies beyond this possibility. It is therefore a perfect spiritualization, in which the possibility that "another law is at war with the law of...the mind" (cf. Rom. 7:23) is completely eliminated. This state which—as is evident—is differentiated essentially (and not

only with regard to degree) from what we experience in earthly life, does not, however, signify any "disincarnation" of the body nor, consequently, a "dehumanization" of man. On the contrary, in fact, it signifies his perfect "realization." In fact, in the composite, psychosomatic being which man is, perfection cannot consist in a mutual opposition of spirit and body, but in a deep harmony between them, in safeguarding the primacy of the spirit. In the "other world," this primacy will be realized and will be manifested in a perfect spontaneity, without any opposition on the part of the body. However, that must not be understood as a definitive "victory" of the spirit over the body. The resurrection will consist in the perfect participation of all that is physical in man in what is spiritual in him. At the same time it will consist in the perfect realization of what is personal in man.

A NEW SPIRITUALIZATION

3. The words of the synoptic Gospels testify that the state of man in the "other world" will not only be a state of perfect spiritualization, but also of fundamental "divinization" of his humanity. The "sons of the resurrection"—as we read in Luke 20:36—are not only "equal to angels," but also "sons of God." The conclusion can be drawn that

the degree of spiritualization characteristic of "eschatological" man will have its source in the degree of his "divinization," incomparably superior to the one that can be attained in earthly life. It must be added that here it is a question not only of a different degree, but, in a way, of another kind of "divinization." Participation in divine nature, participation in the interior life of God Himself, penetration and permeation of what is essentially human by what is essentially divine, will then reach its peak, so that the life of the human spirit will arrive at such fullness which previously had been absolutely inaccessible to it. This new spiritualization will therefore be the fruit of grace, that is, of the communication of God in His very divinity, not only to man's soul, but to his whole psychosomatic subjectivity. We speak here of "subjectivity" (and not only of "nature"), because that divinization is to be understood not only as an "interior state" of man (that is: of the subject) capable of seeing God "face to face," but also as a new formation of the whole personal subjectivity of man in accordance with union with God in His Trinitarian mystery and of intimacy with Him in the perfect communion of persons. This intimacy—with all its subjective intensity—will not absorb man's personal subjectivity, but rather will make it stand out to an incomparably greater and fuller extent.

UNITED WITH
THE VISION OF GOD

4. "Divinization" in the "other world," as indicated by Christ's words, will bring the human spirit such a "range of experience" of truth and love such as man would never have been able to attain in earthly life. When Christ speaks of the resurrection, He proves at the same time that the human body will also take part, in its way, in this eschatological experience of truth and love, united with the vision of God "face to face." When Christ says that those who take part in the future resurrection "neither marry nor are given in marriage" (Mk. 12:25), His words—as has already been pointed out—affirm not only the end of earthly history, bound up with marriage and procreation, but also seem to reveal the new meaning of the body. Is it possible, in this case, to think—at the level of biblical eschatology—of the discovery of the "nuptial" meaning of the body, above all as the "virginal" meaning of being male and female, as regards the body? To answer this question, which emerges from the words reported by the synoptic Gospels, we should penetrate more deeply into the very essence of what will be the beatific vision of the divine Being, a vision of God "face to face" in the future life. It is also necessary to let oneself be guided by that "range of experience" of

truth and love which goes beyond the limits of the cognitive and spiritual possibilities of man in temporality, and in which he will become a participant in the "other world."

IN THE DIMENSION OF THE "OTHER WORLD"

5. This "eschatological experience" of the living God will concentrate in itself not only all man's spiritual energies, but, at the same time, it will reveal to him, in a deep and experiential way, the "self-communication" of God to the whole of creation and, in particular, to man— which is the most personal "self-giving" by God, in His very divinity, to man: to that being who, from the beginning, bears within himself the image and likeness of God. In this way, therefore, in the "other world" the object of the "vision" will be that mystery hidden in the Father from eternity, a mystery which in time was revealed in Christ, in order to be accomplished incessantly through the Holy Spirit. That mystery will become, if we may use the expression, the content of the eschatological experience and the "form" of the entire human existence in the dimension of the "other world." Eternal life must be understood in the eschatological sense, that is, as the full and perfect experience of that grace (charis) of God, in which man becomes a participant through faith

during earthly life, and which, on the contrary, will not only have to reveal itself in all its penetrating depth to those who take part in the "other world," but also will have to be experienced in its beatifying reality.

We suspend here our reflection centered on Christ's words about the future resurrection of the body. In this "spiritualization" and "divinization" in which man will participate in the resurrection, we discover—in an eschatological dimension—the same characteristics that qualified the "nuptial" meaning of the body; we discover them in the meeting with the mystery of the living God, which is revealed through the vision of Him "face to face."

Christ's Words on the Resurrection Complete the Revelation of the Body

General audience of December 16, 1981.

1. "In the resurrection they neither marry nor are given in marriage, but are like angels in heaven" (Mt. 22:30, similarly Mk. 12:25). "...They are equal to angels and are sons of God, being sons of the resurrection" (Lk. 20:36).

The eschatological communion *(communio)* of man with God, constituted thanks to the love of a perfect union, will be nourished by the vision, "face to face," of contemplation of that more perfect communion—because it is purely divine—which is the trinitarian communion of the divine Persons in the unity of the same divinity.

PERFECT SUBJECTIVITY

2. Christ's words, reported by the synoptic Gospels, enable us to deduce that participants in the "other world"—in this union with

the living God which springs from the beatific vision of His unity and trinitarian communion—will not only keep their authentic subjectivity, but will acquire it to a far more perfect extent than in earthly life. In this there will furthermore be confirmed the law of the integral order of the person, according to which the perfection of communion is not only conditioned by the perfection or spiritual maturity of the subject, but also in turn determines it. Those who participate in the "future world," that is, in perfect communion with the living God, will enjoy a perfectly mature subjectivity. If in this perfect subjectivity, while keeping masculinity and femininity in their risen—that is glorious—body, "they neither marry nor are given in marriage," this is explained not only with the end of history, but also—and above all—with the "eschatological authenticity" of the response to that "self-communication" of the divine Subject, which will constitute the beatifying experience of the gift of Himself on God's part, which is absolutely superior to any experience proper to earthly life.

3. The reciprocal gift of oneself to God—a gift in which man will concentrate and express all the energies of his own personal and at the same time psychosomatic subjectivity—will be the response to God's gift of Himself to man.[1] In this mutual gift of himself by man, a gift which will become completely and definitive-

ly beatifying, as a response worthy of a personal subject to God's gift of Himself, "virginity," or rather the virginal state of the body, will be totally manifested as the eschatological fulfillment of the "nuptial" meaning of the body, as the specific sign and the authentic expression of all personal subjectivity. In this way, therefore, that eschatological situation in which "they neither marry nor are given in marriage" has its solid foundation in the future state of the personal subject, when, as a result of the vision of God "face to face," there will be born in him a love of such depth and power of concentration on God Himself, as to completely absorb his whole psychosomatic subjectivity.

UNION OF COMMUNION

4. This concentration of knowledge ("vision") and love on God Himself—a concentration that cannot be other than full participation in the interior life of God, that is, in the very trinitarian reality—will be at the same time the discovery, in God, of the whole "world" of relations, constitutive of His perennial order *(cosmos)*. This concentration will be above all man's rediscovery of himself, not only in the depth of his own person, but also in that union which is proper to the world of persons in their psychosomatic constitution. This is certainly a union of communion. The concentration of

knowledge and love on God Himself in the trinitarian communion of Persons can find a beatifying response in those who become participants in the "other world," only through realizing mutual communion adapted to created persons. And for this reason we profess faith in the "communion of saints" *(communio sanctorum)*, and we profess it in organic connection with faith in the "resurrection of the dead." The words with which Christ affirms that in the other world "they neither marry nor are given in marriage" are at the basis of these contents of our faith, and at the same time they require an adequate interpretation in its light. We must think of the reality of the "other world" in the categories of the rediscovery of a new, perfect subjectivity of everyone and at the same time of the rediscovery of a new, perfect intersubjectivity of all. In this way, this reality signifies the real and definitive fulfillment of human subjectivity, and, on this basis, the definitive fulfillment of the "nuptial" meaning of the body. The complete concentration of created subjectivity, redeemed and glorified, on God Himself will not take man away from this fulfillment; in fact—on the contrary—it will introduce him into it and consolidate him in it. One can say, finally, that in this way eschatological reality will become the source of the perfect realization of the "trinitarian order" in the created world of persons.

REVELATION
OF THE BODY

5. The words with which Christ refers to the future resurrection—words confirmed in a singular way by His own resurrection—complete what in the present reflections we are accustomed to call the "revelation of the body." This revelation penetrates in a way into the very heart of the reality which we are experiencing, and this reality is above all man, his body, the body of "historical" man. At the same time, this revelation enables us to go beyond the sphere of this experience in two directions. In the first place, in the direction of that "beginning" to which Christ refers in His conversation with the Pharisees regarding the indissolubility of marriage (cf. Mt. 19:3-9); in the second place, in the direction of the "other world," to which the Master draws the attention of His listeners in the presence of the Sadducees, who "say that there is no resurrection" (Mt. 22:23). These two "extensions of the sphere" of the experience of the body (if we may say so) are not completely beyond the reach of our understanding (obviously theological) of the body. What the human body is in the sphere of man's historical experience is not completely cut off from those two dimensions of his existence, which are revealed through Christ's words.

SPIRITUAL AND PHYSICAL

6. It is clear that here it is a question not so much of the "body" in abstract, but of man who is at once spiritual and physical. Continuing in the two directions indicated by Christ's words, and linking up again with the experience of the body in the dimension of our earthly existence (therefore in the historical dimension), we can make a certain theological reconstruction of what might have been the experience of the body on the basis of man's revealed "beginning," and also of what it will be in the dimension of the "other world." The possibility of this reconstruction, which extends our experience of man-body, indicates, at least indirectly, the consistency of man's theological image in these three dimensions, which together contribute to the constitution of the theology of the body.

NOTE

1. "In the biblical conception...it is a question of a 'dialogic' immortality (resuscitation!), that is, that immortality does not derive merely from the obvious truth that the indivisible cannot die, but from the saving act of Him who loves, who has the power to do so; therefore man cannot completely disappear, because he is known and

loved by God. If all love postulates eternity, love of God not only wishes it, but actuates it and is it.

"...Since the immortality presented by the Bible does not derive from the power of what is in itself indestructible, but from being accepted in the dialogue with the Creator, for this reason it must be called resuscitation..." (J. Ratzinger, *Risurrezione della carne—aspetto teologico,* in: *Sacramentum Mundi,* vol. 7, Brescia 1977, Morcelliana, pp. 160-161).

New Threshold of the Complete Truth About Man

General audience of January 13, 1982.

"When they rise from the dead, they neither marry nor are given in marriage, but are like angels in heaven" (Mk. 12:25; similarly Mt. 22:30). "...They are equal to angels and are sons of God, being sons of the resurrection" (Lk. 20:36).

The words in which Christ refers to the future resurrection—words confirmed in an extraordinary way by His own resurrection—complete what we are accustomed to call in these reflections the "revelation of the body." This revelation penetrates, so to speak, into the very heart of the reality that we experience, and this reality is above all man, his body: the body of "historical" man. At the same time, this revelation permits us to go beyond the sphere of this experience in two directions. First, in the direction of that "beginning" to which Christ refers in His conversation with the Pharisees concerning the indissolubility of marriage (cf. Mt. 19:3-8); then, in the direction of the "future world," to which the Master addresses the hearts of His listeners in the presence of the Sadducees, who "say that there is no resurrection" (Mt. 22:23).

2. Neither the truth about that "beginning" of which Christ speaks, nor the eschatological truth can be reached by man with empirical and rationalistic methods alone. However, is it not possible to affirm that man bears, in a way, these two dimensions in the depth of the experience of his own being, or rather that he is somehow on his way to them as to dimensions that fully justify the very meaning of his being a body, that is, of his being a "carnal" man? As regards the eschatological dimension, is it not true that death itself and the destruction of the body can confer on man an eloquent significance about the experience in which the personal meaning of existence is realized? When Christ speaks of the future resurrection, His words do not fall in a void. The experience of mankind, and especially the experience of the body, enable the listener to unite with those words the image of his new existence in the "future world," for which earthly experience supplies the substratum and the base. An adequate theological reconstruction is possible.

TRUTH ABOUT MAN

3. To the construction of this image—which, as regards content, corresponds to the article of our profession of Faith: "I believe in the resurrection of the dead"—there greatly contributes the awareness that there exists a connection between earthly experience and the whole dimension of the biblical "beginning" of man in the world. If at the beginning God "created them male and female" (cf. Gn. 1:27); if in this duality concerning the body He envisaged also such a unity that "they become one flesh" (Gn. 2:24); if He linked this unity with the blessing of fertility, that is, of procreation (cf. Gn. 1:29); and if now, speaking before the Sadducees about the future resurrection, Christ explains that "in the resurrection they neither marry nor are given in marriage"— then it is clear that it is a question here of a development of the truth about man himself. Christ indicates his identity, although this identity is realized in eschatological experience in a different way from the experience of the "beginning" itself and of the whole of history. And yet man will always be the same, such as he came from the hands of his Creator and Father. Christ says: "They neither marry nor are given in marriage," but He does not state that this man of the "future world" will no longer be male and female as he was "from the

beginning." It is clear therefore that, as regards the body, the meaning of being male or female in the "future world" must be sought outside marriage and procreation, but there is no reason to seek it outside that which (independently of the blessing of procreation) derives from the very mystery of creation and which subsequently forms also the deepest structure of man's history on earth, since this history has been deeply penetrated by the mystery of redemption.

UNITY OF THE TWO

4. In his original situation man, therefore, is alone and at the same time he *becomes* male and female: unity of the two. In his solitude "he is revealed" to himself as a person, in order to "reveal," at the same time, the communion of persons in the unity of the two. In both states the human being is constituted as an image and likeness of God. From the beginning man is also a body among bodies, and in the unity of the couple he becomes male and female, discovering the "nuptial" meaning of his body as a personal subject. Subsequently, the meaning of being-a-body and, in particular, being male and female in the body, is connected with marriage and procreation (that is, with fatherhood and motherhood). However, the original and fundamental significance of being a body, as well as being, by reason of the body, male

and female—that is precisely that "nuptial" significance—is united with the fact that man is created as a person and called to a life *in communione personarum*. Marriage and procreation in itself did not determine definitively the original and fundamental meaning of being a body or of being, as a body, male and female. Marriage and procreation merely give a concrete reality to that meaning in the dimensions of history.

The resurrection indicates the end of the historical dimension. The words "when they rise from the dead, they neither marry nor are given in marriage" (Mk. 12:25) express univocally not only the meaning which the human body will not have in the "future world," but enable us also to deduce that that "nuptial" meaning of the body in the resurrection to the future life will correspond perfectly both to the fact that man, as a male-female, is a person created in the "image and likeness of God," and to the fact that this image is realized in the communion of persons. That "nuptial" meaning of being a body will be realized, therefore, as a meaning that is perfectly personal and communitarian at the same time.

FACE TO FACE VISION

5. Speaking of the body glorified through the resurrection to the future life, we have in mind man, male-female, in all the truth of his

humanity: man who, together with the eschatological experience of the living God (the "face
to face" vision), will experience precisely this
meaning of his own body. This will be a
completely new experience, and at the same
time it will not be alienated in any way from
what man took part in "from the beginning" nor
from what, in the historical dimension of his
existence, constituted in him the source of the
tension between spirit and body, concerning
mainly the procreative meaning of the body
and sex. The man of the "future world" will
find again in this new experience of his own
body precisely the completion of what he bore
within himself perennially and historically, in a
certain sense, as a heritage and even more as a
duty and objective, as the content of the ethical
norm.

MUTUAL COMMUNICATION

6. The glorification of the body, as the
eschatological fruit of its divinizing spiritualization, will reveal the definitive value of what
was to be from the beginning a distinctive sign
of the created person in the visible world, as
well as a means of mutual communication
between persons and a genuine expression of
truth and love, for which the *communio personarum* is constituted. That perennial meaning of the human body—to which the existence
of every man, weighed down by the heritage of

concupiscence, has necessarily brought a series of limitations, struggles and sufferings—will then be revealed again, and will be revealed in such simplicity and splendor when every participant in the "other world" will find again in his glorified body the source of the freedom of the gift. The perfect "freedom of the sons of God" (cf. Rom. 8:14) will nourish also with that gift each of the communions which will make up the great community of the communion of saints.

DIFFICULT TO ENVISAGE

7. It is all too clear—on the basis of man's experiences and knowledge in his temporal life, that is, in "this world"—that it is difficult to construct a fully adequate image of the "future world." However, at the same time there is no doubt that, with the help of Christ's words, at least a certain approximation to this image is possible and attainable. We use this theological approximation, professing our faith in the "resurrection of the dead" and in "eternal life," as well as faith in the "communion of saints," which belongs to the reality of the "future world."

A NEW THRESHOLD

8. Concluding this part of our reflections, it is opportune to state once more that Christ's words reported by the synoptic Gospels (Mt.

22:30; Mk. 12:25; Lk. 20:34-35) have a decisive meaning not only as regards the words of the book of Genesis (to which Christ refers on another occasion), but also in what concerns the entire Bible. These words enable us, in a certain sense, to read again—that is, in depth—the whole revealed meaning of the body, the meaning of being a man, that is, a person "incarnated," of being male or female as regards the body. These words permit us to understand the meaning, in the eschatological dimension of the "other world," of that unity in humanity, which was constituted "in the beginning" and which the words of Genesis 2:24 ("A man cleaves to his wife, and they become one flesh")—uttered in the act of man's creation as male and female—seemed to direct, if not completely, at least, in any case, especially towards "this world." Since the words of the book of Genesis were almost the threshold of the whole theology of the body—the threshold which Christ took as His foundation in His teaching on marriage and its indissolubility—then it must be admitted that the words reported by the synoptics are, as it were, a new threshold of this complete truth about man, which we find in God's revealed Word. It is indispensable to dwell upon this threshold, if we wish our theology of the body—and also our Christian "spirituality of the body"—to be able to use it as a complete image.

Doctrine of the Resurrection According to St. Paul

General audience of January 27, 1982.

1. During the preceding audiences we reflected on Christ's words about "the other world," which will emerge together with the resurrection of bodies.

Those words had an extraordinarily intense resonance in the teaching of St. Paul. Between the answer given to the Sadducees, transmitted by the synoptic Gospels (cf. Mt. 22:30; Mk. 12:25; Lk. 20:35-36), and Paul's apostolate there took place first of all the fact of the resurrection of Christ Himself and a series of meetings with the risen Christ, among which there must be included, as the last link, the event that occurred in the neighborhood of Damascus. Saul or Paul of Tarsus who, on his conversion, became the "Apostle of the Gentiles," had also his own post-paschal experience, similar to that of the other Apostles. At the basis of his faith in the resurrection, which he expresses above all in the first letter to the Corinthians (ch. 15), there is certainly that meeting with the risen Christ, which became the beginning and foundation of his apostolate.

GOD IS NOT DEAD

2. It is difficult to sum up here and comment adequately on the stupendous and ample argumentation of the fifteenth chapter of the first letter to the Corinthians in all its details. It is significant that, while Christ replied to the Sadducees, who "say that there is no resurrection" (Lk. 20:27), with the words reported by the synoptic Gospels, Paul, on his part, replies or rather engages in polemics (in conformity with his temperament) with those who contest it.[1] Christ, in His (pre-paschal) answer, did not refer to His own resurrection, but appealed to the fundamental reality of the Old Testament covenant, to the reality of the living God, on which the conviction of the possibility of the resurrection is based: the living God "is not God of the dead, but of the living" (Mk. 12:27). Paul in his post-paschal argumentation on the future resurrection, refers above all to the reality and the truth of the resurrection of Christ. In fact, he defends this truth even as the foundation of the Faith in its integrity: "...If Christ has not been raised, then our preaching is in vain and your faith is in

vain.... But, in fact, Christ has been raised from the dead" (1 Cor. 15:14, 20).

GOD OF THE LIVING

3. Here we are on the same line as revelation: the resurrection of Christ is the last and the fullest word of the self-revelation of the living God as "not God of the dead, but of the living" (Mk. 12:27). It is the last and fullest confirmation of the truth about God which is expressed right from the beginning through this revelation. The resurrection, furthermore, is the reply of the God of life to the historical inevitability of death, to which man was subjected from the moment of the breaking of the first covenant and which, together with sin, entered his history. This answer about the victory won over death is illustrated by the first letter to the Corinthians (ch. 15) with extraordinary perspicacity, presenting the resurrection of Christ as the beginning of that eschatological fulfillment, in which, through Him and in Him, everything will return to the Father, everything will be subjected to Him, that is, handed back definitively, "that God may be everything to everyone" (1 Cor. 15:28). And then—in this definitive victory over sin, over what opposed the creature to the Creator—also death will be vanquished: "The last enemy to be destroyed is death" (1 Cor. 15:26).

IMPERISHABLE SOUL

4. The words that can be considered the synthesis of Pauline anthropology concerning the resurrection take their place in this context. And it is on these words that it will be opportune to dwell longer here. We read, in fact, in the first letter to the Corinthians 15:42-46, about the resurrection of the dead: "What is sown is perishable, what is raised is imperishable. It is sown in dishonor, it is raised in glory. It is sown in weakness, it is raised in power. It is sown a physical body, it is raised a spiritual body. If there is a physical body, there is also a spiritual body. Thus it is written, 'The first man Adam became a living being'; the last Adam became a life-giving spirit. But it is not the spiritual which is first but the physical, and then the spiritual."

HISTORICAL EXPERIENCE

5. Between this Pauline anthropology of the resurrection and the one that emerges from the text of the synoptic Gospels (Mt. 22:30; Mk. 12:25; Lk. 20:35-36), there exists an essential consistency; only the text of the first letter to the Corinthians is more developed. Paul studies in depth what Christ had proclaimed, penetrating, at the same time, into the various aspects of that truth which had been expressed concisely and substantially in the

words written by the synoptic Gospels. It is also significant for the Pauline text that man's eschatological perspective, based on faith "in the resurrection of the dead," is united with reference to the "beginning" as well as with deep awareness of man's "historical" situation. The man whom Paul addresses in the first letter to the Corinthians and who (like the Sadducees) is contrary to the possibility of the resurrection, has also his ("historical") experience of the body, and from this experience it emerges quite clearly that the body is "perishable," "weak," "physical," "in dishonor."

MYSTERY
OF CREATION

6. Paul confronts such a man, to whom his words are addressed—either in the community of Corinth or also, I would say, in all times—with the risen Christ, "the last Adam." Doing so, he invites him, in a way, to follow in the footsteps of his own post-paschal experience. At the same time he recalls to him "the first Adam," that is, he induces him to turn to the "beginning," to that first truth about man and the world which is at the basis of the revelation of the mystery of the living God. In this way, therefore, Paul reproduces in his synthesis all that Christ had announced when He had referred, at three different moments, to the

"beginning" in the conversation with the Pharisees (cf. Mt. 19:3-8; Mk. 10:2-9); to the human "heart," as the place of struggle with lusts within man, during the Sermon on the Mount (cf. Mt. 5:27); and to the resurrection as the reality of the "other world," in the conversation with the Sadducees (cf. Mt. 22:30; Mk. 12:25; Lk. 20:35-36).

ENLIVENING OF MATTER

7. It belongs, therefore, to the style of Paul's synthesis that it plunges its roots into the revealed mystery of creation and redemption as a whole, from which it is developed and in the light of which alone it can be explained. The creation of man, according to the biblical narrative, is an enlivening of matter by means of the spirit, thanks to which "the first man Adam became a living being" (1 Cor. 15:45). The Pauline text repeats here the words of the book of Genesis (2:7), that is, of the second narrative of the creation of man (the so-called Jahwist narrative). From the same source it is known that this original "animation of the body" underwent corruption because of sin.

Although at this point of the first letter to the Corinthians the author does not speak directly of original sin, yet the series of definitions which he attributes to the body of historical man, writing that it is "perishable...weak...

physical...in dishonor..." indicates sufficiently what, according to revelation, is the consequence of sin, that which Paul himself will call elsewhere "bondage to decay" (Rom. 8:21). The whole of creation is subjected indirectly to this "bondage to decay" owing to the sin of man, who was placed by the Creator in the midst of the visible world in order to "subdue" it (cf. Gn. 1:28). So man's sin has a dimension that is not only interior, but also "cosmic." And according to this dimension, the body—which Paul (in conformity with his experience) characterizes as "perishable...weak...physical...in dishonor..."—expresses in itself the state of creation after sin. This creation, in fact, "has been groaning in travail together until now" (Rom. 8:22).

However, just as the pains of labor are united with the desire for birth, with the hope of a new man, so, too, the whole of creation "waits with eager longing for the revealing of the sons of God..." and cherishes the hope to "be set free from its bondage to decay, and obtain the glorious liberty of the children of God" (Rom. 8:19-21).

TRY TO UNDERSTAND

8. Through this "cosmic" context of the affirmation contained in the letter to the Romans—in a way, through the "body of all

creatures"—let us try to understand completely the Pauline interpretation of the resurrection. If this image of the body of historical man, so deeply realistic and adapted to the universal experience of men, conceals within itself, according to Paul, not only the "bondage of decay," but also hope, like the hope that accompanies "the pains of labor," that happens because the Apostle grasps in this image also the presence of the mystery of redemption. Awareness of that mystery comes precisely from all man's experiences which can be defined as the "bondage of decay"; and it comes because redemption operates in man's soul by means of the gifts of the Spirit: "...we ourselves, who have the first fruits of the Spirit, groan inwardly as we wait for adoption as sons, the redemption of our bodies" (Rom. 8:23). Redemption is the way to the resurrection. The resurrection constitutes the definitive accomplishment of the redemption of the body.

We will come back to the analysis of the Pauline text in the first letter to the Corinthians in our further reflections.

NOTES

1. Among the Corinthians there were probably movements of thought marked by Platonic dualism and neo-Pythagoreanism of a religious shade, Stoicism and Epicureanism; all Greek philosophies, moreover, denied the resurrection of the body. Paul had already experienced in Athens the reaction of the Greeks to the doctrine of the resurrection, during his address at the Areopagus (cf. Acts 17:32).

The Risen Body Will Be Incorruptible, Glorious, Full of Dynamism, Spiritual

General audience of February 3, 1982.

1. From the words of Christ on the future resurrection of the body, reported by all three synoptic Gospels (Matthew, Mark and Luke), we have passed to the Pauline anthropology of the resurrection. We are analyzing the first letter to the Corinthians, chapter 15, verses 42 to 49.

In the resurrection the human body, according to the words of the Apostle, is seen "incorruptible, glorious, full of dynamism, spiritual." The resurrection is not, therefore, only a manifestation of the life that conquers death —almost a final return to the tree of life, from which man had been separated at the moment of original sin—but is also a revelation of the ultimate destiny of man in all the fullness of his psychosomatic nature and his personal subjectivity. Paul of Tarsus—who, following in the footsteps of the other Apostles, experienced in his meeting with the risen Christ the state of His glorified body—basing himself on this experience, announces in his letter to the Romans "the redemption of the body" (Rom. 8:23) and in his letter to the Corinthians (1 Cor. 15:42-49) the completion of this redemption in the future resurrection.

IN THE PERSPECTIVE OF AN ETERNAL DESTINY

2. The literary method applied here by Paul perfectly corresponds to his style, which uses antitheses that simultaneously bring together those things which they contrast. In this way they are useful in having us understand Pauline thought about the resurrection: both in its "cosmic" dimension and also insofar as it concerns the characteristic of the internal structure itself of the "earthly" and the "heavenly" man. The Apostle, in fact, in contrasting Adam and Christ (risen)—that is, the first Adam with the second Adam—in a certain way shows two poles between which, in the mystery of creation and redemption, man has been placed in the cosmos. One could say that man has been "put in tension" between these two poles in the perspective of his eternal destiny regarding, from beginning to end, his human nature itself. When Paul writes: "The first man was from the earth, a man of dust, the second man is from heaven" (1 Cor. 15:47), he has in mind both

Adam-man and also Christ as man. Between these two poles—between the first and the second Adam—there takes place the process that he expresses in the following words: "As we have borne the image of the man of earth, so we will bear the image of the man of heaven" (1 Cor. 15:49).

MAN COMPLETED

3. This "man of heaven"—the man of the resurrection whose prototype is the risen Christ—is not so much an antithesis and negation of the "man of earth" (whose prototype is the "first Adam"), but is above all his completion and confirmation. It is the completion and confirmation of what corresponds to the psychosomatic makeup of humanity, in the sphere of his eternal destiny, that is, in the thought and in the plan of Him who from the beginning created man in His own image and likeness. The humanity of the "first Adam," the "man of earth," bears in itself, I would say, a particular potential (which is capacity and readiness) to receive all that became the "second Adam," the Man of heaven, namely, Christ: what He became in His resurrection. That humanity which all men, children of the first Adam, share, and which, along with the heritage of sin—being carnal—at the same time is "corruptible," and bears in itself the potentiality of "incorruptibility."

That humanity which in all its psychosomatic makeup appears "ignoble," yet bears within itself the interior desire for glory, that is, the tendency and the capacity to become "glorious," in the image of the risen Christ. Finally, the same humanity about which the Apostle—in conformity with the experience of all men—says that it is "weak" and has an "animal body," bears in itself the aspiration to become "full of dynamism" and "spiritual."

POTENTIAL TO RISE AGAIN

4. We are speaking here of human nature in its integrity, that is, of human nature in its psychosomatic makeup. Paul, however, speaks of the "body." Nevertheless we can admit, on the basis of the immediate context and the remote one, that for him it is not a question only of the body, but of the entire man in his corporeity, therefore also of his ontological complexity. In fact, there is no doubt here that if precisely in the whole visible world (cosmos) that one body which is the human body bears in itself the "potentiality for resurrection," that is, the aspiration and capacity to become definitively "incorruptible, glorious, full of dynamism, spiritual," this happens because, persisting from the beginning in the psychosomatic unity of the personal being, he

can receive and reproduce in this "earthly" image and likeness of God also the "heavenly" image of the second Adam, Christ.

The Pauline anthropology of the resurrection is cosmic and universal at the same time: every man bears in himself the image of Adam and every man is also called to bear in himself the image of Christ, the image of the risen One. This image is the reality of the "other world," the eschatological reality (St. Paul writes: "we *will* bear"). But in the meantime it is already in a certain way a reality of this world, since it was revealed in this world through the resurrection of Christ. It is a reality ingrafted in the man of "this world," a reality that is developing in him toward final completion.

THE VISION OF GOD

5. All the antitheses that are suggested in Paul's text help to construct a valid sketch of the anthropology of the resurrection. This sketch is at the same time more detailed than the one which comes from the text of the synoptic Gospels (Mt. 22:30; Mk. 12:25; Lk. 20:34-35), but on the other hand it is in a certain sense more unilateral. The words of Christ reported by the synoptics open before us the perspective of the eschatological perfection of the body, fully subject to the divinizing profundity of the vision of God "face to face," in which it will find its inexhaustible source of

perpetual "virginity" (united to the nuptial meaning of the body), and of the perpetual "intersubjectivity" of all men, who will become (as males and females) sharers in the resurrection. The Pauline sketch of the eschatological perfection of the glorified body seems to remain rather in the sphere of the very interior structure of the man-person. His interpretation of the future resurrection would seem to link up again with body-spirit "dualism" which constitutes the source of the interior "system of forces" in man.

6. This "system of forces" will undergo a radical change in the resurrection. Paul's words, which explicitly suggest this, cannot however be understood or interpreted in the spirit of dualistic anthropology,[1] which we will try to show in the continuation of our analysis. In fact, it will be suitable to dedicate yet another reflection to the anthropology of the resurrection in the light of the first letter to the Corinthians.

NOTES

1. "Paul takes absolutely no account of the Greek dichotomy between 'soul and body'.... The Apostle resorts to a kind of trichotomy in which the totality of man is body, soul and spirit.... All these terms are alive and the division itself has no fixed limit. He insists on the fact that body and soul are capable of being 'pneumatic,' spiritual" (B. Rigaux, *Dieu l'a ressuscité. Exégèse et Théologie biblique*, Gembloux 1973, Duculot, pp. 406-408).

The Body's Spiritualization Will Be the Source of Its Power and Incorruptibility

General audience of February 10, 1982.

1. From Christ's words on the future resurrection of the body, recorded by all three synoptic Gospels (Matthew, Mark and Luke), our reflections have brought us to what St. Paul wrote on the subject in the first letter to the Corinthians (ch. 15). Our analysis is centered above all on what might be called the "anthropology of the resurrection" according to Saint Paul. The author of the letter contrasts the state of the "earthly" man (i.e., historical) with the state of the risen man, characterizing in a lapidary and at the same time penetrating manner, the interior "system of forces" specific to each of these states.

RADICAL TRANSFORMATION

2. That this interior system of forces should undergo a radical transformation would seem to be indicated, first of all, by the contrast

between the "weak" body and the body "full of power." Paul writes: "What is sown is perishable, what is raised is imperishable. It is sown in dishonor, it is raised in glory. It is sown in weakness, it is raised in power" (1 Cor. 15:42-45). "Weak," therefore, is the description of the body which—in metaphysical terms —rises from the temporal soil of humanity. The Pauline metaphor corresponds likewise to the scientific terminology which defines man's beginning as a body by the use of the same term *(semen,* seed).

If, in the Apostle's view, the human body which arises from earthly seed is "weak," this means not only that it is "perishable," subject to death, and to all that leads to it, but also that it is an "animal body."[1] The body "full of power," however, which man will inherit from the second Adam, Christ, in virtue of the future resurrection, will be a "spiritual" body. It will be imperishable, no longer subject to the threat of death. Thus the antinomy, "weak—full of power," refers explicitly not only to the body considered separately, but also to the whole constitution of man considered in his corporeal nature. Only within the framework of such a constitution can the body become "spiritual"; and this *spiritualization of the body will be the source of its power and incorruptibility* (or immortality).

3. This theme has its origin already in the first chapter of the book of Genesis. It can be said that St. Paul sees the reality of the future resurrection as a certain *restitutio in integrum,* that is, as the reintegration and at the same time as the attaining of the fullness of humanity. It is not truly a restitution, because in that case the resurrection would be, in a certain sense, a return to the state which the soul enjoyed before sin, apart from the knowledge of good and evil (cf. Gn. 1—2). But such a return does not correspond to the internal logic of the whole economy of salvation, to the most profound meaning of the *mystery* of the redemption. *Restitutio in integrum,* linked with the resurrection and the reality of the "other world," can only be an *introduction to a new fullness.* This will be a fullness that presupposes the whole of human history, formed by the drama of the tree of the knowledge of good and evil (cf. Gn. 3) and at the same time permeated by the text of the first letter to the Corinthians.

PERFECT HARMONIZATION

4. According to the text of the first letter to the Corinthians, man, in whom concupiscence—that is, the "animal body" (1 Cor. 15:44)—prevails over the spiritual, is condemned to death. He should rise, however, as a "spiritual body," man in whom the Spirit will

achieve a just supremacy over the body, spirituality over sensuality. It is easy to understand that Paul is here thinking of sensuality as the sum total of the factors limiting human spirituality, that is, as a force that "ties down" the spirit (not necessarily in the Platonic sense) by restricting its own faculty of knowing (seeing) the truth and also the faculty to will freely and to love in truth. Here, however, it cannot be a question of that fundamental function of the senses which serves to liberate spirituality, that is to say, of the simple faculty of knowing and willing proper to the psychosomatic *compositum* of the human subject.

Just as one speaks of the resurrection of the body, that is, of man in his true corporeal nature, consequently the "spiritual body" should mean precisely *the perfect sensitivity of the senses, their perfect harmonization with the activity of the human spirit* in truth and liberty. The "animal body" which is the earthly antithesis of the "spiritual body," indicates sensuality as a force prejudicial to man, precisely because—while living "in the knowledge of good and evil"—he is often attracted and, as it were, impelled towards evil.

INFLUENCE
OF THE HOLY SPIRIT ON MAN

5. It cannot be forgotten that here it is not so much a question of anthropological dualism,

but of a basic antinomy. Constituting it is not only the body (as the Aristotelian *hyle*), but also the soul: or man as a "living being" (cf. Gn. 2:7). Its constituents are: on the one hand, the whole man, the sum total of his psychosomatic subjectivity, inasmuch as he remains under the influence of the vivifying Spirit of Christ; on the other hand, the same man inasmuch as he resists and opposes this Spirit. In the second case man is an "animal body" (and his works are "works of the flesh"). *If, however, he remains under the influence of the Holy Spirit*, man is "spiritual" (and produces the "fruit of the Spirit": Gal. 5:22).

6. Consequently, it can be said that not only in 1 Corinthians 15 are we dealing with the anthropology of the resurrection, but that the whole of St. Paul's anthropology (and ethics) are permeated with the mystery of the resurrection through which we have definitively received the Holy Spirit. Chapter 15 of the first letter to the Corinthians constitutes the Pauline interpretation of the "other world" and of man's state in that world, in which each one, together with the resurrection of the body, will fully participate in the gift of the vivifying Spirit, that is, in the fruit of Christ's resurrection.

CHRIST'S REPLY

7. Concluding the analysis of the "anthropology of the resurrection" according to Paul's first letter to the Corinthians, it is fitting to turn our minds again to Christ's words on the resurrection and on the "other world" which are quoted by the evangelists Matthew, Mark and Luke. We recall that Christ, in His reply to the Sadducees, linked faith in the resurrection with the entire revelation of the God of Abraham, of Isaac, of Jacob and of Moses (Mt. 22:32). At the same time, while rejecting the objection proposed by those who questioned Him, He uttered these significant words: "When they rise from the dead, they neither marry nor are given in marriage" (Mk. 12:25). To these very words, in their immediate context, we devoted our previous reflections, passing on then to the analysis of St. Paul's first letter to the Corinthians (1 Cor. 15).

These reflections have a fundamental significance for the whole theology of the body: for an understanding both of marriage and of celibacy "for the kingdom of heaven." Our further analyses will be devoted to this latter subject.

NOTE

1. The original Greek uses the term *psychikon*. In St. Paul it is found only in the first letter to the Corinthians (2:14; 15:44; 15:46) *and not elsewhere,* probably because of the pre-gnostic tendencies of the Corinthians, and it has a pejorative connotation. As regards its meaning, it corresponds to the term "carnal" (cf. 2 Cor. 1:12; 10:4).

However, in the other Pauline letters, "psyche" and its derivatives signify man in his manifestations, the individual's way of living, and even the human person *in a positive sense* (e.g., to indicate the ideal of life of the ecclesial community: *miâ-i psychê-i* = "in one spirit: Phil. 1:27; *sympsychoi* = "by being of the same mind": Phil. 2:2; *isópsychon* = "like him": Phil. 2:20; cf. R. Jewett, *Paul's Anthropological Terms. A Study of Their Use in Conflict Settings,* Leiden 1971, Brill, pp. 2, 448-449).

Virginity or Celibacy "for the Sake of the Kingdom"

General audience of March 10, 1982.

1. Today we begin to reflect on virginity or celibacy "for the kingdom of heaven."

The question of the call to an exclusive donation of self to God in virginity and in celibacy thrusts its roots deep in the Gospel soil of the theology of the body. To indicate the dimensions proper to it, one must bear in mind Christ's words about the "beginning," and also what He said about the resurrection of the body. The observation: "When they rise from the dead they neither marry nor are given in marriage" (Mk. 12:25), indicates that there is a condition of life without marriage, in which man, male and female, finds at the same time the fullness of personal donation and of the intersubjective communion of persons, thanks to the glorification of his entire psychosomatic being in the eternal union with God. When the call to continence "for the kingdom of heaven" finds an echo in the human soul, in the

conditions of this temporal life, that is, in the
conditions in which persons usually "marry and
are given in marriage" (Lk. 20:34), it is not
difficult to perceive there a particular sen-
sitiveness of the human spirit, which already in
the conditions of the present temporal life
seems to anticipate what man will share in, in
the future resurrection.

CHRIST ON DIVORCE

2. However, Christ did not speak of this
problem, of this particular vocation, in the
immediate context of His conversation with the
Sadducees (cf. Mt. 22:23-30; Mk. 12:18-25;
Lk. 20:27-36), when there was reference to the
resurrection of the body. Instead He had
already spoken of it previously in the context of
His conversation with the Pharisees on marriage and on the grounds of indissolubility, as if
it were a continuation of that conversation (cf.
Mt. 19:3-9). His concluding words concern the
so-called certificate of divorce permitted by
Moses in some cases. Christ says: "For your
hardness of heart Moses allowed you to divorce
your wives, but from the beginning it was not
so. And I say to you: whoever divorces his wife,
except in the case of concubinage, and marries
another, commits adultery" (Mt. 19:8-9). Then
the disciples who—as can be deduced from the
context—were listening attentively to the conversation and particularly to the final words

spoken by Jesus, said to Him: "If such is the case of a man with his wife, it is not expedient to marry" (Mt. 19:10). Christ gives the following reply: "Not all men can receive the precept, but only those to whom it is given. For there are eunuchs who have been so from birth, and there are eunuchs who have been made eunuchs by men, and there are eunuchs who have made themselves eunuchs for the sake of the kingdom of heaven. He who is able to receive this, let him receive it" (Mt. 19:11-12).

CHRIST'S WORDS
ON VOLUNTARY CONTINENCE

3. In regard to this conversation recorded by Matthew one could ask the question: What did the disciples think when, after hearing Jesus' reply to the Pharisees, they remarked: "If such is the case of a man with his wife, it is not expedient to marry"? Anyway, Christ considered it an opportune occasion to speak to them about voluntary continence for the kingdom of heaven. In saying this, He does not directly take a position in regard to what the disciples said, nor does He remain in the line of their reasoning.[1] Hence He does not reply: "it is expedient to marry" or "it is not expedient to marry." The question of continence for the kingdom of heaven is not set in opposition to marriage, nor is it based on a negative judg-

ment in regard to its importance. After all, Christ, speaking previously about the indissolubility of marriage, had referred to the "beginning," that is, to the mystery of creation, thereby indicating the first and fundamental source of its value. Consequently, to reply to the disciples' question, or rather, to clarify the problem placed by them, Christ recurs to another principle. Those who in life choose continence "for the kingdom of heaven" do so, not because "it is inexpedient to marry" or because of a supposed negative value of marriage, but in view of the particular value connected with this choice and which must be discovered and welcomed personally as one's own vocation. And for that reason Christ says: "He who is able to receive this, let him receive it" (Mt. 19:12). But immediately beforehand He says: "Not all men can receive this precept, but only those to whom it is given" (Mt. 19:11).

GRACE NEEDED TO ACCEPT CONTINENCE

4. As can be seen, Christ, in His reply to the disciples' problem, states clearly a rule for the understanding of His words. In the Church's doctrine there exists the conviction that these words do not express a command by which all are bound, but a counsel which concerns only some persons[2]: those precisely

who are able "to receive it." And those able "to receive it" are those "to whom it has been given." The words quoted clearly indicate the importance of the personal choice and also the importance of the particular grace, that is, of the gift which man receives to make such a choice. It may be said that the choice of continence for the kingdom of heaven is a charismatic orientation towards that eschatological state in which men "neither marry nor are given in marriage." However, there is an essential difference between man's state in the resurrection of the body and the voluntary choice of continence for the kingdom of heaven in the earthly life and in the historical state of man fallen and redeemed. The eschatological absence of marriage will be a "state," that is, the proper and fundamental mode of existence of human beings, men and women, in their glorified bodies. Continence for the kingdom of heaven, as the fruit of a charismatic choice, is an exception in respect to the other stage, namely, that state in which man "from the beginning" became and remains a participant during the course of his whole earthly existence.

CONTINENCE IS EXCEPTIONAL

5. It is very significant that Christ does not directly link His words on continence for the kingdom of heaven with His foretelling of

the "other world" in which "they will neither marry nor be given in marriage" (Mk. 12:25). His words, however, are found—as we already said—in the prolongation of the conversation with the Pharisees in which Jesus referred "to the beginning," indicating the institution of marriage on the part of the Creator, and recalling its indissoluble character which, in God's plan, corresponds to the conjugal unity of man and woman.

The counsel and therefore the charismatic choice of continence for the kingdom of heaven are linked, in Christ's words, with the highest recognition of the "historical" order of human existence relative to the soul and body. On the basis of the immediate context of the words on continence for the kingdom of heaven in man's earthly life, one must see in the vocation to such continence a kind of exception to what is rather a general rule of this life. Christ indicates this especially. That such an exception contains within itself the anticipation of the eschatological life without marriage and proper to the "other world" (that is, of the final stage of the "kingdom of heaven"), is not directly spoken of here by Christ. It is a question indeed, not of continence *in* the kingdom of heaven, but of continence *"for* the kingdom of heaven." The idea of virginity or of celibacy as an anticipation and eschatological sign[3] derives from the association of the words spoken here with those which Jesus will utter on another occasion, in the conversation with the Sadducees, when He proclaims the future resurrection of the body.

We shall resume this theme in the course of the following Wednesday reflections.

NOTES

1. On the more detailed problems of the exegesis of this passage, see for example: L. Sabourin, *Il Vangelo di Matteo, Teologia e Esegesi*, vol. II, Roma 1977 (Ed. Paoline), pp. 834-836; *The Positive Values of Consecrated Celibacy*, in "The Way" Supplement 10, summer 1970, p. 51; J. Blinzler, *Eisin eunuchoi, Zur Auslegung von Mt. 19:12*, "Zeitschrift für die Neutestamentliche Wissenschaft" 48 (1957) 268ff.

2. "Likewise the Church's holiness is fostered in a special way by the manifold counsels which the Lord proposes to His disciples in the Gospel for them to observe. Towering among these counsels is that precious gift of divine grace given to some by the Father (cf. Mt. 19:11; 1 Cor. 7:7) to devote themselves to God alone more easily with an undivided heart in virginity or celibacy" (LG, no. 42).

3. Cf. LG, no. 44; *Perfectae caritatis*, no. 12.

eunuchs who have been made eunuchs by

The Vocation to Continence in This Earthly Life

General audience of March 17, 1982.

1. We continue the reflection on virginity or celibacy for the kingdom of heaven—a theme that is important also for a complete theology of the body.

In the immediate context of the words on continence for the kingdom of heaven, Christ makes a very significant comparison; and this confirms us still more in the conviction that He wishes to root the vocation to such continence deep in the reality of the earthly life, thereby gaining an entrance into the mentality of His hearers. He lists, in fact, three categories of eunuchs.

This term concerns the physical defects which render procreation in marriage impossible. These very defects explain the first two categories, when Jesus speaks of both congenital defects: "eunuchs who have been so from birth" (Mt. 19:11), and of acquired defects caused by human intervention: "there are eunuchs who have been made eunuchs by men" (Mt. 19:12). In both cases it is a state of compulsion, and therefore not voluntary. If Christ in His comparison then speaks of those "who have made themselves eunuchs for the sake of the kingdom of heaven" (Mt. 19:12), as of a third category, undoubtedly He makes this distinction to indicate still further its voluntary and supernatural character. Voluntary, because those pertaining to this category "have made themselves eunuchs"; supernatural, because they have done so "for the kingdom of heaven."

CONTINENCE
IN THE OLD TESTAMENT

2. The distinction is very clear and very forceful. Nevertheless, the comparison also is strong and eloquent. Christ speaks to men to whom the tradition of the Old Covenant had not handed down the ideal of celibacy or of virginity. Marriage was so common that only physical impotence could constitute an exception. The reply given to the disciples in Matthew (15:10-12) is at the same time directed, in a certain sense, at the whole tradition of the Old Testament. This is confirmed by a single example taken from the book of Judges to which we refer here not merely because of the event that took place, but also because of the

significant words that accompanied it. "Let it be granted to me...to bewail my virginity" (Jgs. 11:37) the daughter of Jephthah says to her father after learning from him that she was destined to be sacrificed in fulfillment of a vow made to the Lord. (The biblical text explains how such a situation came about.) "Go," the text continues, "and he let her go.... She went with her companions and bewailed her virginity on the mountains. At the end of two months she returned to her father who did with her according to his vow which he had made. She had never known a man" (Jgs. 11:38-39).

3. In the Old Testament tradition, as far as we know, there is no place for this significance of the body, which Christ, in speaking of continence for the kingdom of God, now wishes to present and reveal to His own disciples. Among the personages known to us as spiritual *condottieri* of the people of the Old Covenant, there is not one who would have proclaimed such continence by word or example.[1] Marriage, at that time, was not only a common state, but, still more, in that tradition it had acquired a consecrated significance because of the promise made to Abraham by the Lord: "Behold, my covenant is with you, and you shall be the father of a multitude of nations.... I will make you exceedingly fruitful; and I will make nations of you, and kings shall come forth from you. And I will establish my covenant

between me and you and your descendants after you throughout their generations for an everlasting covenant, to be God to you and to your descendants after you" (Gn. 17:4, 6-7). Hence in the Old Testament tradition, marriage, as a source of fruitfulness and of procreation in regard to descendants, was a *religiously privileged state:* and privileged by revelation itself. Against the background of this tradition, according to which the Messiah should be the "son of David" (Mt. 20:30), it was difficult to understand the ideal of continence. Marriage had everything going in its favor: not only reasons of human nature, but also those of the kingdom of God.[2]

CONTINENCE FOR THE KINGDOM

4. In this environment Christ's words determine a decisive turning point. When He speaks to His disciples for the first time about continence for the kingdom of heaven, one clearly realizes that they, as children of the Old Law tradition, must associate celibacy and virginity with the situation of individuals, especially of the male sex, who because of defects of a physical nature cannot marry ("the eunuchs"), and for that reason He refers directly to them. This reference has a multiple background: both historical and psychological,

as well as ethical and religious. With this reference Jesus—in a certain sense—touches all these backgrounds, as if He wished to say: I know that what I am going to say to you now will cause great difficulty in your conscience, in your way of understanding the significance of the body. In fact, I shall speak to you of continence, and undoubtedly, you will associate this with the state of physical deficiency, whether congenital or brought about by human cause. But I wish to tell you that continence can also be voluntary and chosen by man "for the kingdom of heaven."

5. Matthew, in chapter 19, does not record any immediate reaction of the disciples to these words. We find it later only in the writings of the Apostles, especially in Paul.[3] This confirms that these words were impressed in the conscience of the first generation of Christ's disciples and they repeatedly bore fruit in a manifold way in the generations of His confessors in the Church (and perhaps also outside it). So, from the viewpoint of theology—that is, of the revelation of the significance of the body, completely new in respect to the Old Testament tradition—these words mark a turning point. Their analysis shows how precise and substantial they are, notwithstanding their conciseness. (We will observe it still better when we analyze the Pauline text of the first letter of the Corinthians, chapter 7.) Christ

speaks of continence "for" the kingdom of heaven. In this way He wished to emphasize that this state, consciously chosen by man in this temporal life, in which people usually "marry or are given in marriage," has a singular supernatural finality. Continence, even if consciously chosen or personally decided upon, but without that finality, does not come within the scope of the above-mentioned statement of Christ. Speaking of those who have consciously chosen celibacy or virginity for the kingdom of heaven (that is, "they have made themselves eunuchs"), Christ points out—at least in an indirect way—that this choice during the earthly life is joined to renunciation and also to a determined spiritual effort.

6. The same supernatural finality—"for the kingdom of heaven"—admits of a series of more detailed interpretations which Christ does not enumerate in this passage. It can be said, however, that by means of the lapidary formula which He uses, He indicates indirectly all that is said on the subject in revelation, in the Bible and in Tradition; all that has become the spiritual riches of the Church's experience in which celibacy and virginity for the kingdom of heaven have borne fruit in a manifold way in the various generations of the Lord's disciples and followers.

NOTES

1. It is true that Jeremiah, by explicit command of the Lord, had to observe celibacy (cf. Jer. 16:1-2); but this was a "prophetic sign," which symbolized the future abandonment and destruction of the country and of the people.

2. It is true, as we know from sources outside the Bible, that in the period between the two Testaments, celibacy was maintained in the circles of Judaism by some members of the sect of the Essenes (cf. Josephus Flavius, *Bell. Jud,* II 8, 2: 120-121; Philo Al., *Hypothel,* 11, 14); but this happened on the margin of official Judaism and probably did not continue beyond the beginning of the second century.

In the Qumran community celibacy did not oblige everyone, but some members observed it until death, transferring to the sphere of life during peacetime, the prescription of Deuteronomy (23:10-14) on the ritual purity which was of obligation during the holy war. According to the beliefs of the Qumran community this war lasted always "between the children of light and the children of darkness"; so celibacy was for them the expression of their being ready for the battle (cf. *1 QM* 7, 5-7).

3. Cf. 1 Cor. 7:25-40; see also Rv. 14:4.

Continence for the Sake of the Kingdom—and Its Spiritual Fulfillment

General audience of March 24, 1982.

1. We continue our reflections on celibacy and virginity "for the kingdom of heaven."

Continence for the kingdom of heaven is certainly linked to the revelation of the fact that in the kingdom of heaven people "will no longer marry" (Mt. 22:30). *It is a charismatic sign.* The human being, male and female, who, in the earthly situation where people usually marry (Lk. 20:34), freely chooses continence "for the kingdom of heaven," indicates that in that kingdom, which is the "other world" of the resurrection, people will no longer marry (Mk. 12:25), because God will be "everything to every one" (1 Cor. 15:28).

Such a human being, man and woman, indicates the eschatological "virginity" of the risen man, in whom there will be revealed, I would say, the absolute and eternal nuptial meaning of the glorified body in union with

God Himself through the "face to face" vision of Him; and glorified also through the union of a perfect intersubjectivity, which will unite all who "participate in the other world," men and women, in the mystery of the communion of saints.

Earthly continence for the "kingdom of heaven" is undoubtedly a sign that *indicates* this truth and this reality. It is a sign that the body, whose end is not the grave, is directed to glorification. Already by this very fact, I would say, continence "for the kingdom of heaven" is a witness among men that anticipates the future resurrection. However, this charismatic sign of the "other world" expresses the force and the most authentic dynamics of the mystery of the "redemption of the body": a mystery which Christ has inscribed in man's earthly history and has been deeply rooted by Him in this history. So, then, continence "for the kingdom of heaven" bears, *above all, the imprint of the likeness to Christ,* who, in the work of redemption, did Himself make this choice "for the kingdom of heaven."

THE VIRGINAL MYSTERY

2. Indeed, Christ's whole life, right from the beginning, was a discreet but clear distancing of Himself from that which in the Old Testament had so profoundly determined the

meaning of the body. Christ—as if against the expectations of the whole Old Testament tradition—was born of Mary who, at the moment of the annunciation, clearly says of herself: "How can this be, since I know not man" (Lk. 1:34), and thereby professes her virginity. Though He is born of her like every other man, as a son of his mother, even though His coming into the world is accompanied by the presence of a man who is Mary's spouse and, in the eyes of the law and of men, her husband, nonetheless Mary's maternity is virginal. To this virginal maternity of Mary there corresponds the virginal mystery of Joseph who, following the voice from on high, does not hesitate to "take Mary...for that which is conceived in her is of the Holy Spirit" (Mt. 1:20).

Even though, then, Jesus Christ's virginal conception and birth were hidden from men, even though in the eyes of his contemporaries of Nazareth He was regarded as "the carpenter's son" (Mt. 13:55) *(ut putabatur filius Joseph:* Lk. 3:23), nevertheless the very reality and essential truth of His conception and birth is in itself far removed from what in the Old Testament tradition was exclusively in favor of marriage, and which rendered continence incomprehensible and out of favor. How, therefore, could "continence for the kingdom of heaven" be understood, if the expected Messiah was to be "David's descendant," and as was held, was to be a son of the royal stock "according to the flesh"? Only Mary and Joseph, who had lived the mystery of His conception and birth, became the first witnesses of a fruitfulness different from that of the flesh, that is, of a fruitfulness of the Spirit: "That which is conceived in her is of the Holy Spirit" (Mt. 1:20).

GRADUALLY REVEALED

3. The story of Jesus' birth is certainly in line with that "continence for the kingdom of heaven" of which Christ will speak one day to His disciples. This event, however, remains hidden to the men of that time and also to the disciples. Only gradually will it be revealed to the eyes of the Church on the basis of the witness and texts of the Gospels of Matthew and Luke. The marriage of Mary and Joseph (in which the Church honors Joseph as Mary's spouse, and Mary as his spouse), conceals within itself, at the same time, the *mystery* of the perfect communion of the persons, of the man and the woman in the conjugal pact, and also the mystery of that singular "continence for the kingdom of heaven": a continence that served, in the history of salvation, the most perfect "fruitfulness of the Holy Spirit." Indeed, it was in a certain sense the absolute fullness of that spiritual fruitfulness, since precisely in the

Nazareth conditions of the pact of Mary and Joseph in marriage and in continence, there was realized the gift of the Incarnation of the Eternal Word: the Son of God, consubstantial with the Father, was conceived and born as man from the Virgin Mary.

The grace of the hypostatic union is connected precisely with this—I would say—absolute fullness of supernatural fruitfulness, fruitfulness in the Holy Spirit, participated by a human creature, Mary, in the order of "continence for the kingdom of heaven." Mary's divine maternity is also, in a certain sense, a superabundant revelation of that fruitfulness in the Holy Spirit to which man submits his spirit, when he freely chooses continence "in the body": namely, continence "for the kingdom of heaven."

EXAMPLE OF JESUS

4. This image had to be gradually revealed to the Church's awareness in the ever new generations of confessors of Christ, when —together with the Gospel of the infancy— there was consolidated in them the certainty of the divine maternity of the Virgin, who had conceived by the Holy Spirit. Even though only indirectly—yet essentially and fundamentally —this certainly should *help one to understand*, on the one hand, the sanctity of marriage, and

on the other, the disinterestedness in view "of the kingdom of heaven," of which Christ had spoken to His disciples. Nonetheless, when He spoke to them about it for the first time (as attested by the evangelist Matthew in chapter 19:10-12), that great mystery of His conception and birth was completely unknown to them. It was hidden from them as it was from all the hearers and interlocutors of Jesus of Nazareth.

When Christ spoke of those who "had made themselves eunuchs for the kingdom of heaven" (Mt. 19:12), the disciples could understand it *only on the basis of His personal example*. Such a continence must have impressed itself on their consciousness as a particular trait of likeness to Christ, who had Himself remained celibate "for the kingdom of heaven." The departure from the tradition of the Old Covenant, in which marriage and procreative fruitfulness "in the body" were a religiously privileged condition, had to be effected especially on the basis of the example of Christ Himself. Only little by little did it come to be realized that "for the sake of the kingdom of heaven" attaches a particular meaning to that spiritual and supernatural fruitfulness of man which comes from the Holy Spirit (Spirit of God), and that fruitfulness, in a specific sense and in determined cases, is served precisely by continence "for the kingdom of heaven."

More or less all these elements of Gospel awareness (that is, of an exact consciousness of the New Covenant in Christ) concerning continence are found in Paul. We shall seek to show that at a suitable time.

To sum up, we can say that the principal theme of today's reflection has been the relationship between continence "for the kingdom of heaven," proclaimed by Christ, and the supernatural fruitfulness of the human spirit which comes from the Holy Spirit.

Continence—an Effective and Privileged Way

General audience of March 31, 1982.

1. We continue our reflections on celibacy and on virginity for the kingdom of heaven, on the basis of Matthew's Gospel (Mt. 19:10-12).

Speaking of continence for the kingdom of heaven and basing it on the example of His own life, Christ undoubtedly wished that His disciples should understand it especially in relation to the "kingdom" which He had come to announce and for which He indicated the correct ways. The continence He spoke of is precisely one of these ways and, as appears from the context of Matthew's Gospel, it is a particularly effective and privileged way. Indeed, that preference given to celibacy and virginity "for the kingdom" was an absolute novelty in comparison with the Old Covenant tradition, and had a decisive significance both for the ethos and the theology of the body.

HIS OWN LIFE—A WITNESS

2. Christ, in His statement, points out especially its finality. He says that the way of continence, to which His own life bore witness,

not only exists and not only is it possible, but it is particularly efficacious and important for "the kingdom of heaven." And so should it be, seeing that Christ chose it for Himself. If this way is so efficacious and important, then continence for the kingdom of heaven must have a *special value*. As we have already noted before, Christ did not approach the problem on the same level and according to the same line of reasoning in which it was posed by the disciples when they said: "If such is the case...it is not expedient to marry" (Mt. 19:10). Their words implied a certain utilitarianism. Christ, however, in His reply indicated indirectly that if marriage, true to its original institution by the Creator (we recall that the Master at this very point spoke of the "beginning"), is fully appropriate and of a value that is fundamental, universal and ordinary, then continence, on its part, possesses a particular and "exceptional" value for this kingdom. It is obviously a question of continence consciously chosen for supernatural motives.

3. If Christ in His statement points out, before all else, the supernatural finality of that continence, He does so, not only in an objective sense, but also in a sense explicitly subjective— that is to say, He indicates the necessity of a motivation that corresponds adequately and fully to the objective finality implied by the expression "for the kingdom." To achieve the

end in question—that is, to rediscover in continence that particular spiritual fruitfulness which comes from the Holy Spirit—then continence must be willed and chosen by virtue of a deep faith which does not merely show us the kingdom of God in its future fufillment, but permits us and makes it possible for us to identify ourselves in a special way with the truth and reality of that kingdom, such as it is revealed by Christ in His Gospel message and especially by the personal example of His life and manner of behavior. Hence, it was said above that continence "for the kingdom of heaven"—as an unquestionable sign of the "other world"—bears in itself especially the interior dynamism of the mystery of the redemption of the body (cf. Lk. 20:35), and in this sense it possesses also the characteristic of a particular likeness to Christ. He who consciously chooses such continence, chooses, in a certain sense, a special participation in the mystery of the redemption (of the body). He wishes in a particular way to complete it, so to say, in his own flesh (cf. Col. 1:24), finding thereby also the imprint of a likeness to Christ.

RIGHT MOTIVATION

4. All this refers to the motivation of the choice (or to its finality in the subjective sense). In choosing continence for the kingdom of

heaven, man "should" let himself be guided precisely by this motivation. Christ, in the case in question, does not say that man is obliged to it (in any event it is certainly not a question of a duty deriving from a commandment). However, without any doubt, His concise words on continence "for the kingdom of heaven" place in bold relief its precise motivation. And they point that out (that is, they indicate the finality of which the subject is well aware), both in the first part of the entire statement, and also in the second part, by indicating that here it is a question of a particular choice—a choice that is proper to a rather exceptional vocation, and not one that is universal and ordinary.

At the beginning, in the first part of His statement, Christ speaks of an understanding ("not all men can understand it, but only those to whom it is given": Mt. 19:11); and it is not a question of an "understanding" in the abstract, but such as to influence the decision, the personal choice, in which the "gift," that is, the grace should find an adequate response in the human will. Such an "understanding" involves the motivation. Subsequently, the motivation influences the choice of continence, accepted after having understood its significance "for the kingdom of heaven." Christ, in the second part of His statement, declares then that a man "makes himself" a eunuch when he chooses continence for the kingdom of heaven and makes it the fundamental situation or state of his whole earthly life. In such a firm decision there exists a supernatural motivation, from which the decision itself originated. It subsists by renewing itself, I would say, continually.

VIEWED IN THE MYSTERY OF REDEMPTION

5. Previously we have already turned our attention to the particular significance of the final assertion. If Christ, in the case quoted, speaks of "making oneself" a eunuch, not only does He place in relief the specific importance of this decision which is explained by the motivation born of a deep faith, but He does not even seek to conceal the anguish that such a decision and its enduring consequences can have for a man for the normal (and on the other hand noble) inclinations of his nature.

The reference to "the beginning" in the problem of marriage enabled us to discover all the original beauty of that vocation of man, male and female: a vocation that comes from God and corresponds to the twofold constitution of man, as well as to the call to the "communion of persons." In preaching continence for the kingdom of God, Christ not only takes a stand against the whole tradition of the Old Covenant, according to which marriage and procreation were, as we have said, religiously privileged, but He expresses Himself, in a certain sense, even in opposition to that "beginning" to which He Himself had appealed and perhaps also for this He nuances His words with that particular "rule of understanding" to which we referred above. The analysis of the "beginning" (especially on the basis of the Jahwist text) had demonstrated in fact that, even though it be possible to conceive man as solitary before God, however God Himself draws him from this "solitude" when He says: "It is not good that the man should be alone; I will make him a helper fit for him" (Gn. 2:18).

6. So, then, the double aspect, male and female, proper to the very constitution of humanity, and the unity of the two which is based on it, remain "from the beginning," that is, to their ontological depth, the work of God. Christ, speaking of continence "for the kingdom of heaven," has before Him this reality. Not without reason does He speak of it (according to Matthew) in the most immediate context in which He refers precisely "to the beginning," that is, to the divine beginning of marriage in the very constitution of man.

On the strength of Christ's words it can be asserted that not only does marriage help us to understand continence for the kingdom of heaven, but also continence itself sheds a particular light on marriage viewed in the mystery of creation and redemption.

"Superiority" of Continence Does Not Devaluate Marriage

General audience of April 7, 1982.

Today's meeting falls during Holy Week, that is, during the central period of the liturgical year, which calls us to relive the so very important and basic events in the redemption brought about by Christ: the Last Supper, when Christ instituted the Sacrament of the Eucharist, mystically anticipating and passing down by means of the priesthood the sacrifice of the cross; the passion of Jesus Christ, beginning with the agony of Gethsemane up to the cruel crucifixion and death on the cross; and finally the glorious resurrection on the joyful Sunday of Easter.

They are moving, touching days, filled with a special atmosphere that all Christians know and feel. Therefore, they must be days of interior silence, of more intense prayer and special meditation on the extraordinary historical events which mark mankind's redemption and which give true meaning to our existence.

I therefore urge you to live intensely these holy days with great love, and to take part in the liturgical functions in order to penetrate more deeply into the content of the Faith so that you may draw from it resolutions for an authentic commitment to a consistently Christian life. Let us accompany the holy Virgin along the road of Christ's passion, looking on the tragedy of Good Friday in the light of a victorious Easter, in order to learn that all suffering must be accepted and interpreted in the perspective of the glorious resurrection and, most of all, to unite ourselves to Christ, who loved us so much that He gave Himself for us (cf. Gal. 2:20).

1. With our gaze fixed on Christ the Redeemer, let us now continue our reflections on celibacy and virginity "for the kingdom of heaven," according to the words of Christ recorded in the Gospel of Matthew (Mt. 19:10-12).

MAN "ALONE" BEFORE GOD

In proclaiming continence "for the kingdom of heaven," Christ fully accepts all that from the beginning was wrought and instituted by the Creator. Consequently, on the one hand, continence must demonstrate that man, in his deepest being, is not only "dual," but also (in this duality) "alone" before God, with God. Nevertheless, on the other hand, what is an invitation to solitude for God in the call to continence for the kingdom of heaven at the same time respects both the "dual nature of mankind" (that is, his masculinity and femininity), and the dimension of communion of existence that is proper to the person. Whoever, in compliance with Christ's words, correctly "comprehends" the call to continence for the kingdom of heaven and responds to it, thereby preserves the integral truth of his own humanity, without losing along the way any of the essential elements of the vocation of the person created in "God's image and likeness." This is important to the idea itself, or rather, to the idea of continence, that is, for its objective content, which appears in Christ's teachings as radically new. It is equally important to the accomplishment of that ideal; that is, in order for the actual decision taken by man or woman to live in celibacy or virginity for the kingdom of heaven (he who "makes himself" a eunuch, to use Christ's words) to be fully sincere in its motivation.

"BREAKING AWAY FROM"

2. From the context of the Gospel according to Matthew (Mt. 19:10-12), it can be seen sufficiently clearly that here it is not a question of diminishing the value of matrimony in favor of continence, nor of lessening the value of one

in comparison with the other. Instead, it is a question of "breaking away from," with full awareness, that which in man, by the Creator's will, causes him to marry, and to move toward continence, which reveals itself to the concrete man, masculine or feminine, as a call and gift of particular eloquence and meaning "for the kingdom of heaven." Christ's words (Mt. 19:11-12) arise from the reality of man's condition and, with the same realism, lead him out towards the call in which, in a new way even though remaining "dual" by nature (that is, directed as man towards woman, and as woman, towards man), he is capable of discovering in his solitude, which never ceases to be a personal dimension of everyone's dual nature, a new and even fuller form of intersubjective communion with others. This guidance of the call explains explicitly the expression "for the kingdom of heaven"; indeed, the achievement of this kingdom must be found along the line of the authentic development of the image and likeness of God in its trinitarian meaning, that is, precisely "of communion." By choosing continence for the kingdom of heaven, man has the knowledge of being able in that way to fulfill himself "differently" and, in a certain way, "more" than through matrimony, becoming a "true gift to others" (GS 24).

3. Through the words recorded in Matthew (Mt. 19:11-12), Christ makes us under-

stand clearly that that "going" towards continence for the sake of the kingdom of heaven is
linked with a voluntary giving up of matrimony, that is, of the state in which man and
woman (according to the meaning the Creator
gave to their union "in the beginning") become
gifts to one another through their masculinity
and femininity, also through their physical
union. Continence means a conscious and voluntary renouncement of that union and all that
is connected to it in the full meaning of life and
human society. The man who renounces matrimony also gives up procreation as the foundation of the family, concessive renouncements
and voluntary children. The words of Christ to
which we refer indicate without doubt this kind
of renunciation, although they do not go into
detail. And the way in which these words were
stated leads us to assume that Christ understood the importance of such a sacrifice, and
that He understood it not only in view of the
opinions on the subject prevailing in Jewish
society at that time. He understood the importance of this sacrifice also in relationship to the
good which matrimony and the family in themselves constitute due to their divine institution.
Therefore, through the way in which He states
the words He makes it understood that breaking away from the circle of the good that He
Himself calls "for the sake of the kingdom of
heaven," is connected with a certain self-

sacrifice. That break also becomes the beginning of successive self-sacrifices that are indispensable if the first and fundamental choice must be consistent in the breadth of one's entire earthly life; and thanks only to such consistency that choice is internally reasonable and not contradictory.

CONCUPISCENCE REMAINS

4. In this way, in the call to continence as it was stated by Christ—concisely but at the same time very precisely—the outline and dynamism of the mystery of the redemption emerge, as has previously been stated. It is the same profile under which Jesus, in His Sermon on the Mount, pronounced the words about the need to guard against concupiscence, against the desire that begins with "looking at" and becomes at that very moment "adultery in the heart." Behind Matthew's words, both in chapter 19 (verses 11-12) and in chapter 5 (verses 27-28), are found the same anthropology and the same ethos. In the invitation to voluntary continence for the kingdom of heaven, the prospects of this ethos are enlarged upon; in the overall view of the words of the Sermon on the Mount is found the anthropology of "historical" man. In the overall view of the words on voluntary continence, essentially the same anthropology remains, but illuminated by the

prospect of the "kingdom of heaven," in other words, of the future anthropology of the resurrection. Nonetheless, along the path of this voluntary continence during earthly life, the anthropology of the resurrection does not replace the anthropology of "historical" man, in whom remains at the same time the heritage of threefold concupiscence, the heritage of sin together with the heritage of redemption, who must take the decision about continence "for the kingdom of heaven." He must put this decision into effect, subjugating the sinfulness of his human nature to the forces that spring from the mystery of the redemption of the body. He must do so just as any other man does who has not taken a similar decision and whose way remains that of matrimony. The only difference is the type of responsibility for the good chosen, just as the type of good chosen is different.

EXCEPTIONAL CALL

5. In His pronouncement, does Christ perhaps suggest the superiority of continence for the kingdom of heaven to matrimony? Certainly, He says that this is an "exceptional" vocation, not a "common" one. In addition He affirms that it is particularly important and necessary to the kingdom of heaven. If we understand superiority to matrimony in this

sense, we must admit that Christ set it out implicitly; however, He does not express it directly. Only Paul will say of those who choose matrimony that they do "well"; and about those who are willing to live in voluntary continence, he will say that they do "better" (1 Cor. 7:38).

6. That is also the opinion of the whole of Tradition, both doctrinal and pastoral. The "superiority" of continence to matrimony in the authentic Tradition of the Church never means disparagement of matrimony or belittlement of its essential value. It does not even mean a shift, even implicit, on the Manichean positions, or a support of ways of evaluating or acting based on the Manichean understanding of the body and sexuality, matrimony and procreation. The evangelical and authentically Christian superiority of virginity and continence is, consequently, dictated by the motive of the kingdom of heaven. In Christ's words recorded in Matthew (Mt. 19:11-12) we find a solid basis for admitting only this superiority, while we do not find any basis whatever for any disparagement of matrimony which, however, could have been present in the recognition of that superiority.

Marriage and Continence Complement Each Other

General audience of April 14, 1982.

Beloved brothers and sisters!

The solemnity of Easter, just passed, fills our souls during this week, and will fill them during all of Easter time with that joy which comes from the commemoration of Christ's glorious resurrection. We have traveled the tortured way of His passion, from the Last Supper up to the agony and death on the cross; and we have awaited in the deep silence of Holy Saturday the joyful peal of the "Blessed Night" of the Vigil.

Easter must not remain only on the emotional level or in our memories; it must leave a mark, it must continuously be felt in our lives, every day it must encourage us to consistently give Christian witness.

Easter is to the Christian an invitation to live "a new life": "If then you have been raised with Christ, seek the things that are above, where Christ is seated at the right hand of God. Set your minds on things that are above..." (Col. 3:1-2).

During life's happy or sad moments, at work, in one's profession, at school, the Christian must bear witness that Christ is truly risen, following Him with courage and love, placing all his faith and every hope in Him.

I wish from my heart that the memory of the Easter festivities will accompany you all and make you feel the joyful presence of the risen Christ.

NO REFERENCE
TO INFERIORITY OF MARRIAGE

1. Let us now continue our reflections of the previous weeks on the words about continence "for the sake of the kingdom of heaven" which, according to the Gospel of Matthew (19:10-12), Christ addressed to His disciples.

Let us say once more that these words, as concise as they are, are admirably rich and precise, rich with a number of implications both of doctrinal and pastoral nature. At the same time they establish a proper limit on the subject. Therefore, any kind of Manichaean interpretation decidedly goes beyond that limit, so that, according to what Christ said in the Sermon on the Mount, there is lustful desire "in the heart" (Mt. 5:27-28).

In Christ's words on continence "for the kingdom of heaven" there is no reference to the "inferiority" of marriage with regard to the "body," or in other words with regard to the essence of marriage, consisting in the fact that man and woman join together in marriage, thus becoming "one flesh" (Gn. 2:24: "The two will become one flesh"). Christ's words recorded in Matthew 19:11-12 (as also the words of Paul in his first letter to the Corinthians, chapter 7) give no reason to assert the "inferiority" of marriage, nor the "superiority" of virginity or celibacy inasmuch as by their nature virginity and celibacy consist in abstinence from the conjugal "union in the body." Christ's words on this point are quite clear. He proposes to His disciples the ideal of continence and the call to it, not by reason of inferiority, nor with prejudice against conjugal "union of the body," but only "for the sake of the kingdom of heaven."

RELATIONSHIP BETWEEN MARRIAGE AND CONTINENCE

2. In this light a deeper clarification of the very expression "for the sake of the king-

dom of heaven" is particularly useful, and this is what we shall try to do in the following, at least briefly. However, with regard to the correct understanding of the relationship between marriage and continence that Christ speaks about, and the understanding of that relationship as the whole of Tradition has understood it, it is worthwhile to add that "superiority" and "inferiority" fall within the limits of the same complementarity of marriage and continence for the kingdom of God.

Marriage and continence are neither opposed to each other, nor do they divide the human (and Christian) community into two camps (let us say, those who are "perfect" because of continence and those who are "imperfect" or "less perfect" because of the reality of married life). But these two basic situations, it is true, as it is often said, these two "states," in a certain sense explain and complete each other as regards the existence and life (Christian) of this community, which in its entirety and in each of its members is fulfilled in the dimension of the kingdom of God and has an eschatological orientation, which is precisely of that kingdom. So, with regard to this dimension and this orientation—in which the entire community, that is, all of those who belong to it, must share in the faith—continence "for the kingdom of heaven" has a particular importance and a special eloquence for those who live a married life. Besides, it is known that these constitute the majority.

3. It therefore seems that a complementarity understood in this way finds its foundation in the words of Christ according to Matthew 19:11-12 (and also 1 Cor. 7). On the other hand there is no basis for a presumed counterposition according to which celibates (or unmarried persons), only by reason of their continence, would make up the class of those who are "perfect," and, to the contrary, married persons would make up a class of those who are "imperfect" (or "less perfect"). If, according to a certain theological tradition, one speaks of a state of perfection *(status perfectionis)*, it is done not by reason of continence in itself, but with regard to the entirety of a life based on the evangelical counsels (poverty, chastity and obedience), since this life corresponds to Christ's call to perfection ("If you would be perfect...": Mt. 19:21). Perfection of the Christian life, instead, is measured with the rule of charity. It follows that a person who does not live in the "state of perfection" (that is, in an Institute that bases its life plan on vows of poverty, chastity and obedience), or, in other words, who does not live in a religious institute but in the "world," can *de facto* reach a superior degree of

perfection—whose measure is charity—in comparison to the person who lives in the "state of perfection" with a lesser degree of charity. In any case, the evangelical counsels undoubtedly help us to achieve a fuller charity. Therefore, whoever achieves it, even if he does not live in an institutionalized "state of perfection," reaches that perfection which flows from charity, through fidelity to the spirit of those counsels. Such perfection is possible and accessible to every man, both in a "religious institute" and in the "world."

COMPLEMENTARITY

4. It seems then that the complementarity of marriage and continence for "the kingdom of heaven," in their significance and manifold importance, adequately corresponds to Christ's words recorded in Matthew (19:11-12). In the life of an authentically Christian community the attitudes and values proper to the one and the other state—that is, to one or the other essential and conscious choice as a vocation for one's entire earthly life and in the perspective of the "heavenly Church"—complete and in a certain sense interpenetrate each other. Perfect conjugal love must be marked by that fidelity and that donation to the only Spouse (and also of the fidelity and donation of the Spouse to the only Bride), on

which religious profession and priestly celibacy are founded. Finally, the nature of one and the other love is "conjugal," that is, expressed through the total gift of oneself. Both types of love tend to express that conjugal meaning of the body which "from the beginning" has been inscribed in the personal make-up of man and woman.

We shall return to this point at a later date.

EACH HAS HIS SPECIAL GIFT

5. On the other hand, conjugal love which finds its expression in continence "for the kingdom of heaven" must lead in its normal development to "paternity" or "maternity" in a spiritual sense (in other words, precisely to that "fruitfulness of the Holy Spirit" that we have already spoken about), in a way analogous to conjugal love, which matures in physical paternity and maternity, and in this way confirms itself as conjugal love. For its part, physical procreation also fully responds to its meaning only if it is completed by paternity and maternity in the spirit, whose expression and fruit is all the educative work of the parents in regard to the children born of their conjugal corporeal union.

As can be seen, there are many aspects and spheres of the complementarity between the vocation, in an evangelical sense, of those who "marry and are given in marriage" (Lk. 20:34), and of those who knowingly and voluntarily choose continence "for the kingdom of heaven" (Mt. 19:12).

In his first letter to the Corinthians (which we will analyze later in our considerations), St. Paul will write on this subject: "Each has his special gift from God, one of one kind and one of another" (1 Cor. 7:7).

The Value of Continence
Is Found in Love

General audience of April 21, 1982.

1. Let us continue our reflections on Christ's words about continence "for the sake of the kingdom of heaven."

It is impossible to understand fully the significance and the nature of continence if the last phrase of Christ's statement, "for the sake of the kingdom of heaven," is not complete in its adequate, concrete and objective content. We have previously said that this phrase expresses the motive, or in a certain sense places in relief, the subjective purpose of Christ's call to continence. However, the expression in itself has an objective character, indicating, in fact, an objective reality for which individual persons, men and women, can "make themselves" (as Christ says) eunuchs. The reality of the "kingdom" in Christ's statement according to Matthew (19:11-12) is defined in a precise, but at the same time general way, so as to be able to include all the determinations and particular meanings that are proper to it.

TEMPORAL ESTABLISHMENT

2. The "kingdom of heaven" means the "kingdom of God," which Christ preached in its final, that is, eschatological, completion. Christ preached this kingdom in its temporal realization or establishment, and at the same time He foretold it in its eschatological completion. The temporal establishment of the kingdom of God is at the same time its beginning and its preparation for definitive fulfillment. Christ calls to this kingdom and, in a certain sense, invites everyone to it (cf. the parable of the wedding banquet: Mt. 22:1-14). If He calls some to continence "for the sake of the kingdom of heaven," it follows from the content of that expression that He calls them to participate in a singular way in the establishment of the kingdom of God on earth, through which the definitive phase of the "kingdom of heaven" is begun and prepared.

KINGDOM FOR ALL

3. In this sense we have said that this call bears in itself the particular sign of the very dynamism of the mystery of the redemption of the body. So, therefore, in continence for the

sake of the kingdom of God there is manifested, as we have already mentioned, the renunciation of one's self, taking up one's cross every day, and following Christ (cf. Lk. 9:23), which can reach the point of implying the renunciation of marriage and a family of one's own. All this arises from the conviction that in this way it is possible to contribute more greatly to the realization of the kingdom of God in its earthly dimension with the prospect of eschatological completion. In His statement according to Matthew (19:11-12), Christ says generically that the voluntary renunciation of marriage has this purpose, but He does not say so specifically. In His first statement on this subject, He still does not specify through what concrete obligation this voluntary continence is necessary and even indispensable for the realization of the kingdom of God on earth and for its preparation for future fulfillment. We will hear something further on this point from Paul of Tarsus (1 Cor.) and the rest will be completed by the life of the Church in her historical development, borne by the current of authentic Tradition.

4. In Christ's statement on continence "for the sake of the kingdom of heaven" we do not find any more detailed indication about how to understand that very "kingdom"—with regard to its earthly realization and its definitive

completion—in its specific and "exceptional" relation with those who voluntarily "make themselves eunuchs" for it.

Neither is it said through which particular aspect of the reality that constitutes the kingdom are those associated to it who freely are made "eunuchs." In fact, we know that the kingdom of heaven is for everybody: those who "marry and are given in marriage" also are in a relation with it on earth (and in heaven). For everybody it is the "Lord's vineyard" in which they must work here on earth; and it is subsequently the "Father's house" in which they must be in eternity. Therefore, what is that kingdom for those who choose voluntary continence in view of it?

CLEAR EXPRESSION OF CHRIST'S TEACHING

5. For now, we do not find any answer to this question in Christ's statement as reported by Matthew (19:11-12). It seems that this is in keeping with the character of the whole statement. Christ answers His disciples in such a way as not to keep in line with their thought and their evaluation, in which is contained, at least indirectly, a utilitarian attitude regarding marriage ("If this is the case...it is better not to marry" Mt. 19:10). The Master explicitly evades these general lines of the problem, and

therefore, speaking about continence "for the sake of the kingdom of heaven," He does not indicate in this way why the renunciation of marriage is worthwhile, so that the "it is better" would not be understood by His disciples in any utilitarian sense. He says only that this continence is at times required, if not indispensable, for the kingdom of God. And with this He points out that continence, in the kingdom which Christ preaches and to which He calls, constitutes a particular value in itself. Those who voluntarily choose it must do so with regard to that value it has, and not as a result of any other calculation whatever.

6. This essential tone of Christ's answer, which refers directly to continence itself "for the sake of the kingdom of heaven," can also be referred indirectly to the previous problem of marriage (cf. Mt. 19:3-9). Therefore, taking into consideration His statement as a whole, according to Christ's basic intention, the answer would be as follows: if anyone chooses marriage, he must choose it just as it was instituted by the Creator "from the beginning." He must seek in it those values that correspond to God's plan. If on the other hand anyone decides to pursue continence for the kingdom of heaven, he must seek in it the values proper to such a vocation. In other words, *one must act in conformity with his chosen vocation.*

SEEK VALUES PROPER
TO VOCATION

7. The "kingdom of heaven" is certainly the definitive fulfillment of the aspirations of all men, to whom Christ addresses His message: it is the fullness of the good that the human heart desires beyond the limits of all that can be his lot in this earthly life; it is the maximum fullness of God's bounty toward man. In His conversation with the Sadducees (Mt. 22:24-30; Mk. 12:18-27; Lk. 20:27-40), which we have previously analyzed, we find other details about that "kingdom," or rather about that "other world." There are still more in the whole New Testament. Therefore, it seems that in order to clarify what the kingdom of heaven is for those who choose voluntary continence for the sake of it, the revelation of the nuptial relationship of Christ with the Church has a particular significance. Among the other texts, however, a decisive one is that from the letter to the Ephesians 5:25ff., on which it will be especially well to rely when we take into consideration the question of the sacramentality of marriage.

That text is equally valid both for the theology of marriage and for the theology of continence "for the sake of the kingdom," that is, the theology of virginity or celibacy. It seems that in that very text we find almost

concretized what Christ had said to His disciples, inviting them to voluntary continence "for
the sake of the kingdom of heaven."

8. In this analysis it has already been sufficiently emphasized that Christ's words—with
all their great conciseness—are fundamental,
full of essential content and also characterized
by a certain severity. There is no doubt that
Christ puts out His call to continence in the
perspective of the "other world," but in this call
He puts the emphasis on everything in which
there is expressed the temporal realism of the
decision for such continence, a decision bound
with the will to share in the redeeming work of
Christ.

So, therefore, in the light of Christ's respective words reported by Matthew (19:11-12),
there emerge above all the depth and the
gravity of the decision to live in continence "for
the sake of the kingdom," and the importance
of the renunciation that such a decision implies
finds its expression. Undoubtedly, throughout
all this, through the gravity and depth of the
decision, through the severity and the responsibility that it bears with it, love appears and
shines through: love as the readiness to give the
exclusive gift of oneself for the sake of "the
kingdom of God." However, in Christ's words
this love seems to be veiled by what is put in
the foreground instead. Christ does not conceal
from His disciples the fact that the choice of

continence "for the sake of the kingdom of heaven" is—viewed in the light of temporal categories—a renunciation. That way of speaking to His disciples, which clearly expresses the truth of His teaching and of the demands contained in it, is significant through the whole Gospel; and it is precisely this that confers on it, among other things, so convincing a mark and power.

Celibacy Is a Particular Response to the Love of the Divine Spouse

General audience of April 28, 1982.

1. "There are others who have made themselves eunuchs for the sake of the kingdom of heaven." This is how Christ expresses Himself in St. Matthew's Gospel (Mt. 19:12).

It is natural for the human heart to accept demands, even difficult ones, in the name of love for an ideal, and above all in the name of love for a person (love, in fact, is by its very nature directed toward a person). Therefore in that call to continence "for the sake of the kingdom of heaven," first the disciples themselves, and then the whole living Tradition of the Church, will soon discover the love that is referred to Christ Himself as the Spouse of the Church, the Spouse of souls, to whom He has given Himself to the very limit, in paschal and Eucharistic mystery.

GIVING OF ONESELF

In this way, continence "for the sake of the kingdom of heaven," the choice of virginity or celibacy for one's whole life, has become in the experience of Christ's disciples and followers the act of a particular response of love for the divine Spouse, and therefore has acquired the significance of an act of nuptial love, that is, a nuptial giving of oneself for the purpose of reciprocating in a particular way the nuptial love of the Redeemer; a giving of oneself understood as renunciation, but made above all out of love.

2. In this way we obtained all the wealth of the meaning contained in the very concise, but at the same time very profound, statement of Christ about continence "for the sake of the kingdom of heaven." But now it is fitting that we direct our attention to the significance that these words have for the theology of the body, just as we tried to present and reconstruct the biblical foundations for it "from the beginning." This very analysis of that biblical "beginning," to which Christ refers in His conversation with the Pharisees on the subject of marriage, its unity and indissolubility (cf. Mt. 19:3-9)— shortly *before* addressing to His disciples the words about continence "for the sake of the kingdom of heaven" *(ibid.,* 19:10-12)—this

analysis allows us to recall the profound truth about the nuptial meaning of the human body in its masculinity and femininity, as we deduced at that time from the analysis of the first chapters of Genesis (particularly from 2:23-25). It was in just this way that it was necessary to formulate and specify what we find in those ancient texts.

"IN THE BEGINNING"

3. The modern mentality is accustomed to thinking and speaking about the sexual instinct, transferring onto the level of human reality what is proper to the world of living beings, of animals. Now deep reflection on the concise text of the first and second chapters of Genesis permits us to establish with certainty and conviction that right "from the beginning" a very clear and univocal boundary is laid down in the Bible between the world of animals (*animalia*) and the man created in the image and likeness of God. In that text, though relatively very brief, there is nevertheless enough to demonstrate that man has a clear awareness of what essentially distinguishes him from all other living beings (*animalia*).

4. Therefore, applying to man this substantially naturalistic category that is contained in the concept and in the expression of "sexual

instinct," is not at all appropriate and adequate. It is obvious that such application can become the basis for a certain analogy. In fact, the particular characteristic of man compared with the whole world of living beings *(animalia)* is such that man, understood from the viewpoint of species, can not even basically qualify as an *animal,* but a *rational animal.* Therefore, despite this analogy, applying the concept of "sexual instinct" to man—given the dual nature in which he exists as male or female—nevertheless greatly limits, and in a certain sense "diminishes," what is the very masculinity-femininity in the personal dimension of human subjectivity. It limits and "diminishes" even what for both of them, man and woman, unite to become one flesh (cf. Gn. 2:24). In order to express this in an appropriate and adequate way, we must use also an analysis different from the naturalistic one. And it is precisely the study of the biblical "beginning" that obliges us to do this convincingly. The truth about the nuptial meaning of the human body in its masculinity and femininity, deduced from the first chapters of Genesis (particularly from 2:23-25), that is, the discovery at the time of the nuptial meaning of the body in the personal makeup of the subjectivity of man and woman, seems to be a key concept in this area, and at the same time the only appropriate and adequate one.

THE FREEDOM OF THE GIFT

5. Well now, precisely in relation to this concept, to this truth about the nuptial meaning of the human body, it is necessary to reread and understand Christ's words about continence "for the sake of the kingdom of heaven," spoken in the immediate context of that reference to "the beginning," on which He based His teaching about the unity and indissolubility of marriage. At the basis of Christ's call to continence there is not only the "sexual instinct," in the category, I would say, of a naturalistic necessity, but also the consciousness of the freedom of the gift, which is organically connected with the profound and mature knowledge of the nuptial meaning of the body, in the total makeup of the personal subjectivity of man and woman. Only in relation to such a meaning of the masculinity and femininity of the human person does the call to voluntary continence "for the sake of the kingdom of heaven" find full warranty and motivation. Only and exclusively in this perspective does Christ say, "He who is able to receive this, let him receive it" (Mt. 19:12). With this, He indicates that such continence—although in each case it is above all a "gift"—can be also "received," that is, drawn and deduced from the concept that man has his own psychosomatic "I" in its entirety, and particu-

larly the masculinity and femininity of this "I" in the reciprocal relationship which is as though "by nature" inscribed in every human subjectivity.

6. As we recall from the previous analyses, developed on the basis of the book of Genesis (Gn. 2:23-25), that reciprocal relationship of masculinity and femininity, that reciprocal "for" of man and woman, can be understood in an appropriate and adequate way only in the overall dynamics of the personal subject. Christ's words in Matthew (19:11-12) consequently show that this "for," present "from the beginning" at the basis of marriage, can also be at the basis of continence "for" the kingdom of heaven! Based on the same disposition of the personal subject, thanks to which man fully rediscovers himself through a sincere gift of himself (cf. GS 24), man (male and female) is capable of choosing the personal gift of his very self, made to another person in a conjugal pact in which they become "one flesh," and he is also capable of freely renouncing such a giving of himself to another person, so that, choosing continence "for the sake of the kingdom of heaven," he can give himself totally to Christ. On the basis of the same disposition of the personal subject and on the basis of the same nuptial meaning of the being as a body, male or female, there can be formed the love that commits man to marriage for the whole dura-

tion of his life (cf. Mt. 19:3-10), but there can be formed also the love that commits man to a life of continence "for the sake of the kingdom of heaven" (cf. Mt. 19:11-12). It is precisely about this that Christ is speaking in His overall statement addressed to the Pharisees (cf. Mt. 19:3-10) and then to the disciples (cf. Mt. 19:11-12).

THE NUPTIAL MEANING OF THE BODY

7. It is evident that the choice of marriage, just as it was instituted by the Creator "from the beginning," supposes the learning and the interior acceptance of the nuptial meaning of the body, bound up with the masculinity and femininity of the human person. In fact, this very thing is expressed concisely in the verses of the book of Genesis. In listening to Christ's words addressed to the disciples about continence "for the sake of the kingdom of heaven" (cf. Mt. 19:11-12), we cannot think that this second kind of choice can be made consciously and freely without reference to one's masculinity or femininity and to that nuptial meaning which is proper to man precisely in the masculinity or femininity of his being as a personal subject. Furthermore, in the light of Christ's words, we must admit that this second kind of choice, namely, continence

for the sake of the kingdom of God, comes about also in relation to the masculinity or femininity proper to the person who makes such a choice. It comes about on the basis of full consciousness of that nuptial meaning which masculinity and femininity contain in themselves. If this choice should come about by way of some artificial "prescinding" from this real wealth of every human subject, it would not appropriately and adequately correspond to the content of Christ's words in Matthew 19:11-12.

Here Christ explicitly requires full understanding when He says, "He who is able to receive this, let him receive it" (Mt. 19:12).

Celibacy for the Kingdom Affirms Marriage

General audience of May 5, 1982.

1. In answering the Pharisees' questions about marriage and its indissolubility, Christ referred to the "beginning," that is, to its original institution on the part of the Creator. Since those with whom He was speaking recalled the law of Moses, which provided for the possibility of the so-called "decree of divorce," He answered, "Because of the hardness of your hearts Moses permitted you to divorce your wives, but it was not so from the beginning" (Mt. 19:8).

After the conversation with the Pharisees, Christ's disciples addressed the following words to Him: "'If this is the case of a man with his wife, it is not expedient to marry.' He answered them, 'Not all men can receive this precept, but only those to whom it is given. For there are eunuchs who have been so from birth, and there are eunuchs who have been made

128

eunuchs by men, and there are eunuchs who have made themselves eunuchs for the sake of the kingdom of heaven. He who is able to receive this, let him receive it'" (Mt. 19:10-12).

UNDERSTANDING VALUES

2. Christ's words undoubtedly allude to a conscious and voluntary renunciation of marriage. This renunciation is possible only when one admits an authentic knowledge of that value that is constituted by the nuptial disposition of masculinity and femininity to marriage. In order for man to be fully aware of what he is choosing (continence for the sake of the kingdom), he must also be fully aware of what he is renouncing (it is a question here really of the knowledge of the value in an "ideal" sense; nevertheless this knowledge is after all "realistic"). In this way, Christ certainly demands a mature choice. The form in which the call to continence for the sake of the kingdom of heaven is expressed proves this without a doubt.

RENUNCIATION NOT ENOUGH

3. But a renunciation made with full awareness of the above-mentioned value is not enough. In the light of Christ's words, and also in the light of the whole authentic Christian Tradition, it is possible to deduce that this

renunciation is at the same time a particular form of affirmation of that value from which the unmarried person consistently abstains, following the evangelical counsel. This can seem paradoxical. Nevertheless, it is known that many statements in the Gospel are paradoxical, and those are often the most eloquent and profound. Accepting such a meaning of the call to continence "for the sake of the kingdom of heaven," we draw a correct conclusion, holding that the realization of this call serves also—and in a particular way—to confirm the nuptial meaning of the human body in its masculinity and femininity. The renunciation of marriage for the kingdom of God at the same time highlights that meaning in all its interior truth and personal beauty. We can say that this renunciation on the part of individual persons, men and women, is in a certain sense indispensable, so that the very nuptial meaning of the body can be more easily recognized in all the ethos of human life and above all in the ethos of conjugal and family life.

ASPECTS TO CONSIDER

4. So, therefore, although continence "for the sake of the kingdom of heaven" (virginity, celibacy) orients the life of persons who freely choose it toward the exclusion of the common way of conjugal and family life, nevertheless it

is not without significance for this life: for its style, its value and its evangelical authenticity. Let us not forget that the only key to understanding the sacramentality of marriage is the spousal love of Christ for the Church (cf. Eph. 5:22-23): Christ, the Son of the Virgin, who was Himself a virgin, that is, a "eunuch for the sake of the kingdom of heaven," in the most perfect meaning of the term. It will be convenient for us to take up this point again at a later time.

5. At the end of these reflections there still remains a concrete problem: In what way is this call formed in man, to whom the call to continence for the sake of the kingdom "has been given," on the basis of the knowledge of the nuptial meaning of the body in its masculinity and femininity, and further, as the fruit of such knowledge? In what way is it formed, or rather "transformed"? This question is equally important, both from the viewpoint of the theology of the body, and from the viewpoint of the development of the human personality, which has a personalistic and charismatic character at the same time. If we should want to answer this question exhaustively—in the measure of all the aspects and all the concrete problems that it includes—it would be necessary to make a study based on the relationship between marriage and virginity and between marriage and celibacy. This however would go beyond the limits of the present considerations.

VALUE IN THIS LIFE

6. Remaining within the sphere of Christ's words according to Matthew (19:11-12), we must conclude our reflections with the following affirmation. First, if continence "for the sake of the kingdom of heaven" undoubtedly signifies a renunciation, this renunciation is at the same time an affirmation: an affirmation that arises from the discovery of the "gift," that is, at the same time from the discovery of a new perspective of the personal realization of oneself "through a sincere gift of oneself" (GS 24). This discovery still lies in a profound interior harmony with the significance of the nuptial meaning of the body, bound "from the beginning" to the masculinity or femininity of man as a personal subject. Second, although continence "for the sake of the kingdom of heaven" is identified with the renunciation of marriage, which in the life of a man and woman gives rise to the family, in no way can one see in this a denial of the essential value of marriage. On the contrary, continence serves indirectly to highlight what is most lasting and most profoundly personal in the vocation to marriage, that which in the dimensions of temporality (and at the same time in the perspective of the "other world") corresponds to the dignity of the personal gift, bound to the nuptial meaning of the body in its masculinity or femininity.

CAPITAL SIGNIFICANCE

7. In this way, Christ's call to continence "for the sake of the kingdom of heaven," rightly associated to the reference to the future resurrection (cf. Mt. 21:24-30; Mk. 12:18-27; Lk. 20:27-40), has a capital significance not only for Christian ethos and spirituality, but also for anthropology and for the whole theology of the body, which we discover at its foundation. We remember that Christ, referring to the resurrection of the body in the "other world," said, according to the version of the three synoptic Gospels, "When they rise from the dead...they will neither marry nor be given in marriage..." (Mk. 12:25). These words, already analyzed before, form part of our overall considerations on the theology of the body and contribute to building up this theology.

Voluntary Continence Derives from a Counsel, Not from a Command

General audience of June 23, 1982.

1. Having analyzed Christ's words reported in Matthew's Gospel (Mt. 19:10-12), it is now fitting to pass on to Paul's treatment of the subject of virginity and marriage.

Christ's statement about continence for the sake of the kingdom of heaven is concise and fundamental. In Paul's teaching, as we will soon be convinced, we can distinguish a correlating of the words of the Master. However, the significance of his statement (1 Cor. 7) taken as a whole is assessed in a different way. The greatness of Paul's teaching consists in the fact that in presenting the truth proclaimed by Christ in all its authenticity and identity, he gives it a stamp of his own, in a certain sense his own "personal" interpretation, but which is drawn primarily from the experiences of his apostolic missionary activity, and perhaps directly from the necessity to answer the concrete questions of the men to whom this activity was directed. And so in Paul we encounter the question of the mutual relationship between marriage and celibacy or virginity, the subject that troubled the minds of the first generation of Christ's confessors, the generation of disciples, of apostles, of the first Christian communities. This happened through the converts from hellenism, therefore from paganism, more than through the converts from Judaism. And this can explain the fact that the subject appears precisely in a letter addressed to the community in Corinth, the first.

2. The tone of the whole statement is without doubt a magisterial one. However, the tone as well as the language is also pastoral. Paul teaches the doctrine handed down by the Master to the Apostles, and at the same time he engages in a continuous conversation on the subject in question with the recipients of his letter. He speaks as a classical teacher of morality, facing and resolving problems of conscience, and therefore moralists love to turn preferably to the explanations and resolutions of this first letter to the Corinthians (chapter 7). It is necessary, however, to remember that the ultimate basis for those resolutions is sought in the life and teaching of Christ Himself.

VIRGINITY—A COUNSEL

3. The Apostle emphasizes with great clarity that virginity, or voluntary continence, derives exclusively from a counsel and not from a commandment: "With regard to virgins, I have no command from the Lord, but I give my opinion." Paul gives this opinion "as one who has obtained mercy from the Lord and merits your trust" (1 Cor. 7:25). As is seen from the words quoted, the Apostle, just as the Gospel (cf. Mt. 19:11-12), distinguishes between counsel and commandment. On the basis of the "doctrinal" rule of understanding proclaimed teaching, he wants to counsel, he wishes to give his personal opinions to the men who turned to him. So, therefore, in the first letter to the Corinthians (chapter 7), the "counsel" clearly has two different meanings. The author states that virginity is a counsel and not a commandment, and at the same time he gives his opinions to persons already married and also to those who still must make a decision in this regard, and finally to those who have been widowed. The problem is substantially the same as the one which we meet in the whole statement of Christ reported by Matthew (19:2-12): first on marriage and its indissolubility, and then on voluntary continence for the sake of the kingdom of heaven. Nevertheless, the style of this problem is totally his own: it is Paul's.

4. "If however someone thinks he is not behaving properly with regard to his betrothed, if his passions are strong, and it has to be, let him do as he wishes: he does not sin. Let them marry! But whoever is firmly established in his heart, being under no necessity but having his desire under control, and has determined this in his heart, to keep her as his betrothed, he will do well. So then, he who marries his betrothed does well, and he who refrains from marriage does better" (1 Cor. 7:36-38).

VOLUNTARY CONTINENCE IS BETTER

5. The one who had sought advice could have been a young man who found himself faced with the decision to take a wife, or perhaps a newlywed who in the face of the current asceticism existing in Corinth was reflecting on the direction to give to his marriage. It could have even been a father, or the guardian of a girl, who had posed the question of her marriage. In any case, it would deal directly with the decision that derives from their rights as guardians. In fact, Paul is writing at a time when decisions in general belonged more to parents and guardians than to the young people themselves. Therefore, in answering in this way the question that was addressed to him, he tried to explain very

precisely that the decision about continence, that is, about the life of virginity, must be voluntary, and that only such continence is better than marriage. The expressions, "he does well," "he does better," are completely univocal in this context.

6. So then the Apostle teaches that virginity, or voluntary continence, the young woman's abstention from marriage, derives exclusively from a counsel, and given the appropriate circumstances, it is better than marriage. The question of sin does not enter in any way: "Are you bound to a wife? Do not seek to be free. Are you free from a wife? Do not seek marriage. But if you marry, you do not sin, and if a girl marries, she does not sin" (1 Cor. 7:27-28). Solely on the basis of these words, we certainly cannot make judgments on what the Apostle was thinking or teaching about marriage. This subject will indeed be partially explained in the context of the first letter to the Corinthians (chapter 7) and more fully in the letter to the Ephesians (Eph. 5:21-33). In our case, he is probably dealing with the answer to the question of whether marriage is a sin; and one could also think that in such a question there might be some influence from dualistic prognostic currents, which later become encratism and Manichaeism. Paul answers that the question of sin absolutely

does not enter into play here. It is not a question of the difference between "good" and "evil," but only between "good" and "better." He later goes on to justify why one who chooses marriage "will do well" and one who chooses virginity, or voluntary continence, "will do better."

We will treat of Paul's argumentation in our next reflection.

"The Unmarried Person Is Anxious To Please the Lord!"

General audience of June 30, 1982.

1. St. Paul, in explaining in the seventh chapter of his first letter to the Corinthians the question of marriage and virginity (or continence for the sake of the kingdom of God), tries to give the reason why one who chooses marriage does "well," while one who decides on a life of continence or virginity does "better." This is what he writes: "I tell you this, brothers: the time is already short. From now on, let those who have wives live as though they had none...." And then: "...those who buy, as though they had no goods; those who deal with the world, as though they had no dealings with it: for the form of this world is passing away! I want you to be free from anxieties..." (1 Cor. 7:29-32).

TRUE CONJUGAL LOVE

2. The last words of the text just quoted show that in his argumentation, Paul is referring also to his own experience, which makes his reasoning more personal. He not only formulates the principle and seeks to justify it as such, but he ties it in with personal reflections and convictions arising from his practice of the evangelical counsel of celibacy. The individual expressions and phrases testify to their persuasive power. The Apostle not only writes to his Corinthians: "I wish that all were as I myself am" (1 Cor. 7:7), but he goes further when, referring to men who contract marriage, he writes: "Yet they will have troubles in the flesh, and I would want to spare you that" (1 Cor. 7:28). However, this personal conviction of his was already expressed in the first words of the seventh chapter of the same letter, referring to, in order to modify it as well, this opinion of the Corinthians: "Now concerning the matters about which you wrote, it is well for a man not to touch a woman..." (1 Cor. 7:1).

3. We can ask here: What "troubles in the flesh" did Paul have in mind? Christ spoke only of suffering (or "afflictions"), which a woman experiences when she is to deliver a child, emphasizing, however, the joy (cf. Jn. 16:21) that fills her as a reward for these

sufferings after the birth of her child: the joy of motherhood. Paul, rather, writes of the "tribulations of the body" which spouses expect. Would this be an expression of the Apostle's personal aversion with regard to marriage? In this realistic observation we must see a just warning for those who—as at times young people do—hold that conjugal union and living together must bring them only happiness and joy. The experience of life shows that spouses are not rarely disappointed in what they were greatly expecting. The joy of the union brings with it also those "troubles in the flesh" that the Apostle writes about in his letter to the Corinthians. These are often "troubles" of a moral nature. If by this he intends to say that true conjugal love—precisely that love by virtue of which "a man...cleaves to his wife and the two become one flesh" (Gn. 2:24)—is also a difficult love, he certainly remains on the grounds of evangelical truth and there is no reason here to see symptoms of the attitude that later was to characterize Manichaeism.

A MATURE RESPONSE

4. In his words about continence for the sake of the kingdom of God, Christ does not in any way try to direct His listeners to celibacy or virginity by pointing out to them the "troubles" of marriage. We see rather that He tries to

highlight various aspects, humanly painful, of deciding on continence: both the social reason and reasons of a subjective nature lead Christ to say about the man who makes such a decision, that he makes himself a "eunuch," that is, he voluntarily embraces continence. But precisely thanks to this, there very clearly springs forth the whole subjective significance, the greatness and exceptional character of such a decision: the significance of a mature response to a particular gift of the Spirit.

5. In the letter to the Corinthians, St. Paul does not understand the counsel of continence differently, but he expresses it in a different way. In fact, he writes: "I tell you this, brothers: the time is already short..." (1 Cor. 7:29); and a little later on, "the form of this world is passing away..." (1 Cor. 7:31). This observation about the perishability of human existence and the transience of the temporal world, in a certain sense about the accidental nature of all that is created, should cause "those who have wives to live as though they had none" (1 Cor. 7:29; cf. 7:31) and at the same time should prepare the ground for the teaching on continence. At the center of his reasoning, in fact, Paul places the key phrase that can be joined to Christ's statement, one of its own kind, on the subject of continence for the sake of the kingdom of God (cf. Mt. 19:12).

"ANXIOUS ABOUT
THE AFFAIRS OF THE LORD"

6. While Christ emphasizes the greatness of the renunciation, inseparable from such a decision, Paul demonstrates above all what the "kingdom of God" must mean in the life of the man who has renounced marriage in view of it. And while the triple parallelism of Christ's statement reaches its climax in the word that signifies the greatness of the renunciation voluntarily made ("and there are others who have become eunuchs for the sake of the kingdom of heaven": Mt. 19:12), Paul describes the situation with only one word: the "unmarried" *(agamos);* further on, however, he expresses the whole content of the expression "kingdom of heaven" in splendid synthesis. He says: "The unmarried person is anxious about the affairs of the Lord, how to please the Lord" (1 Cor. 7:32).

Each word of this statement deserves a special analysis.

7. The context of the word "to be anxious" or "to try" in the Gospel of Luke, Paul's disciple, indicates that one must truly seek only the kingdom of God (cf. Lk. 12:31), that which constitutes "the better part," the *unum necessarium* (one thing necessary) (cf. Lk. 10:41). And Paul himself speaks directly about his

"anxiety for all the Churches" (2 Cor. 11:28), about his search for Christ through his concern for the problems of the brethren, for the members of the Body of Christ (cf. Phil. 2:20-21; 1 Cor. 12:25). Already from this context there emerges the whole vast field of the "anxiety" to which the unmarried can totally dedicate his mind, his toil, his heart. Man, in fact, can "be anxious" only about what is truly in his heart.

8. In Paul's statement, the unmarried person is anxious about the affairs of the Lord *(ta tou kyriou)*. With this concise expression, Paul embraces the entire objective reality of the kingdom of God. "The earth is the Lord's and everything in it," he himself will say a little further on in this letter (1 Cor 10:26; cf. Ps. 23[24]:1).

The object of the Christian's concern is the whole world! But Paul, with the name "Lord," describes first of all Jesus Christ (cf. Phil. 2:11), and therefore the "affairs of the Lord" signify in the first place the "kingdom of Christ," His Body which is the Church (cf. Col. 1:18) and all that contributes to its growth. The unmarried person is anxious about all this, and therefore Paul, being in the full sense of the term the "Apostle of Jesus Christ" (1 Cor. 1:1) and minister of the Gospel (cf. Col. 1:23), writes to the Corinthians: "I wish that all of you were as I myself am" (1 Cor. 7:7).

9. Nevertheless, apostolic zeal and most fruitful activity do not yet exhaust what is contained in the Pauline motivation for continence. We could even say that their root and source is found in the second part of the sentence, which demonstrates the subjective reality of the kingdom of God: "The unmarried person is anxious...how to please the Lord." This observation embraces the whole field of man's personal relationship with God. "To please God"—the expression is found in ancient books of the Bible (cf. Dt. 13:19)—is synonymous with life in God's grace and expresses the attitude of one who seeks God, of one who behaves according to His will so as to please Him. In one of the last books of Sacred Scripture this expression becomes a theological synthesis of sanctity. St. John applies it only once to Christ: "I always do what is pleasing to him [the Father]" (Jn. 8:29). St. Paul observes in his letter to the Romans that Christ "did not please himself" (Rom. 15:3).

Between these two observations there is contained all that makes up the content of "pleasing God," understood in the New Testament as following in the footsteps of Christ.

10. It seems that both parts of the Pauline expression overlap: in fact, to be anxious about what "pertains to the Lord," about the "affairs of the Lord," must "please the Lord." On the

other hand, one who pleases God cannot be closed in upon himself, but is open to the world, to everything that is to be led to Christ. These evidently are only two aspects of the same reality of God and His kingdom. Paul nevertheless had to distinguish them in order to show more clearly the nature and the possibility of continence "for the sake of the kingdom of heaven."

Everyone Has His Own Gift from God, Suited to Each One's Vocation

General audience of July 7, 1982.

1. During last Wednesday's meeting, we tried to investigate the reasoning St. Paul uses in his first letter to the Corinthians to convince them that he who chooses marriage does "well," while he who chooses virginity (or continence according to the spirit of the evangelical counsel) does "better" (1 Cor. 7:38). Continuing this meditation today, let us remember that according to Paul, "the unmarried person is anxious...how to please the Lord" (1 Cor. 7:32).

"To please the Lord" has love as its foundation. This foundation arises from a further comparison: the unmarried person is anxious about how to please God, while the married man is anxious also about how to please his wife. In a certain sense, there is apparent here the spousal character of "continence for the sake of the kingdom of God." Man always tries to please the person he loves. "To please God," therefore, is not without this character that distinguishes the interpersonal relationship between spouses. On the one hand, it is an effort of the man who is inclined toward God and seeks the way to please Him, that is, to actively express his love. On the other hand, there corresponds to this aspiration an approval by God, who by accepting man's efforts crowns His own work by giving a new grace: right from the beginning, in fact, this aspiration has been His gift. "Being anxious how to please God" is therefore a contribution of man in the continual dialogue of salvation that has been begun by God. Evidently, every Christian who lives his faith takes part in this dialogue.

INTERIOR INTEGRATION

2. However, Paul observes that the man who is bound by the marriage bond "is divided" (1 Cor. 7:34) by reason of his family obligations (cf. 1 Cor. 7:34). From this remark it apparently follows that the unmarried person would be characterized by an interior integration, by a unification that would allow him to dedicate himself completely to the service of the kingdom of God in all its dimensions. This attitude presupposes abstention from marriage, exclusively "for the sake of the kingdom of God," and a life uniquely directed to this goal. In a

different way the "division" can also sneak into the life of an unmarried person who, being deprived of married life on the one hand, and on the other, of a clear goal for which he should renounce marriage, could find himself faced with a certain emptiness.

3. The Apostle seems to know all this very well, and takes pains to specify that he does not want to "lay any restraint" on one whom he advises not to marry, but he gives this advice to direct him to what is worthy and keeps him united to the Lord without any distractions (cf. 1 Cor. 7:35). These words bring to mind what Christ says to His Apostles during the Last Supper, according to the Gospel of Luke: "You are those who have continued with me in my trials [literally, 'in temptations'], and I prepare a kingdom for you, as the Father has prepared for me" (Lk. 22:28-29). The unmarried person, "being united to the Lord," can be certain that his difficulties will be met with understanding: "For we do not have a high priest who is unable to sympathize with our weaknesses, but one who in every respect has been tempted as we are, yet without sinning" (Heb. 4:15). This allows the unmarried person not so much to immerse himself exclusively in possible personal problems, but rather to include them in the great stream of the sufferings of Christ and of His Body, the Church.

4. The Apostle shows how one can be "united to the Lord": what can be attained by aspiring to a constant remaining with Him, to a rejoicing in His presence *(eupáredron),* without letting himself be distracted by nonessential things *(aperispástos)* (cf. 1 Cor. 7:35).

Paul explains this thought even more clearly when he speaks of the situation of the married woman and of one who has chosen virginity or is widowed. While the married woman must be anxious about "how to please her husband," the unmarried woman "is anxious about the affairs of the Lord, in order to be holy in body and spirit" (1 Cor. 7:34).

5. In order to grasp adequately the whole depth of Paul's thought, we must note that "holiness," according to the biblical concept, is a state rather than an action. It has first of all an ontological character and then also a moral one. Especially in the Old Testament it is a "separation" from what is not subject to God's influence, from what is "profane," in order to belong exclusively to God. "Holiness in body and spirit," therefore, signifies also the sacredness of virginity or celibacy accepted "for the sake of the kingdom of God." And at the same time, what is offered to God must be distinguished by moral purity and therefore presupposes behavior "without spot or wrinkle," "holy

and immaculate," according to the virginal example of the Church in the presence of Christ (Eph. 5:27).

In this chapter of his letter to the Corinthians, the Apostle touches upon the problems of marriage and celibacy or virginity in a way that is deeply human and realistic, keeping in mind the mentality of his audience. Paul's reasoning is to a certain extent *ad hominem*. The new world, the new order of values that he proclaims, must, in the ambience of his audience in Corinth, encounter another "world" and another order of values different even from the one that the words addressed by Christ reached.

UNDERSTANDING MARRIAGE IN CONFORMITY WITH EVANGELICAL VALUES

6. If Paul, with his teaching about marriage and continence, refers also to the transience of the world and human life in it, he certainly does so in reference to the ambience which in a certain sense was programmed for the "use of the world." From this viewpoint, how significant is his appeal to "those who make use of the world" that they·do it "as though they had no dealings with it" (1 Cor. 7:31). From the immediate context it follows that even marriage, in this ambience, was

understood as a way of "making use of the world"—differently from how it had been in the whole Jewish tradition (despite some perversions, which Jesus pointed out in His conversation with the Pharisees and in His Sermon on the Mount). Undoubtedly, all this explains the style of Paul's answer. The Apostle is well aware that by encouraging abstinence from marriage he, at the same time, had to stress a way of understanding marriage that would be in conformity with the whole evangelical order of values. And he had to do it with the greatest realism—that is, keeping before his eyes the ambience to which he was addressing himself, the ideas and the ways of evaluating things that were predominant in it.

7. To men who lived in an ambience where marriage was considered above all one of the ways of "making use of the world," Paul therefore expresses himself with the significant words about virginity or celibacy (as we have seen), and also about marriage itself: "To unmarried persons and to widows I say, 'It is good for them to remain as I am. But if they cannot live in continence, let them marry. It is better to marry than to burn'" (1 Cor. 7:8-9). Almost the same idea had already been expressed by Paul before: "Now concerning the matters about which you wrote, it is well for a man not to touch a woman. But because of the danger of incontinence, each man should have

his own wife and each woman her own husband" (1 Cor. 7:1-2).

8. Does the Apostle, in his first letter to the Corinthians, perhaps look upon marriage exclusively from the viewpoint of a "remedy for concupiscence," as used to be said in traditional theological language? The statements mentioned a little while ago would seem to verify this. However, right next to the statements quoted, we read a passage that leads us to see differently Paul's teaching as a whole, contained in the seventh chapter of his first letter to the Corinthians: "I wish that all were as I myself am; (he repeats his favorite argument for abstaining from marriage)—but each has his own special gift from God, one of one kind, and one of another" (1 Cor. 7:7). Therefore even those who choose marriage and live in it receive a "gift" from God, his "own gift," that is, the grace proper to this choice, to this way of living, to this state. The gift received by persons who live in marriage is different from the one received by persons who live in virginity and choose continence for the sake of the kingdom of God. All the same, it is a true "gift from God," "one's own" gift, intended for concrete persons, and "specific," that is, suited to their vocation in life.

9. We can therefore say that while the Apostle, in his characterization of marriage on the human side (and perhaps still more in view

of the local situation that prevailed in Corinth) strongly emphasizes the reason concerning concupiscence of the flesh, he at the same time, with no less strength of conviction, stresses also its sacramental and "charismatic" character. With the same clarity with which he sees man's situation in relation to concupiscence of the flesh, he sees also the action of grace in every person—in one who lives in marriage no less than in one who willingly chooses continence, keeping in mind that "the form of this world is passing away."

Man's Eternal Destiny—
the Kingdom of God,
Not the World,

General audience of July 14, 1982.

1. During our previous considerations in analyzing the seventh chapter of the first letter to the Corinthians, we have been striving to gather together and understand the teachings and advice that St. Paul gives to the recipients of his letter about the questions concerning marriage and voluntary continence (or abstention from marriage). Declaring that one who chooses marriage "does well" and one who chooses virginity "does better," the Apostle makes reference to the passing away of the world—that is, of everything that is temporal.

It is easy to see that the argument from the perishable and transient nature of what is temporal speaks with much greater force in this case than reference to the reality of the "other world." Although the Apostle here expresses himself with some difficulty, we can nevertheless agree that at the basis of the Pauline interpretation of the subject of "marriage-virginity" there is found not so much the very metaphysics of accidental being (therefore fleeting), but rather the theology of a great expectation, of which Paul was a fervent champion. It is not the "world" that is man's eternal destiny, but the kingdom of God. Man cannot become too attached to the goods that are linked to a perishable world.

"PLEASING THE LORD"

2. Marriage also is tied in with the "form of this world" which is passing away. Here we are in a certain sense very close to the perspective opened by Christ in His statement about the future resurrection (cf. Mt. 22:23-32; Mk. 12:18-27; Lk. 20:27-40). Therefore the Christian, according to Paul's teaching, must live marriage from the point of view of his definitive vocation. And while marriage is tied in with the form of this world which is passing away and therefore in a certain sense imposes the necessity of "being locked" in this transiency, abstention from marriage, on the other hand, could be said to be free of this necessity. It is for this very reason that the Apostle declares that one who chooses continence "does better." Although his argumentation follows this course, nevertheless he decidedly stresses

above all (as we have already seen) the question of "pleasing the Lord" and "being anxious about the affairs of the Lord."

3. It can be admitted that the same reasons speak in favor of what the Apostle advises women who are widowed: "A wife is bound to her husband as long as he lives. If the husband dies, she is free to be married to whom she wishes, only in the Lord. But in my judgment she is happier if she remains as she is. And I think that I have the Spirit of God" (1 Cor. 7:39-40). Therefore, she should remain a widow rather than contract a new marriage.

THE REALITY OF GOD'S GIFT

4. Through what we discover from a thoughtful reading of the letter to the Corinthians, especially chapter seven, the whole realism of the Pauline theology of the body is revealed. If in the letter the Apostle proclaims that "your body is a temple of the Holy Spirit who is in you" (1 Cor. 6:19), at the same time he is fully aware of the weakness and sinfulness to which man is subjected, precisely by reason of the concupiscence of the flesh.

However, this awareness in no way obscures for him the reality of God's gift, which is shared by those who abstain from marriage and also by those who take a wife or husband. In the seventh chapter of the first letter to the Corinthians we find clear encouragement for abstention from marriage, the conviction that he "does better" who decides on this abstention. But we do not find, however, any foundation for considering those who live in marriage as "carnal" and those who instead choose continence for religious motives as "spiritual." In fact, in both the one and the other way of living—today we would say in one and the other vocation—there is operative that "gift" that each one receives from God, that is, the grace that makes the body a "temple of the Holy Spirit," and this remains, in virginity (in continence) as well as in marriage, if the person remains faithful to his gift and, according to his state, does not "dishonor" this "temple of the Holy Spirit," which is his body.

5. In Paul's teaching, contained above all in the seventh chapter of the first letter to the Corinthians, we find no introduction to what will later be called "Manichaeism." The Apostle is fully aware that—insofar as continence for the sake of the kingdom of God is always worthy of recommendation—at the same time grace, that is, "one's own gift from God," also helps married couples in that common life in which (according to the words of Gn. 2:24) they are so closely united that they become "one body." This carnal common life is therefore subject to the power of their "own gift from God." The Apostle writes about it with the

same realism that marks his whole reasoning in the seventh chapter of this letter: "The husband should give to his wife her conjugal rights, and likewise the wife to her husband. For the wife does not rule over her own body, but the husband does; likewise, the husband does not rule over his own body, but the wife does" (verses 3-4).

6. It can be said that these statements are a clear comment in the New Testament on the words scarcely recorded in the book of Genesis (Gn. 2:24). Nevertheless, the words used here, especially the expressions "rights" and "does not rule," cannot be explained apart from the proper context of the marriage covenant, as we have tried to clarify in analyzing the texts of the book of Genesis. We will attempt to do it even more fully when we speak about the sacramentality of marriage, drawing on the letter to the Ephesians (cf. Eph. 5:22-33). At the proper time it will be necessary to return to these significant expressions, which have passed from Paul's vocabulary into the whole theology of marriage.

STRENGTHENING THE MUTUAL PERSONAL BOND

7. For now we will continue to direct our attention to the other sentences in the same passage of the seventh chapter of the first let-

ter to the Corinthians, in which the Apostle addresses these words to married couples: "Do not refuse one another except perhaps by agreement for a season, that you may devote yourselves to prayer; but then come together again, lest Satan tempt you through lack of self-control. I say this by way of concession, not of command" (1 Cor. 7:5-6). This is a very significant text, and it will perhaps be necessary to refer to it again in the context of our meditations on the other subjects.

Very significant is the fact that the Apostle, who in all of his argumentation about marriage and continence makes a clear distinction, as Christ does, between the commandment and the evangelical counsel, feels the need to refer also to "concession," as to an additional rule, above all precisely in reference to married couples and their mutual common life. St. Paul clearly says that conjugal common life and the voluntary and periodic abstinence by the couple must be the fruit of this "gift of God" which is their "own," and that the couple themselves, by knowingly cooperating with it, can maintain and strengthen that mutual personal bond and also that dignity conferred on the body by the fact that it is a "temple of the Holy Spirit who is in them" (cf. 1 Cor. 6:19).

8. It seems that the Pauline rule of "concession" indicates the need to take into consideration all that in some way corresponds to

the very different subjectivity of the man and the woman. Everything in this subjectivity that is not only of a spiritual but also of a psychosomatic nature, all the subjective richness of man which, between his spiritual being and his corporeal, is expressed in the sensitivity whether for the man or for the woman—all this must remain under the influence of the gift that each one receives from God, a gift that is one's own.

As is evident, in the seventh chapter of the first letter to the Corinthians, St. Paul interprets Christ's teaching about continence for the sake of the kingdom of heaven in that very pastoral way that is proper to him, not sparing on this occasion entirely personal accents. He interprets the teaching on continence, on virginity, along parallel lines with the doctrine on marriage, keeping the realism that is proper to a pastor, and at the same time the proportions that we find in the Gospel, in the words of Christ Himself.

9. In Paul's statement we can find again that fundamental structure containing the revealed doctrine about man, that even with his body he is destined for "future life." This supporting structure is at the basis of all the Gospel teaching about continence for the sake of the kingdom of God (cf. Mt. 19:12)—but at the same time there also rests on it the definitive (eschatological) fulfillment of the Gospel

doctrine on marriage (cf. Mt. 22:30; Mk. 12:25; Lk. 20:36). These two dimensions of the human vocation are not opposed to each other, but are complementary. Both furnish a full answer to one of man's fundamental questions, the question about the significance of "being a body," that is, about the significance of masculinity and femininity, of being "in the body" a man or a woman.

10. What we usually define here as theology of the body is shown to be something truly fundamental and constitutive for all anthropological hermeneutics—and at the same time equally fundamental for ethics and for the theology of the human ethos. In each one of these fields we must listen attentively not only to the words of Christ, in which He recalls the "beginning" (Mt. 19:4) or the "heart" as the interior, and at the same time "historical," place of meeting with the concupiscence of the flesh—but we must listen attentively also to the words through which Christ recalled the resurrection in order to implant in the same restless heart of man the first seeds of the answer to the question about the significance of being "flesh" in the perspective of the "other world."

Mystery of the Body's Redemption

General audience of July 21, 1982.

1. "We ourselves, who have the first fruits of the Spirit, groan inwardly as we await...the redemption of our body" (Rom. 8:23). In his letter to the Romans, St. Paul sees this "redemption of the body" in both an anthropological and a cosmic dimension. Creation "in fact was subjected to futility" (Rom. 8:20). All visible creation, all the universe, bears the effects of man's sin. "The whole creation has been groaning in travail together until now" (Rom. 8:22). And at the same time, the whole "creation awaits with eager longing the revelation of the sons of God" and "nourishes the hope of also being freed from the slavery of corruption, to obtain the glorious liberty of the children of God" (Rom. 8:19, 20-21).

THE OBJECT OF HOPE

2. According to Paul, the redemption of the body is the object of hope. This hope was

implanted in the heart of man in a certain sense immediately after the first sin. Suffice it to recall the words of the book of Genesis, which is traditionally called the *"protoevangelium"* (cf. Gn. 3:15), and we could therefore also call them the beginning of the Good News, the first announcement of salvation. The redemption of the body, according to the words of the letter to the Romans, is connected precisely with this hope in which, as we read, "we have been saved" (Rom. 8:24). Through the hope that arises at man's very origin, the redemption of the body has its anthropological dimension: it is the redemption of man. At the same time it radiates, in a certain sense, on all creation, which from the beginning has been bound in a particular way to man and subordinated to him (cf. Gn. 1:28-30). The redemption of the body is therefore the redemption of the world: it has a cosmic dimension.

AWAITING REDEMPTION

3. Presenting in his letter to the Romans the "cosmic" image of redemption, Paul of Tarsus places man at its very center, just as "in the beginning" he had been placed at the very center of the image of creation. It is precisely man, they are men, those who "have the first fruits of the Spirit," who groan inwardly, await-

ing the redemption of their body (cf. Rom. 8:23). Christ, who came to reveal man to man fully by making him aware of his sublime vocation (cf. GS 22), speaks in the Gospel from the divine depths of the mystery of redemption, which finds its specific "historical" subject precisely in Christ Himself. Christ therefore speaks in the name of that hope that had already been implanted in the heart of man in the *"proto-evangelium."* Christ gives fulfillment to this hope, not only with the words of His teaching, but above all with the testimony of His death and resurrection. So therefore the redemption of the body has already been accomplished in Christ. In Him has been confirmed that hope in which "we have been saved." And at the same time, that hope has been opened anew to its definitive eschatological fulfillment. "The revelation of the sons of God" in Christ has been definitively directed toward that "glorious liberty" that is to be definitively shared by the "children of God."

AUTHENTIC THEOLOGY

4. To understand all that "the redemption of the body" implies according to Paul's letter to the Romans, an authentic theology of the body is necessary. We have tried to construct this theology by referring first of all to the words of Christ. The constitutive elements of

the theology of the body are contained in what Christ says, recalling "the beginning," concerning the question about the indissolubility of marriage (cf. Mt. 19:8), in what He says about concupiscence, referring to the human heart in His Sermon on the Mount (cf. Mt. 5:28), and also in what He says in reference to the resurrection (cf. Mt. 22:30). Each one of these statements contains a rich content of an anthropological and ethical nature. Christ is speaking to man—and He is speaking about man: about man who is "body" and who has been created male and female in the image and likeness of God. He is speaking about man whose heart is subject to concupiscence, and finally, about man before whom is opened the eschatological prospect of the resurrection of the body.

"Body," according to the book of Genesis, means the visible aspect of man and his belonging to the visible world. For St. Paul it means not only this belonging, but sometimes also the alienation of man by the influence of the Spirit of God. Both the one meaning and the other are in relation to the "resurrection of the body."

SERMON ON THE MOUNT

5. Since in the previously analyzed texts Christ is speaking from the divine depths of the mystery of redemption, His words serve that

very hope which is spoken of in the letter to the Romans. "The redemption of the body," according to the Apostle, is ultimately what "we await." So we await precisely the eschatological victory over death, to which Christ gave testimony above all by His resurrection. In the light of the paschal mystery, His words about the resurrection of the body and about the reality of the "other world," recorded by the synoptic Gospels, have acquired their full eloquence. Christ, and then Paul of Tarsus, proclaimed the call for abstention from marriage "for the sake of the kingdom of heaven" precisely in the name of this eschatological reality.

6. However, the "redemption of the body" is expressed not only in the resurrection as victory over death. It is present also in Christ's words addressed to "historical" man, when they confirm the principle of the indissolubility of marriage as a principle coming from the Creator Himself, and also when, in the Sermon on the Mount, Christ calls man to overcome concupiscence, even in the uniquely interior movements of the human heart. The key to both the one and the other of these statements must be to say that they refer to human morality, they have an ethical meaning. Here it is a question not of the eschatological hope of the resurrection, but of the hope of victory over sin, which can be called the hope of every day.

STRENGTH TO CONQUER EVIL

7. In his daily life man must draw from the mystery of the redemption of the body the inspiration and the strength to overcome the evil that is dormant in him under the form of threefold concupiscence. Man and woman, bound in marriage, must daily undertake the task of the indissoluble union of that covenant which they have made between them. But also a man or a woman who has voluntarily chosen continence for the sake of the kingdom of heaven must daily give living witness of fidelity to that choice, heeding the directives of Christ in the Gospel and those of Paul the Apostle in his first letter to the Corinthians. In each case it is a question of the hope of every day, which in proportion to the normal duties and difficulties of human life helps to overcome "evil with good" (Rom. 12:21). In fact, "in hope we have been saved": the hope of every day manifests its power in human works and even in the very movements of the human heart, clearing a path, in a certain sense, for the great eschatological hope bound with the redemption of the body.

VICTORY OVER SIN

8. Penetrating daily life with the dimension of human morality, the redemption of the body helps first of all to discover all this

good in which man achieves the victory over sin and concupiscence. Christ's words, which spring from the divine depths of the mystery of redemption, permit us to discover and strengthen that bond that exists between the dignity of the human being (man or woman) and the nuptial meaning of his body. They permit us to understand and put into practice, on the basis of that meaning, the mature freedom of the gift, which in one way is expressed in indissoluble marriage and in another way through abstention from marriage for the sake of the kingdom of God. In these different ways Christ fully reveals man to man, making him aware of "his sublime vocation." This vocation is inscribed in man according to all his psycho-physical makeup, precisely through the mystery of the redemption of the body.

Everything we have tried to do in the course of our meditations in order to understand Christ's words has its ultimate foundation in the mystery of the redemption of the body.

Marital Love Reflects God's Love for His People

General audience of July 28, 1982.

1. Today we begin a new chapter on the subject of marriage, reading the words of St. Paul to the Ephesians:

"Wives, be subject to your husbands as to the Lord. For the husband is the head of the wife as Christ is the head of the Church, his body, and is himself its savior. As the Church is subject to Christ, so let wives also be subject in everything to their husbands.

"Husbands, love your wives, as Christ loved the Church and gave himself up for her, that he might sanctify her, having cleansed her by the washing of water with the word, that he might present the Church to himself in splendor, without spot or wrinkle or any such thing, that she might be holy and without blemish. Even so husbands should love their wives as their own bodies. He who loves his wife loves himself. For no man ever hates his own flesh, but nourishes and cherishes it, as Christ does the Church, because we are members of his body. 'For this reason a man shall leave his father and mother and be joined to his wife, and the two shall become one.' This is a great mystery, and I mean in reference to Christ and the Church. However, let each one of you love his wife as himself, and let the wife see that she respects her husband" (Eph. 5:22-33).

SIMPLE AND FUNDAMENTAL

2. We should now subject to deep analysis the quoted text contained in this fifth chapter of the letter to the Ephesians, just as we have previously analyzed the individual words of Christ that seem to have a key significance for the theology of the body. The analysis dealt with the words with which Christ recalled "the beginning" (Mt. 19:4; Mk. 10:6), the human "heart," in the Sermon on the Mount (Mt. 5:28), and the future resurrection (cf. Mt. 22:30; Mk. 12:25; Lk. 20:35). What is contained in the passage of the letter to the Ephesians constitutes almost a "crowning" of those other concise key words. If there has emerged from them the theology of the body along its evangelical lines, simple and at the same time fundamental, it is in a certain sense necessary to presuppose that theology in interpreting the above-mentioned passage of the letter to the Ephesians. Therefore if we want to

interpret that passage, we must do so in the light of what Christ told us about the human body. He spoke not only reminding historical man, and therefore man himself, always "contemporary," about concupiscence (in his "heart"), but also revealing, on the one hand, the prospectives of "the beginning" or original innocence or justice, and on the other hand, the eschatological prospectives of the resurrection of the body, when "they will neither marry nor be given in marriage" (cf. Lk. 20:35). All of this is a part of the theological viewpoint of the "redemption of our body" (Rom. 8:23).

MEANINGS CONVERGE

3. Even the words of the author of the letter to the Ephesians[1] are centered on the body, and that is in both its metaphorical meaning, namely the Body of Christ which is the Church, and its concrete meaning, namely the human body in its perennial masculinity and femininity, in its perennial destiny for union in marriage, as the book of Genesis says: "The man will leave his father and his mother and will cling to his wife and the two will be one flesh" (Gn. 2:24).

In what way do these two meanings of the body appear together and converge in the passage of the letter to the Ephesians? And why do they appear together and converge there? These are the questions we must ask, expecting not so much immediate and direct answers, but possibly studied and long-term answers for which we have been prepared by our previous analyses. In fact, that passage from the letter to the Ephesians cannot be correctly understood except in the full biblical context, considering it as the "crowning" of the themes and truths which, through the Word of God revealed in Sacred Scripture, ebb and flow like long waves. They are central themes and essential truths. And therefore the quoted text from the letter to the Ephesians is also a key and "classic" text.

4. It is a text that is well known in the liturgy, in which it always appears in relation to the sacrament of marriage. The Church's *lex orandi* sees in it an explicit reference to this sacrament: and the *lex orandi* presupposes and at the same time always expresses the *lex credendi*. Admitting this premise, we must immediately ask ourselves: In this "classic" text of the letter to the Ephesians, how does the truth about the sacramentality of marriage emerge? In what way is it expressed and confirmed there? It will become clear that the answers to these questions cannot be immediate and direct, but gradual and "long-term." This is proved even at first glance at this text, which brings us back to the book of Genesis and therefore to "the beginning," and which, in the

description of the relationship between Christ and the Church, takes from the writings of the Old Testament prophets the well-known analogy of the spousal love between God and His chosen people. Without examining these relationships it would be difficult to answer the question about how the sacramentality of marriage is dealt with in the letter to the Ephesians. We will also see how the answer we are seeking must pass through the whole sphere of the questions previously analyzed, that is, through the theology of the body.

BODY ENTERS INTO DEFINITION OF SACRAMENT

5. The sacrament or the sacramentality—in the more general sense of this term—meets with the body and presupposes the "theology of the body." In fact, the sacrament, according to the generally known meaning, is a "visible sign." The "body" also signifies that which is visible; it signifies the "visibility" of the world and of man. Therefore, in some way, even if in the most general way, the body enters the definition of sacrament, being "a visible sign of an invisible reality," that is, of the spiritual, transcendent, divine reality. In this sign—and through this sign—God gives Himself to man in His transcendent truth and in His love. The sacrament is a sign of grace, and it is an

efficacious sign. Not only does the sacrament indicate grace and express it in a visible way, but it also produces it, and effectively contributes to having grace become part of man, and to realizing and fulfilling in him the work of salvation, the work begun by God from all eternity and fully revealed in Jesus Christ.

6. I would say that already this first glance at the "classic" text of the letter to the Ephesians points out the direction in which our further analyses must be developed. It is necessary that these analyses begin with the preliminary understanding of the text itself. However, they must subsequently lead us, so to say, beyond their limits, in order to understand possibly "to the very depths" how much richness of the truth revealed by God is contained in the scope of that wonderful page. Using the well-known expression from the Constitution *Gaudium et spes,* we can say that the passage we have selected from the letter to the Ephesians, "reveals—in a particular way—man to man, and makes him aware of his lofty vocation" (GS 22), inasmuch as he shares in the experience of the incarnate person. In fact, God, creating him in His image, from the very beginning created him "male and female" (Gn. 1:27).

During the subsequent analyses we will try—above all in the light of the quoted text from the letter to the Ephesians—to understand more deeply the sacrament (particularly, marriage as a sacrament): first in the dimension of the covenant and grace, and afterwards in the dimension of the sacramental sign.

NOTE

1. The question of Pauline authorship of the letter to the Ephesians, acknowledged by some exegetes and denied by others, can be resolved by means of a median supposition which we accept here as a working hypothesis: namely, that St. Paul entrusted some concepts to his secretary, who then developed and refined them.

It is this provisional solution of the question that we have in mind when we speak of "the author of the letter to the Ephesians," the "Apostle," and "St. Paul."

The Call To Be Imitators of God and To Walk in Love

General audience of August 4, 1982.

1. After an introductory glance at this classical text, Ephesians (vv. 22-23), one should examine the way in which this passage—so important both for the mystery of the Church and of the sacramental character of marriage—is situated in the immediate context of the whole letter.

While realizing that there are a number of problems discussed among biblical scholars as regards those to whom the letter was addressed, as regards the authorship and also the date of its composition, one must note that the letter to the Ephesians has a very significant structure. The author begins this letter by presenting the eternal plan of the salvation of man in Jesus Christ.

"God the Father of our Lord Jesus Christ... has chosen us in him that we should be holy and blameless before him. He destined us in love to be his sons through Jesus Christ according to the purpose of his will, to the praise of his glorious grace which he freely bestowed on us in the Beloved. In him we have redemption through his blood, the forgiveness of our trespasses, according to the riches of his grace...as a plan for the fullness of time to unite all things in him..." (Eph. 1:3, 4-7, 10).

The author of the letter to the Ephesians, after having presented in words full of gratitude the plan which, from eternity, is in God, and at a certain time is already fulfilled in the life of humanity, beseeches the Lord that men (and directly those to whom the letter is addressed) may fully know Christ as head: "...he has made him the head over all things for the Church, which is his body, the fullness of him who fills all in all" (1:22-23).

Sinful humanity is called to a new life in Christ, in which the pagans and the Hebrews should join together as in a temple (cf. 2:11-21). The Apostle preaches the mystery of Christ among the pagans, to whom he especially addresses himself in his letter, bending "the knee before the Father" and asking him to grant them "according to the riches of his glory to be strengthened with might through his Spirit in the inner man" (3:14, 16).

VOCATION FLOWING FROM THE DIVINE PLAN

2. After this profound and moving revelation of Christ in the Church, the author passes,

in the second part of the letter, to more detailed instructions aimed at defining the Christian life as a vocation flowing from the divine plan, of which we have previously spoken, namely, from the mystery of Christ in the Church. Here also the author touches various questions which are always valid for the Christian life. He makes an exhortation for the preservation of unity, underlining at the same time, that this unity is constructed on the multiplicity and diversity of Christ's gifts. To each one is given a different gift, but all, as Christians, must "put on the new nature created after the likeness of God in true righteousness and holiness" (4:24). To this is linked the categorical summons to overcome vices and to acquire the virtues corresponding to the vocation which all have obtained through Christ (cf. 4:25-32). The author writes: "Therefore be imitators of God, as beloved children. And walk in love, as Christ loved us and gave himself up for us...in sacrifice" (5:1-2).

CONDEMNS PAGAN ABUSES

3. In the fifth chapter of the letter to the Ephesians these directives become more detailed. The author severely condemns pagan abuses, writing: "For once you were darkness, but now you are light in the Lord; walk as children of light" (5:8). And then: "Therefore do not be foolish but understand what the will

of the Lord is. And do not get drunk with wine (referring to the book of Proverbs 23:31)...but be filled with the Spirit, addressing one another in psalms and hymns and spiritual songs, singing and making melody to the Lord with all your heart" (5:17-19). The author of the letter wishes to illustrate in these words the climate of spiritual life which should animate every Christian community. At this point he then goes on to consider the domestic community, namely, the family. He writes: "Be filled with the Spirit...always and for everything giving thanks in the name of our Lord Jesus Christ, to God the Father. Be subject to one another out of reverence for Christ" (5:20-21). And thus we enter precisely into that passage of the letter which will be the theme of our special analysis. We might easily observe that the essential content of this classical text appears at the meeting of the two principal guidelines of the entire letter to the Ephesians: the first, that of the mystery of Christ which, as the expression of the divine plan for the salvation of man, is realized in the Church; the second, that of the Christian vocation as the model of life of the baptized individual, and of the single communities, corresponding to the mystery of Christ, or to the divine plan for the salvation of man.

4. In the immediate context of the passage quoted, the author of the letter seeks to explain in what way the Christian vocation thus under-

stood should be realized and manifested in the relations between all members of the family; therefore, not merely between the husband and wife (treated of precisely in the passage, 5:22-23 which we have chosen), but also between parents and children. The author writes: "Children, obey your parents in the Lord, for this is right. Honor your father and mother (this is the first commandment with a promise) that it may be well with you and that you may live long on the earth. Fathers, do not provoke your children to anger but bring them up in the discipline and instruction of the Lord" (6:1-4). Following upon that, he speaks of the duty of servants in regard to their masters and, vice versa, of masters in regard to servants, that is, in regard to the slaves (cf. 6:5-9), and this is to be referred also to the directives concerning the family in the broad sense. The family, indeed, comprised not only the parents and children (according to the succession of generations), but included also in the wide sense, the servants or slaves of both sexes.

MORAL OBLIGATIONS

5. Thus, then, the text of the letter to the Ephesians which we proposed as the object of a deeper analysis, is found in the immediate context of the teaching on the moral obligations of the family society (the so-called *Haustaflen*

or domestic codes according to Luther's definition). We find similar instructions also in other letters (e.g., in the letter to the Colossians, chapter 3:18-24, and in the first letter of Peter, 2:13; 3:7). Moreover, this immediate context forms part of our passage, inasmuch as the classical text which we have chosen treats of the reciprocal duties of husbands and wives. However, one must note that *per se* the passage 5:22-23 of the letter to the Ephesians deals exclusively with married couples and marriage, and what regards the family also in the broad sense is already found in the context. First, however, before undertaking a more detailed analysis of the text, it should be added that the whole letter ends with a stupendous encouragement to the spiritual battle (cf. 6:10-20), with brief recommendations (cf. 6:21-22) and with a final farewell (cf. 6:23-24). That call to the spiritual battle seems to be based logically on the line of argument of the entire letter. It is, as it were, the explicit fulfillment of its principal guidelines.

Having thus before our eyes the overall structure of the entire letter to the Ephesians, we shall seek in the first analysis to clarify the meaning of the words: "Be subject to one another out of reverence for Christ" (5:21), addressed to husbands and to wives.

Reverence for Christ— the Basis of Relationship Between Spouses

General audience of August 11, 1982.

1. Today we begin a more detailed analysis of the passage of the letter to the Ephesians 5:21-23. The author, addressing husbands and wives, recommends them to be "subject to one another out of reverence for Christ" (5:21).

Here it is a question of a relationship of a double dimension or degree: reciprocal and communitarian. One clarifies and characterizes the other. The mutual relations of husband and wife should flow from their common relationship with Christ. The author of the letter speaks of the "reverence for Christ" in a sense analogous to that when he speaks of the "fear of God." In this case it is not a question of fear which is a defensive attitude before the threat of evil, but it is above all a case of respect for holiness, for the *sacrum*. It is a question of *pietas,* which, in the language of the Old Testament, was expressed by the term "fear of God" (cf., e.g., Ps. 103:11; Prv. 1:7; 23:17; Sir.

1:11-16). In fact, this *pietas,* arising from a profound awareness of the mystery of Christ, should constitute the basis of the reciprocal relations between husbands and wives.

MORAL INSTRUCTION

2. The text chosen by us, as likewise the immediate context, has a "parenetic" character, that is, of moral instruction. The author of the letter wishes to indicate to husbands and wives the basis of their mutual relationship and their entire conduct. He deduces the relative indications and directives from the mystery of Christ presented at the beginning of the letter. This mystery should be spiritually present in the mutual relationship of spouses. The mystery of Christ, penetrating their hearts, engendering in them that holy "reverence for Christ" (namely, *pietas),* should lead them to "be subject to one another": the mystery of Christ, that is, the mystery of the choice from eternity of each of them in Christ "to be the adoptive sons" of God.

HUSBAND NOT THE "LORD"

3. The opening expression of our passage of Ephesians 5:21-23, which we have approached by an analysis of the remote and immediate context, has quite a special eloquence. The author speaks of the mutual

subjection of the spouses, husband and wife, and in this way he explains the words which he will write afterwards on the subjection of the wife to the husband. In fact we read: "Wives, be subject to your husbands, as to the Lord" (5:22). In saying this, the author does not intend to say that the husband is the "lord" of the wife and that the interpersonal pact proper to marriage is a pact of domination of the husband over the wife. Instead, he expresses a different concept: that is, that the wife can and should find in her relationship with Christ —who is the one Lord of both the spouses—the motivation of that relationship with her husband which flows from the very essence of marriage and of the family. Such a relationship, however, is not one of one-sided domination. Marriage, according to the letter to the Ephesians, excludes that element of the pact which was a burden and, at times, does not cease to be a burden on this institution. The husband and the wife are in fact "subject to one another," and are mutually subordinated to one another. The source of this mutual subjection is to be found in Christian *pietas,* and its expression is love.

NO ONE-SIDED DOMINATION

4. The author of the letter underlines this love in a special way, in addressing himself to husbands. He writes: "You husbands love your

wives...," and by expressing himself in this way, he removes any fear that might have arisen (given the modern sensitivity) from the previous phrase: "Wives, be subject to your husbands." Love excludes every kind of subjection whereby the wife might become a servant or a slave of the husband, an object of unilateral domination. Love makes the husband simultaneously subject to the wife, and thereby subject to the Lord Himself, just as the wife to the husband. The community or unity which they should establish through marriage, is constituted by a reciprocal donation of self, which is also a mutual subjection. Christ is the source and at the same time the model of that subjection, which, being reciprocal "out of reverence for Christ," confers on the conjugal union a profound and mature character. In this source and before this model many elements of a psychological or moral nature are so transformed as to give rise, I would say, to a new and precious "fusion" of the bilateral relations and conduct.

5. The author of the letter to the Ephesians does not fear to accept those concepts which were characteristic of the mentality and of the customs of the times. He does not fear to speak of the subjection of the wife to the husband; he does not fear (also in the last verse of the text quoted by us) to recommend to the wife, that "she respect her husband" (5:33). It

is certain, in fact, that when the husband and wife are subject to one another "out of reverence for Christ," there will be established a just balance, such as to correspond to their Christian vocation in the mystery of Christ.

"OUT OF REVERENCE"

6. Nowadays our contemporary sensitivity is certainly different; quite different, too, are the mentality and customs, and also the social position of women in regard to men. Nevertheless, the fundamental moral principle which we find in the letter to the Ephesians remains the same and produces the same results. The mutual subjection "out of reverence for Christ"—a subjection arising from the basis of Christian *pietas*—produces always that profound and solid structure of the community of the spouses in which there is constituted the true "communion" of the person.

A GREAT ANALOGY

7. The author of the text to the Ephesians, who began his letter with a magnificent vision of God's eternal plan in regard to humanity, does not limit himself to emphasizing merely the traditional aspects of morality or the ethical aspects of marriage, but he goes beyond the scope of teaching, and writing on the reciprocal relationship of the spouses, he discovers therein

the dimension of the very mystery of Christ of which he is the herald and the apostle: "Wives, be subject to your husbands as to the Lord. For the husband is the head of the wife as Christ is the Head of the Church, His Body, and is Himself its Savior. As the Church is subject to Christ, so let wives also be subject in everything to their husbands. Husbands, love your wives, as Christ loved the Church and gave himself up for her..." (5:22-25). In this way, the teaching of this "paranaetic" part of the letter is inserted, in a certain sense, into the very reality of the mystery hidden from eternity in God and revealed to mankind in Jesus Christ. In the letter to the Ephesians we are, I would say, witnesses of a particular meeting of that mystery with the very essence of the vocation to marriage. How are we to understand this meeting? In the text of the letter to the Ephesians it is presented above all as a great analogy. There we read: "Wives, be subject to your husbands *as* to the Lord..."; here we have the first component of the analogy. "For the husband is the head of the wife *as* Christ is the head of the Church...": and here we have the second component which clarifies and motivates the first. "As the Church is subject to Christ, *so* let wives also be subject to their husbands...": the relationship of Christ to the Church, presented previously, is now expressed as a relationship of the Church to

Christ, and here there is contained the successive component of the analogy. Finally: "Husbands, love your wives, as Christ loved the Church and gave Himself up for her...": and this is the ultimate component of the analogy. The remainder of the text of the letter develops the fundamental thought contained in the passage just now quoted; and the entire text of the letter to the Ephesians in chapter 5 (vvs. 21-23) is completely permeated with the same analogy. That is to say, the mutual relationship between the spouses, husband and wife, is to be understood by Christians in the light of the relationship between Christ and the Church.

Deeper Understanding
of the Church and Marriage

General Audience of August 18, 1982.

1. Analyzing the respective components of the letter to the Ephesians we established last Wednesday that the reciprocal relationship between husband and wife is to be understood by Christians as an image of the relationship between Christ and the Church.

This relationship is a revelation and a realization in time of the mystery of salvation, of the election of love, hidden from eternity in God. In this revelation and realization the mystery of salvation includes the particular aspect of conjugal love in the relationship of Christ to the Church, and thus one can express it most adequately by applying the analogy of the relationship which exists—which should exist—between husband and wife in marriage. Such an analogy clarifies the mystery, at least to a certain degree. Indeed, it seems, according to the author of the letter to the Ephesians, that this analogy serves as a complement to that of the "Mystical Body" (cf. Eph. 1:22-23) when we attempt to express the mystery of the relationship of Christ to the Church—and, going back even further, the mystery of the eternal love of God for man and for humanity, that mystery which is expressed and is realized in time through the relationship of Christ to the Church.

UNDERSTANDING RECIPROCAL LOVE

2. If—as has been said—this analogy illuminates the mystery, it in its turn *is illuminated by that mystery*. The conjugal relationship which unites husband and wife should help us—according to the author of the letter to the Ephesians—to understand the love which unites Christ to the Church, that reciprocal love between Christ and the Church in which is realized the divine eternal plan for the salvation of man. Yet the content of meaning of the analogy does not end here. The analogy used in the letter to the Ephesians, illuminating the mystery of the relationship between Christ and the Church, contemporaneously unveils the essential truth about marriage: that is, that marriage corresponds to the vocation of Christians only when it reflects the love which Christ the Bridegroom gives to the Church His Bride, and which the Church (resembling the "sub-

ject" wife, that is, completely given) attempts to return to Christ. This is redeeming love, love as salvation, the love with which man from eternity has been loved by God in Christ: "even as he chose us in him before the foundation of the world, that we should be holy and blameless before him..." (Eph. 1:4).

ANALOGY FOLLOWS TWO DIRECTIONS

3. Marriage corresponds to the vocation of Christians as spouses only if, precisely, that love is reflected and effected therein. This will become clear if we attempt to reread the Pauline analogy inversely, that is, beginning with the relationship of Christ to the Church and turning next to the relationship of husband and wife in marriage. In the text, an exhortative tone is used: "As the Church is subject to Christ, so let wives also be subject in everything to their husbands." And, on the other hand: "Husbands, love your wives, as Christ loved the Church...." These expressions make it clear that what is involved is a moral obligation. Yet, in order to recommend such an obligation one must admit that in the very essence of marriage a particle of the same mystery is captured. Otherwise, the entire analogy would hang suspended in a void. The call of the author of the letter to the Ephesians

directed the spouses, that they model their reciprocal relationship on the relationship of Christ to the Church *("as—so")*, would be without a real basis, as if it had no ground beneath its feet. Such is the logic of the analogy used in the cited text to the Ephesians.

4. As we can see, the analogy operates in two directions. If, on the one hand, it helps us better to understand the essence of the relationship between Christ and the Church, on the other, at the same time, it helps us to see more deeply into the essence of marriage to which Christians are called. The analogy shows, in a certain sense, the way in which this marriage, in its deepest essence, emerges from the mystery of God's eternal love for man and for humanity: from that salvific mystery which is fulfilled in time through the spousal love of Christ for the Church. Beginning with the words of the letter to the Ephesians (5:22-33), we can move on to develop the thought contained in the great Pauline analogy in two directions: either in the direction of a deeper understanding of the Church, or in the direction of a deeper understanding of marriage. In our considerations, we will pursue first of all the latter, mindful that, at the basis of an understanding of marriage in its very essence is the spousal relationship of Christ to the Church. That relationship will be analyzed even more precisely in order to establish—

presupposing the analogy with marriage—in
what way the latter becomes a visible sign of
the divine eternal mystery, as an image of the
Church united with Christ. In this way the
letter to the Ephesians leads us to the very
foundations of the sacramentality of marriage.

MENTALITY OF THE TIME

5. Let us undertake, then, a detailed analysis of the text. When we read in the letter to
the Ephesians that "the husband is the head of
the wife as Christ is the head of the Church, his
body, and is himself its Savior" (Eph. 5:23), we
can presume that the author, who has already
explained that the submission of the wife to the
husband as head is intended as reciprocal
submission "out of reverence for Christ," goes
back to the concept rooted in the mentality of
the time, to express first of all the truth
concerning the relationship of Christ to the
Church, that is, that Christ is the Head of the
Church. He is Head as "Savior of his body."
The Church is exactly that Body which—being submissive in everything to Christ as its
Head—receives from Him all that through
which it becomes and is His Body: that is, the
fullness of salvation as the gift of Christ, who
"gave himself up for her" to the last. Christ's
"giving himself up" to the Father by obedience
unto death on the cross acquired here a strictly

ecclesiological sense: "Christ loved the Church and gave himself up for her" (Eph. 5:25). Through a total giving up of Himself because of His love He formed the Church as His Body and continually builds her up, becoming her Head. As Head He is the Savior of His Body, and, at the same time, as Savior He is Head. As Head and Savior of the Church, He is also Bridegroom of His Bride.

FRUIT OF CHRIST'S LOVE

6. Inasmuch as the Church is herself, so, as Body, she receives from Christ her Head the entire gift of salvation as fruit of Christ's love and of His giving Himself up for the Church: fruit of His giving Himself up to the last. That gift of Himself to the Father by obedience unto death (cf. Phil. 2:8) is contemporaneously, according to the letter to the Ephesians, a "giving himself up for the Church." In this expression, redeeming love is transformed, I would say, into spousal love: Christ, giving Himself up for the Church, through the same redeeming act is united once and for all with her, as bridegroom with the bride, as husband with his wife, giving Himself through all that which is once and for all contained in His "giving Himself up" for the Church. In this way, the mystery of the redemption of the body conceals within itself, in

a certain sense, the mystery "of the marriage of the Lamb" (cf. Rv. 19:7). Because Christ is the Head of the Body, the entire salvific gift of the redemption penetrates the Church as the Body of that Head, and continually forms the most profound, essential substance of her life. It is the spousal form, given that in the cited text the analogy of body-head becomes an analogy of groom-bride, or rather of husband-wife. This is demonstrated by the subsequent passages of the text, which will be considered next.

St. Paul's Analogy of Union of Head and Body Does Not Destroy the Individuality of the Person

General audience of August 25, 1982.

1. In the preceding reflections on the fifth chapter of the letter to the Ephesians (5:21-23), we drew attention particularly to the analogy of the relationship which exists between Christ and the Church, and of that which exists between husband and wife united by the bond of marriage. Before undertaking the analysis of the further passages of the text in question, we must take note of the fact that within the range of the fundamental Pauline analogy—Christ and the Church, on the one hand, and man and woman as spouses on the other— there is a supplementary analogy: the analogy of the head and of the body. And it is precisely this analogy that confers a chiefly ecclesiological significance on the statement analyzed by

us: the Church as such is formed by Christ; it is constituted by Him in its essential part, as the body is by the head. The union of the body with the head is above all of an organic nature; it is, to put it simply, the somatic union of the human organism. On this organic union there is founded directly the biological union, inasmuch as it can be said that the body lives by the head (even if at the same time, though in a different way, the head lives by the body). And besides, in the case of man, there is founded on this organic union also the psychic union, understood in its integrity, and, in fine, the integral unity of the human person.

ESCHATOLOGICAL PERSPECTIVE

2. As already stated (at least in the passage analyzed), the author of the letter to the Ephesians has introduced the supplementary analogy of the head and the body within the limits of the analogy of marriage. He even seems to have conceived the first analogy: "head-body," in a more central manner from the point of view of the truth about Christ and the Church proclaimed by him. However, one must equally affirm that he has not place it alongside or outside of the analogy of marriage as a conjugal bond. Quite the contrary. In the

whole text of the letter to the Ephesians (5:22-33), and especially in the first part with which we are dealing (5:22-23), the author speaks as if in marriage also the husband is "head of the wife," and the wife "the body of the husband," as if the married couple formed one organic union. This can find its basis in the text of Genesis which speaks of one flesh (Gn. 2:24), or in that same text to which the author of the letter to the Ephesians will shortly refer in the context of this great analogy. Nevertheless, in the text of the book of Genesis it is made clear that the man and the woman are two distinct personal subjects who knowingly decide on their conjugal union, defined by that archaic text with the words "one flesh." This is equally clear also in the letter to the Ephesians. The author makes use of a twofold analogy: head-body, husband-wife, for the purpose of illustrating clearly the nature of the union between Christ and the Church. In a certain sense, especially in the first part of the text to the Ephesians 5:22-23, the ecclesiological dimension seems decisive and dominant.

PARTICULAR RELATIONSHIP

3. "Wives, be subject to your husbands, as to the Lord. For the husband is the head of the wife as Christ is the head of the Church, his body, and is himself its Savior. As the

Church is subject to Christ, so let wives also be subject in everything to their husbands. Husbands, love your wives, as Christ loved the Church, and gave himself up for her..." (Eph. 5:22-25). This supplementary analogy "head-body" indicates that within the limits of the entire passage of the letter to the Ephesians 5:22-23, we are dealing with two distinct subjects which, in virtue of a particular reciprocal relationship, become in a certain sense, a single subject. The head, together with the body, constitutes a subject (in the physical and metaphysical sense), an organism, a human person, a being. There is no doubt that Christ is a subject different from the Church; however, in virtue of a particular relationship, He is united with her, as in an organic union of head and body: the Church is so strongly, so essentially herself in virtue of a union with Christ (mystical). Is it possible to say the same thing of the spouses, of the man and the woman united by the marriage bond? If the author of the letter to the Ephesians sees also in marriage the analogy of the union of head and body, this analogy in a certain sense seems to apply to marriage in consideration of the union which Christ constitutes with the Church, and the Church with Christ. Therefore, the analogy regards, above all, marriage itself as that union through which "the two become one flesh" (Eph. 5:31; cf. Gn. 2:24).

BI-SUBJECTIVITY

4. This analogy however does not blur the individuality of the subjects: that of the husband and that of the wife, that is, the essential bi-subjectivity which is at the basis of the image of "one single body." Rather, the essential bi-subjectivity of the husband and wife in marriage, which makes of them in a certain sense "one single body" passes, within the limits of the whole text we are examining (Eph. 5:22-33), to the image of Church-Body united with Christ as Head. This is seen especially in the continuation of this text where the author describes the relationship of Christ to the Church precisely by means of the image of the relationship of the husband to the wife. In this description the Church-Body of Christ appears clearly as the second subject of the spousal union to which the first subject, Christ, manifests the love with which He has loved her by giving Himself for her. That love is an image and above all a model of the love which the husband should show to his wife in marriage, when the two are subject to each other "out of reverence for Christ."

TWO BECOME ONE FLESH

5. In fact we read: "Husbands, love your wives, as Christ loved the Church and gave himself up for her, that he might sanctify her,

having cleansed her by the washing of water with the word, that he might present the Church to himself in splendor, without spot or wrinkle or any such thing, that she might be holy and without blemish. Even so husbands should love their wives as their own bodies. He who loves his wife loves himself. For no man ever hates his own flesh, but nourishes and cherishes it, as Christ does the Church, because we are members of his body. 'For this reason a man should leave his father and mother and be joined to his wife, and the two shall become one flesh'" (Eph. 5:25-31).

AIM IS SANCTIFICATION

6. It is easy to perceive that in this part of the text of the letter to the Ephesians (5:22-23), bi-subjectivity clearly dominates. It is manifested both in the relationship Christ-Church, and also in the relationship husband-wife. This does not mean to say that the image of a single subject disappears: the image of "a single body." It is preserved also in the passage of our text, and in a certain sense it is better explained there. This will be seen more clearly when we submit to a detailed analysis the above-quoted passage. Thus the author of the letter to the Ephesians speaks of the love of Christ for the Church by explaining the way in which that love is expressed, and by pre-

senting at the same time both that love and its expressions as a model which the husband should follow in regard to his wife. The love of Christ for the Church has essentially, as its scope, her sanctification, "Christ loved the Church and gave himself up for her that he might sanctify her" (5:25-26). As a principle of this sanctification there is baptism, the first and essential fruit of Christ's giving Himself for the Church. In this text baptism is not called by its own proper name, but is defined as purification "by the washing of water with the word" (5:26). This washing, with the power that derives from the redemptive giving of Himself by Christ for the Church, brings about the fundamental purification through which Christ's love for the Church acquires, in the eyes of the author of the letter, a spousal character.

7. It is known that the sacrament of baptism is received by an individual subject in the Church. The author of the letter, however, beyond the individual subject of baptism sees the whole Church. The spousal love of Christ is applied to her, the Church, every time that a single person receives in her the fundamental purification by means of baptism. He who receives baptism becomes at the same time—by the virtue of the redemptive love of Christ—a participant in His spousal love for the Church. In our text "the washing of water with the

word" is an expression of the spousal love in the sense that it prepares the Bride (Church) for the Bridegroom, it makes the Church the spouse of Christ, I would say, *in actu primo*. Some biblical scholars observe that in this text quoted by us, the washing with water recalls the ritual ablution which preceded the wedding—something which constituted an important religious rite also among the Greeks.

ECCLESIOLOGICAL DIMENSION

8. As the sacrament of baptism, "the washing of water with the word" (Eph. 5:26) renders the Church a spouse not only *in actu primo* but also in the more distant perspective, in the eschatological perspective. This opens up before us when, in the letter to the Ephesians we read that "the washing of water" serves, on the part of the groom "to present the Church to himself in splendor without spot or wrinkle or any such thing, that she might be holy and without blemish" (Eph. 5:27). The expression "to present to himself" seems to indicate that moment of the wedding in which the bride is led to the groom, already clothed in the bridal dress and adorned for the wedding. The text quoted indicates that the Christ-spouse Himself takes care to adorn the spouse-Church; He is concerned that she should be beautiful with the beauty of grace,

beautiful by virtue of the gift of salvation in its fullness, already granted from the moment of the sacrament of baptism. But baptism is only the beginning from which the figure of the glorious Church (as we read in the text) will emerge, as a definitive fruit of the redemptive and spousal love, only with the final coming of Christ *(parousia)*.

We see how profoundly the author of the letter to the Ephesians examines the sacramental reality, proclaiming its grand analogy: both the union of Christ with the Church, and the conjugal union of man and woman in marriage are in this way illuminated by a particular supernatural light.

The Sacredness of the Human Body and Marriage

General audience of September 1, 1982.

1. The author of the letter to the Ephesians, proclaiming the analogy between the spousal bond which unites Christ and the Church, and that which unites the husband and wife in marriage, writes as follows: "Husbands, love your wives, as Christ loved the church and gave himself up for her, that he might sanctify her, having cleansed her by the washing of water with the word, that he might present the church to himself in splendor, without spot or wrinkle or any such thing, that she might be holy and without blemish" (Eph. 5:25-27).

2. It is significant that the image of the Church "in splendor" is presented, in the text quoted, as a bride all beautiful in her body. Certainly this is a metaphor; but it is very eloquent, and it shows how deeply important is the body in the analogy of spousal love. The

Church "in splendor" is that "without spot or wrinkle." "Spot" can be understood as a sign of ugliness, "wrinkle" as a sign of old age or senility. In the metaphorical sense, both terms indicate moral defects, sin. It may be added that in St. Paul the "old man" signifies sinful man (cf. Rom. 6:6). Christ therefore with His redemptive and spousal love ensures that the Church not only becomes sinless, but remains "eternally young."

BRIDEGROOM—BRIDE

3. The scope of the metaphor is, as may be seen, quite vast. The expressions which refer directly and immediately to the human body, characterizing it in the reciprocal relationships between husband and wife, indicate at the same time attributes and qualities of the moral, spiritual and supernatural order. This is essential for such analogy. Therefore the author of the letter can define the state of the Church "in splendor" in relation to the state of the body of the bride, free from signs of ugliness or old age ("or any such thing"), simply as holiness and absence of sin: such is the Church "holy and without blemish." It is obvious then what kind of beauty of the bride is in question, in what sense the Church is the Body of Christ, and in what sense that Body-Bride welcomes the gift of the Bridegroom who "has

loved the Church and has given himself for her." Nevertheless it is significant that St. Paul explains all this reality, which is essentially spiritual and supernatural, by means of the resemblance of the body and of the love whereby husband and wife become "one flesh."

4. In the entire passage of the text cited, the principle of bi-subjectivity is clearly preserved: Christ-Church, Bridegroom-Bride (husband-wife). The author presents the love of Christ for the Church—that love which makes the Church the Body of Christ of which He is the Head—as the model of the love of the spouses and as the model of the marriage of the bridegroom and the bride. Love obliges the bridegroom-husband to be solicitous for the welfare of the bride-wife, it commits him to desire her beauty and at the same time to appreciate this beauty and to care for it. Here it is a case of visible beauty, of physical beauty. The bridegroom examines his bride with attention as though in a creative, loving anxiety to find everything that is good and beautiful in her and which he desires for her. That good which he who loves creates, through his love, in the one that is loved, is like a test of that same love and its measure. Giving himself in the most disinterested way, he who loves does so only within the limits of this measure and of this control.

UNITY THROUGH LOVE

5. When the author of the letter to the Ephesians—in the succeeding verses of the text (5:28-29)—turns his mind exclusively to the spouses themselves, the analogy of the relationship of Christ to the Church is still more profound and impels him to express himself thus: "Husbands should love their wives as their own bodies" (Eph. 5:28). Here there returns again the motive of "one flesh," which in the above-mentioned phrase and in the subsequent phrases is not only taken up again, but also clarified. If husbands should love their wives as their own bodies, this means that uni-subjectivity is based on bi-subjectivity and has not a real character but only intentional: the wife's body is not the husband's own body, but it must be loved like his own body. It is therefore a question of unity, not in the ontological sense, but in the moral sense: unity through love.

6. "He who loves his wife loves himself" (Eph. 5:28). This phrase confirms still more that character of unity. In a certain sense, love makes the "I" of the other person his own "I": the "I" of the wife, I would say, becomes through love the "I" of the husband. The body is the expression of that "I" and the foundation of its identity. The union of husband and wife in love is expressed also by means of the body.

It is expressed in the reciprocal relationship, even though the author of the letter indicates it especially from the part of the husband. This results from the structure of the total image. Even though the spouses should be "subject to one another out of reverence for Christ" (this was already made evident in the first verse of the text quoted: Eph. 5:22-23), however, later on, the husband is above all, *he who loves* and the wife, on the other hand, is *she who is loved*. One could even hazard the idea that the wife's "submission" to her husband, understood in the context of the entire passage (5:22-23) of the letter to the Ephesians, signifies above all the "experiencing of love." All the more so since this "submission" is related to the image of the submission of the Church to Christ, which certainly consists in experiencing His love. The Church, as bride, being the object of the redemptive love of Christ-Bridegroom, becomes His Body. The wife, being the object of the spousal love of the husband, becomes "one flesh" with him: in a certain sense, his "own" flesh. The author will repeat this idea once again in the last phrase of the passage analyzed here: "However, let each one of you love his wife as himself" (Eph. 5:33).

7. This is a moral unity, conditioned and constituted by love. Love not only unites the two subjects, but allows them to be mutually

interpenetrated, spiritually belonging to one another to such a degree that the author of the letter can affirm: "He who loves his wife loves himself" (Eph. 5:28). The "I" becomes in a certain sense the "you" and the "you" the "I" (in a moral sense, that is). And therefore the continuation of the text analyzed by us reads as follows: "For no man ever hates his own flesh, but nourishes and cherishes it, as Christ does the Church, because we are members of his body" (Eph. 5:29-30). The phrase, which initially still refers to the relationships of the married couple, returns successively in an explicit manner to the relationship Christ-Church, and so, in the light of that relationship, it leads us to define the sense of the entire phrase. The author, after explaining the character of the relationship of the husband to his own wife by forming "one flesh" wishes to reinforce still more his previous statement ("he who loves his wife loves himself"), and in a certain sense, to maintain it by the negation and exclusion of the opposite possibility ("no man ever hates his own flesh": Eph. 5:29). In the union through love the body of the "other" becomes "one's own" in the sense that one cares for the welfare of the other's body as he does for his own. The above-mentioned words, characterizing the "carnal" love which should unite the spouses, express, it may be said, the most general and at the same time, the most essential content. They seem to speak of this love above all in the language of "agape."

8. The expression according to which man "nourishes and cherishes his own flesh"—that is, that the husband "nourishes and cherishes" the flesh of his wife as his own—seems rather to indicate the solicitude of the parents, the protective relationship, instead of the conjugal tenderness. The motivation of this character should be sought in the fact that the author here passes distinctly from the relationship which unites the spouses to the relationship between Christ and the Church. The expressions which refer to the care of the body, and in the first place to its nourishment, to its sustenance, suggest to many Scripture scholars a reference to the Eucharist with which Christ in His spousal love nourishes the Church. If these expressions, even though in a minor key, indicate the specific character of conjugal love, especially of that love whereby the spouses become "one flesh," they help us at the same time to understand, at least in a general way, the dignity of the body and the moral imperative to care for its good: for that good which corresponds to its dignity. The comparison with the Church as the Body of Christ, the Body of His redemptive and at the same time spousal love, should leave in the minds of those to whom the letter to the Ephesians was destined

(5:22-23) a profound sense of the "sacredness" of the human body in general, and especially in marriage, as the "situation" in which this sense of the sacred determines in a particularly profound way, the reciprocal relationships of the persons and, above all, those of the man with the woman, inasmuch as she is wife and mother of their children.

Christ's Redemptive Love Has a Spousal Nature

General audience of September 8, 1982.

1. The author of the letter to the Ephesians writes: "No man ever hates his own flesh, but nourishes and cherishes it, as Christ does the Church, because we are members of his body" (Eph. 5:29-30). After this verse the author deems it opportune to cite that which in the entire Bible can be considered the fundamental text on marriage, the text contained in Genesis 2:24: "for this reason a man shall leave his father and mother and be joined to his wife, and the two shall become one" (Eph. 5:31; Gn. 2:24). It is possible to deduce from the immediate context of the letter to the Ephesians that the citation from the book of Genesis (2:24) is necessary here not so much to recall the unity of the spouses, determined from the beginning in the work of creation, but to present the mystery of Christ with the Church from which the author deduces the truth about

the unity of the spouses. This is the most important point of the whole text, in a certain sense, the keystone. The author of the letter to the Ephesians sums up in these words all that he has said previously, tracing the analogy and presenting the similarity between the unity of the spouses and the unity of Christ with the Church. Citing the words of the book of Genesis (2:24), the author points out that the bases of this analogy are to be sought in the line which, in God's salvific plan, unites marriage, as the most ancient revelation ("manifestation") of the plan in the created world, with the definitive revelation and "manifestation," the revelation that "Christ loved the Church and gave himself up for her" (Eph. 5:25), conferring on His redemptive love a spousal character and meaning.

MYSTERY OF CHRIST
AND THE CHURCH

2. So then this analogy which permeates the text of the letter to the Ephesians (5:22-33) has its ultimate basis in God's salvific plan. This will become still more clear and evident when we place the passage of this text analyzed by us in the overall context of the letter to the Ephesians. Then one will more easily understand why the author, after citing the words of the book of Genesis (2:24), writes: "This is a

great mystery, and I mean in reference to Christ and the Church" (Eph. 5:32).

In the overall context of the letter to the Ephesians and likewise in the wider context of the words of Holy Scripture, which reveal God's salvific plan "from the beginning," one must admit that here the term *mystèrion* signifies the mystery, first of all hidden in God's mind, and later revealed in the history of man. Indeed, it is a question of a "great" mystery, given its importance: that mystery, as God's salvific plan in regard to humanity, is in a certain sense the central theme of the whole of revelation, its central reality. It is this that God, as Creator and Father, wishes above all to transmit to mankind in His Word.

THE WORK OF SALVATION

3. It is a question not only of transmitting the "Good News" of salvation, but of initiating at the same time the work of salvation, as a fruit of grace which sanctifies man for eternal life in union with God. Precisely along the line of this revelation-accomplishment, St. Paul sets in relief the continuity between the most ancient covenant which God established by constituting marriage in the very work of creation, and the definitive covenant in which Christ, after having loved the Church and given Himself up for her, is united to her in a

spousal way, corresponding to the image of spouses. This continuity of God's salvific initiative constitutes the essential basis of the great analogy contained in the letter to the Ephesians. The continuity of God's salvific initiative signifies the continuity and even the identity of the mystery, of "the great mystery," in the different phases of its revelation—therefore in a certain sense, of its "manifestation"—and at the same time of its accomplishment: in its "most ancient" phase from the point of view of the history of man and salvation, and in the phase "of the fullness of time" (Gal. 4:4).

UNDERSTANDING THAT "GREAT MYSTERY"

4. Is it possible to understand that "great mystery" as "a sacrament"? Is the author of the letter to the Ephesians speaking perchance, in the text quoted by us, of the sacrament of marriage? If he is not speaking of it directly, in the strict sense—here one must be in agreement with the sufficiently widespread opinion of Biblical scholars and theologians—however it seems that in this text he is speaking of the bases of the sacramentality of the whole of Christian life and in particular of the bases of the sacramentality of marriage. He speaks then of the sacramentality of the whole of Christian existence in the Church and in particular of

marriage in an indirect way, but in the most fundamental way possible.

SACRAMENT AND MYSTERY

5. Is not "sacrament" synonymous with "mystery"?[1] The mystery indeed remains "occult"—hidden in God Himself—in such wise that even after its proclamation (or its revelation) it does not cease to be called "mystery," and it is also preached as a mystery. The sacrament presupposes the revelation of the mystery and presupposes also its acceptance by means of faith on the part of man. At the same time, however, it is something more than the proclamation of the mystery and its acceptance by faith. The sacrament consists in the "manifesting" of that mystery in a sign which serves not only to proclaim the mystery, but also to accomplish it in man. The sacrament is a visible and efficacious sign of grace. Through it, there is accomplished in man that mystery hidden from eternity in God, of which the letter to the Ephesians speaks at the very beginning (cf. Eph. 1:9)—the mystery of God's call of man in Christ to holiness, and the mystery of his predestination to become His adopted son. This becomes a reality in a mysterious way, under the veil of a sign; nonetheless that sign is always a "making visible" of the supernatural mystery which it works in man under its veil.

MYSTERY HIDDEN IN GOD

6. Taking into consideration the passage of the letter to the Ephesians analyzed here, and in particular the words: "this is a great mystery, and I mean in reference to Christ and the Church," one must note that the author of the letter writes not only of the great mystery hidden in God, but also—and above all—of the mystery which is accomplished by the fact that Christ, who with an act of redemptive love, loved the Church and gave Himself up for her, is by the same act united with the Church in a spousal manner, as the husband and wife are reciprocally united in marriage instituted by the Creator. It seems that the words of the letter to the Ephesians provide sufficient motivation for what is stated at the very beginning of the Constitution *Lumen gentium:* "The Church is in Christ in the nature of a sacrament—a sign and instrument, that is, of communion with God and of unity among all men" (LG 1). This text of Vatican II does not say: "the Church is a sacrament," but "it is in the nature of a sacrament," thereby indicating that one must speak of the sacramentality of the Church in a manner which is analogical and not identical in regard to what we mean when we speak of the seven sacraments administered by the Church by Christ's institution. If there are bases for speaking of the Church as in the

nature of a sacrament, such bases for the greater part have been indicated precisely in the letter to the Ephesians.

MISSION TO SANCTIFY

7. It may be said that this sacramentality of the Church is constituted by all the sacraments by means of which she carries out her mission of sanctification. It can also be said that the sacramentality of the Church is the source of the sacraments and in particular of Baptism and the Eucharist, as can be seen from the passage, already analyzed, of the letter to the Ephesians (cf. Eph. 5:25-30). Finally it must be said that the sacramentality of the Church remains in a particular relationship with marriage: the most ancient sacrament.

NOTES

1. "Sacrament," a central concept for our reflections, has traveled a long way in the course of the centuries. The semantic history of the term "sacrament" must begin with the Greek term *"mystèrion"* which, truth to tell, in the book of Judith still means the king's military plans ("secret plan," cf. Jdt. 2:2), but already in the book of Wisdom (2:22) and in the prophecy of Daniel (2:27) signifies the creative plans of God and the purpose which He assigns to the world, and which are revealed only to faithful confessors.

In this sense *"mystèrion"* appears only once in the Gospels: "To you has been given the secret of the kingdom of God" (Mk. 4:11 and par.). In the great letters of St. Paul, this term is found seven times, reaching its climax in the letter to the Romans: "...according to my gospel and the preaching of Jesus Christ, according to the revelation of the mystery which was kept secret for long ages, but is now disclosed..." (Rom. 16:25-26).

In the later letters we find the identification of "*mystèrion*" with the Gospel (cf. Eph. 6:19) and even with Jesus Christ Himself (cf. Col. 2:2; 4:3; Eph. 3:4), which marks a turning point in the meaning of the term: "*mystèrion*" is no longer merely God's eternal plan, but the accomplishment on earth of that plan revealed in Jesus Christ.

Therefore, in the Patristic period, the term "*mystèrion*" begins to be applied also to the historical events by which the divine will to save man was manifested. Already in the second century in the writings of St. Ignatius of Antioch, Sts. Justin and Meliton, the mysteries of the life of Jesus, the prophecies and the symbolic figures of the Old Testament are defined with the term "*mystèrion.*"

In the third century there begin to appear the most ancient Latin versions of Sacred Scripture in which the Greek term is translated, both by "*mystèrion*" and by "sacramentum" (e.g., Wis. 2:22; Eph. 5:32), perhaps to distance themselves explicitly from the pagan mystery rites and from the Neo-Platonic gnostic mystagogy.

However, "sacramentum" originally meant the military oath taken by the Roman legionaries. Given that in it there can be distinguished the aspect of "initiation to a new form of life," "commitment without reserve," "faithful service even at the risk of death," Tertullian points out these dimensions in the Christian sacraments of Baptism, Confirmation and the Eucharist. In the third century, therefore, the term "sacramentum" is applied both to the mystery of God's salvific plan in Christ (cf., e.g., Eph. 5:32), and to its concrete accomplishment by means of the seven sources of grace which are today called "sacraments of the Church."

St. Augustine, making use of various meanings of the term sacrament, applied it to religious rites both of the old and the new covenant, to biblical symbols and figures as well as to the revealed Christian religion. All these "sacraments," according to St. Augustine, pertain to the great sacrament: the mystery of Christ and the Church. St. Augustine influenced the further clarification of the term "sacrament," emphasizing that the sacraments are sacred signs; that they contain in themselves a resemblance to what they signify and that they confer what they signify. By his analyses, he therefore contributed to the elaboration of the concise scholastic definition of sacrament: *"signum efficax gratiae."*

St. Isidore of Seville (7th century) later stressed another aspect: the mysterious nature of the sacrament which, under the veils of material species, conceals the action of the Holy Spirit in the human soul.

The theological Summae of the 12th and 13th centuries already formulate the systematic definitions of the sacraments, but a special signification belongs to the definition of St. Thomas: *"Non omne signum rei sacrae est sacramentum, sed solum ea quae significant perfectionem sanctitatis humanae"* (3a qu. 60 a.2).

From then on, "sacrament" was understood exclusively as one of the seven sources of grace and theological studies were directed to a deeper understanding of the essence and of the action of the seven sacraments, by elaborating in a systematic way the principal lines contained in the scholastic tradition.

Only in the last century was attention paid to the aspects of the sacrament which had been neglected in the course of the centuries, for example, to the ecclesial dimension and to the personal encounter with Christ, which have found expression in the *Constitution on the Sacred Liturgy* (no. 59). However, the Second Vatican Council returns above all to the original significance of "sacramentum-mysterium," calling the Church "the universal sacrament of salvation" (LG 48), sacrament, or "sign and instrument of communion with God and of unity among all men" (LG 1).

Here sacrament is understood—in conformity with its original meaning—as the accomplishment of God's eternal plan in regard to the salvation of mankind.

Moral Aspects
of the Christian's Vocation

General audience of September 15, 1982.

1. We have before us the text of the letter to the Ephesians 5:22-23, which we have already been analyzing for some time because of its importance in regard to marriage and the sacrament. In the whole of its content, beginning from the first chapter, the letter treats above all of the mystery "for ages" "hidden in God" as a gift eternally destined for mankind "Blessed be the God and Father of our Lord Jesus Christ, who has blessed us in Christ with every spiritual blessing in the heavenly places, even as he chose us in him before the foundation of the world, that we should be holy and blameless before him. He destined us in love to be his sons through Jesus Christ, according to the purpose of his will, to the praise of his glorious grace which he freely bestowed on us in the Beloved" (Eph. 1:3-6).

FULFILLMENT
OF THE MYSTERY

2. Until now the letter speaks of the mystery hidden "for ages" (Eph. 3:9) in God. The subsequent phrases introduce the reader to the phase of fulfillment of this mystery in the history of man: the gift, destined for him "for ages" in Christ, becomes a real part of man in the same Christ: "...in him we have redemption through his blood, the forgiveness of our trespasses, according to the riches of his grace, which he lavished upon us. For he has made known to us in all wisdom and insight the mystery of his will, according to his purpose which he set forth in Christ, as a plan for the fullness of time, to unite all things in him, things in heaven and things on earth" (Eph. 1:7-10).

3. And so the eternal mystery passed from the mystery of "being hidden in God" to the phase of revelation and actualization. Christ, in whom humanity was "for ages" chosen and blessed "with every spiritual blessing of the Father"—Christ, destined according to the eternal "plan" of God, so that in Him, as in a head "all things might be united, things in heaven and things on earth" in the eschatological perspective—reveals the eternal mystery and accomplishes it among men. Therefore the author of the letter to the Ephesians, in the

remainder of the same letter, exhorts those who have received this revelation, and those who have accepted it in faith, to model their lives in the spirit of the truth they have learned. And to the same end he exhorts in a particular way Christian couples, husbands and wives.

THE VOCATION
OF A CHRISTIAN

4. For the greater part of the context the letter becomes instruction or *parenesis*. The author seems to speak, above all, of the moral aspects of the vocation of Christians, while however making continuous reference to the mystery, which is already at work in them, by virtue of the redemption of Christ—and efficaciously works in them especially by virtue of Baptism. He writes in fact: "In him you also, who have heard the word of truth, the gospel of your salvation, and have believed in him, were sealed with the promised Holy Spirit" (Eph. 1:13). Thus then the moral aspects of the Christian vocation remain linked not only with the revelation of the eternal divine mystery in Christ and with its acceptance through faith, but also with the sacramental order, which although not placed in the forefront in the whole letter, seems however to be present in a discreet manner. Anyway, it could not be otherwise seeing that the Apostle is writing to

Christians who, through Baptism, had become members of the ecclesial community. From this point of view, the passage of the letter to the Ephesians, chapter 5:22-23, analyzed up to the present, seems to have a special importance. Indeed, it throws a special light on the essential relationship of the mystery with the sacrament and especially on the sacramentality of matrimony.

5. At the heart of the mystery there is Christ. In Him—precisely in Him—humanity has been eternally blessed "with every spiritual blessing." In Him—in Christ—humanity has been chosen "before the creation of the world," chosen "in love" and predestined to the adoption of sons. When later, in the "fullness of time" this eternal mystery is accomplished in time, this is brought about also in Him and through Him: in Christ and through Christ. Through Christ there is revealed the mystery of divine love. Through Him and in Him it is accomplished: in Him "we have redemption through his blood, the forgiveness of our trespasses..." (Eph. 1:7). In this manner men who through faith accept the gift offered to them in Christ, really become participants in the eternal mystery, even though it works in them under the veils of faith. This supernatural conferring of the fruits of redemption accomplished by Christ acquires, according to the

letter to the Ephesians 5:22-23, the character of a spousal donation of Christ Himself to the Church similar to the spousal relationship between husband and wife. Therefore, not only the fruits of redemption are a gift, but above all, Christ Himself is a gift: He gives Himself to the Church as to His spouse.

6. We should ask the question whether in this matter such analogy does not permit us to penetrate more profoundly and with greater exactitude the essential content of the mystery. We should ask ourselves this question with all the greater reason because this "classical" passage of the letter to the Ephesians (5:22-23) does not appear in the abstract and isolated, but constitutes a continuity, in a certain sense a continuation of the statements of the Old Testament, which presented the love of God-Yahweh for His chosen people Israel according to the same analogy. We are dealing in the first place with the texts of the prophets who, in their discourses, introduced the similarity of spousal love in order to characterize in a particular way the love which Yahweh has for Israel, a love which on the part of the chosen people was not understood and reciprocated; rather it encountered infidelity and betrayal. That infidelity and betrayal was expressed especially in idolatry, a worship given to strange gods.

THE LOVE WHICH UNITES

7. Truth to tell, in the greater part of the cases, the prophets were pointing out in a dramatic manner that very betrayal and infidelity which were called the "adultery" of Israel. However, at the basis of all these statements of the prophets, there is the explicit conviction that the love of Yahweh for the chosen people can and should be compared to the love which unites husband and wife. Here one could quote numerous passages from Isaiah, Hosea, Ezekiel (some of these were already quoted previously when we were analyzing the concept of "adultery" against the background of Christ's words in the Sermon on the Mount). One cannot forget that to the patrimony of the Old Testament belongs also the Song of Solomon in which the image of spousal love is traced—it is true—without the typical analogy of the prophetic texts, which presented in that love, the image of the love of Yahweh for Israel, but also without that negative element which, in the other texts, constitutes the motive of "adultery" or infidelity. Thus then the analogy of the spouses, which enabled the author of the letter to the Ephesians to define the relationship of Christ to the Church, possesses an abundant tradition in the books of the Old Testament. In analyzing this analogy in the

"classic" text of the letter to the Ephesians, we cannot but refer to that tradition.

8. To illustrate this tradition we will limit ourselves for the moment to citing a passage of the text of Isaiah. The prophet says: "Fear not, for you will not be ashamed; be not confounded, for you will not be put to shame; for you will forget the shame of your youth and the reproach of your widowhood you will remember no more. For your Maker is your husband, the Lord of hosts is his name; and the Holy One of Israel is your redeemer, the God of the whole earth he is called. For the Lord has called you like a wife forsaken and grieved in spirit, like a wife of youth when she is cast off, says your God. For a brief moment I forsook you, but with great compassion I will gather you...but my steadfast love shall not depart from you, and my covenant of peace shall not be removed, says the Lord, who has compassion on you" (Is. 54:4-7, 10).

During our next meeting we shall begin the analysis of the text cited from Isaiah.

Relationship of Christ to the Church Connected with Tradition of the Prophets

General audience of September 22, 1982.

1. The letter to the Ephesians, by means of a comparison of the relation between Christ and the Church with the spousal relationship of husband and wife, refers to the tradition of the prophets of the Old Testament. To illustrate it we recall again the following passage of Isaiah:

"Fear not, for you will not be ashamed; be not confounded, for you will not be put to shame; for you will forget the shame of your youth, and the reproach of your widowhood you will remember no more. For your Maker is your husband, the Lord of hosts is his name; and the Holy One of Israel is your redeemer, the God of the whole earth he is called. For the Lord has called you like a wife forsaken and grieved in spirit, like a wife of youth when she is cast off, says your God. For a brief moment I forsook you, but with great compassion I will gather you. In overflowing wrath for a moment I hid my face from you, but with everlasting love, I will have compassion on you, says the Lord, your redeemer. For this is like the days of Noah to me: as I swore that the waters of Noah should no more go over the earth, so I have sworn that I will not be angry with you and will not rebuke you. For the mountains may depart and the hills be removed, but my steadfast love shall not depart from you, and my covenant of peace shall not be removed, says the Lord, who has compassion on you" (Is. 54:4-10).

BACK TO THE MYSTERY HIDDEN IN GOD

2. The text of Isaiah in this case does not contain the reproaches made to Israel as an unfaithful spouse, which echo so strongly in the other texts, in particular of Hosea and Ezekiel. Thanks to this, the essential content of the biblical analogy becomes more evident: the love of God-Yahweh for the chosen people-Israel is expressed as the love of the man-spouse for the woman chosen to be his wife by means of the marriage alliance. In this way Isaiah explains the events which make up the course of Israel's history, going back to the mystery hidden as it were in the very heart of God. In a certain sense, he leads us in the same

direction in which, after many centuries, the author of the letter to the Ephesians will lead us. The latter—basing himself on the redemption already accomplished in Christ—will reveal much more fully the depth of the mystery itself.

3. The text of the prophet has all the coloring of the tradition and the mentality of the people of the Old Testament. The prophet, speaking in the name of God and as it were, with His words, addresses Israel as a husband would address the wife chosen by him. These words brim over with an authentic ardor of love and at the same time place in relief the whole specific character both of the situation and of the outlook proper to that age. They underline that the choice on the part of the man takes away the woman's "dishonor," which, according to the opinion of society, seems connected with the marriageable state, whether original (virginity), or secondary (widowhood), or finally that deriving from repudiation of a wife who is not loved (cf. Dt. 24:1) or in the case of an unfaithful wife. However, the text quoted does not mention infidelity; it indicates however the motive of the "love of compassion,"[1] indicating thereby not merely the social nature of marriage in the Old Testament, but also the very character of the gift, which is the love of God for the spouse-Israel: a gift which derives entirely from God's initiative. In other words:

indicating the dimension of grace, which from the beginning is contained in that love. This is perhaps the strongest "declaration of love" on God's part, linked up with the solemn oath of faithfulness forever.

CREATOR AND LORD

4. The analogy of the love which unites spouses is brought out strongly in this passage. Isaiah says: "...for your Maker is your husband, the Lord of hosts is his name; and the Holy One of Israel is your redeemer, the God of the whole earth he is called" (Is. 54:5). So, then, in that text God Himself, in all His majesty as Creator and Lord of creation, is explicitly called "spouse" of the chosen people. This "spouse" speaks of His great "compassion," which will not "depart" from Israel-spouse, but will constitute a stable foundation of the "alliance of peace" with Him. Thus the motif of spousal love and of marriage is linked with the motif of alliance. Besides the "Lord of hosts" calls Himself not only "creator," but also "redeemer." The text has theological content of extraordinary richness.

CONTINUITY OF ANALOGY

5. Comparing the text of Isaiah with the letter to the Ephesians and noting the continuity regarding the analogy of spousal love

and of marriage, we should point out at the same time a certain diversity of theological viewpoint. The author of the letter already in the first chapter speaks of the mystery of love and of election, whereby "God the Father of our Lord Jesus Christ" embraces mankind in His Son, especially as a mystery "hidden in the mind of God." This is a mystery of eternal love, the mystery of election to holiness ("to be holy and blameless before him": Eph. 1:4) and of adoption as sons in Christ ("he destined us to be his adopted sons through Jesus Christ": Eph. 1:5). In this context, the deduction of the analogy concerning marriage which we have found in Isaiah ("for your Maker is your husband, the Lord of hosts is his name": Is. 54:5), seems to be a foreshortened view constituting a part of the theological perspective. The first dimension of love and of election, as a mystery hidden for ages in God, is a paternal and not a "conjugal" dimension. According to the letter to the Ephesians the first characteristic note of that mystery remains connected with the very paternity of God, set out in relief particularly by the prophets (cf. Hos. 11:1-4; Is. 63:8-9; 64:7; Mal. 1:6).

THEOLOGICAL PERSPECTIVE

6. The analogy of spousal love and of marriage appears only when the "Creator" and the "Holy One of Israel" of the text of Isaiah is

manifested as "redeemer." Isaiah says: "for your Maker is your husband, the Lord of hosts is his name; and the Holy One of Israel is your redeemer" (Is. 54:5). Already in this text it is possible, in a certain sense, to read the parallelism between the "spouse" and the "redeemer." Passing to the letter to the Ephesians we should observe that this thought is fully developed there. The figure of the Redeemer[2] is already delineated in the first chapter as proper to Him who is the first "beloved Son" of the Father (Eph. 1:6), beloved from eternity: of Him, in whom all of us have been loved by the Father "for ages." It is the Son of the same substance of the Father, "in whom we have redemption through his blood, the forgiveness of our trespasses according to the riches of his grace" (Eph. 1:7). The same Son, as Christ (or as the Messiah) "has loved the Church and has given himself up for her" (Eph. 5:25).

This splendid formulation of the letter to the Ephesians summarizes in itself and at the same time sets in relief the elements of the Canticle on the Servant of Yahweh and of the Canticle of Sion (cf. e.g., Is. 42:1; 53:8-12; 54:8).

And thus the giving of Himself up for the Church is equivalent to carrying out the work of redemption. In this way the "Creator Lord of hosts" of the text of Isaiah becomes the "Holy One of Israel," of the new Israel, as Redeemer.

In the letter to the Ephesians the theological perspective of the prophetic text is preserved and at the same time deepened and transformed. There enter new revealed moments: the trinitarian, Christological[3] and finally the eschatological moment.

HIS SALVIFIC LOVE

7. Thus St. Paul, writing the letter to the People of God of the New Covenant and precisely to the Church of Ephesus, will no longer repeat: "your Maker is your husband," but will show in what way the "redeemer," who is the firstborn Son and for ages "beloved of the Father," reveals contemporaneously His salvific love which consists in giving Himself up for the Church, as spousal love whereby He espouses the Church and makes it His own Body. Thus the analogy of the prophetic texts of the Old Testament (in this case especially of the book of Isaiah) remains preserved in the letter to the Ephesians and at the same time obviously transformed. To the analogy there corresponds a mystery which is expressed and, in a certain sense, explained by means of it. In the text of Isaiah this mystery is scarcely outlined, "half-open" as it were; in the letter to the Ephesians, however, it is fully revealed (but of course without ceasing to be a mystery). In the letter to the Ephesians there is explicitly clear the eternal dimension of the mystery

inasmuch as it is hidden in God ("Father of our Lord Jesus Christ") and the dimension of its historical fulfillment, according to its Christological and at the same ecclesiological dimension. The analogy of marriage refers especially to the second dimension. Also in the prophets (in Isaiah) the analogy of marriage referred directly to an historical dimension: it was linked with the history of the chosen people of the old covenant, with the history of Israel; on the other hand the Christological and the ecclesiological dimension, in the Old Testament fulfillment of the mystery, was found only as an embryo: it was only foretold.

Nonetheless it is clear that the text of Isaiah helps us to understand better the letter to the Ephesians and the great analogy of the spousal love of Christ and the Church.

NOTES

1. In the Hebrew text we have the words *hesed-rahamim* which appear together on more than one occasion.

2. Even though in the most ancient biblical books the word "redeemer" (Hebrew *Go'el*) signified the person bound by blood relationship to vindicate a relative who had been killed (cf. e.g., Nm. 35:19), to help a relative who was unfortunate (e.g., Ru. 4:6) and especially to ransom him from servitude (cf. e.g., Lv. 25:48), with the passage of time this analogy was applied to Yahweh, "who redeemed Israel from the house of bondage, from the hand of Pharaoh, king of Egypt" (Dt. 7:8). Particularly in the Deutero-Isaiah the accent changes from the act of redemption to the Person of the

Redeemer who personally saves Israel as though merely by His very presence, "not for price or reward" (Is. 45:13).

Therefore the passage from the "redeemer" of the prophecy of Isaiah chapter 54, to the letter to the Ephesians, has the same motivation of the application, in the said letter, of the texts of the Canticle on the Servant of Yahweh (cf. Is. 53:10-12; Eph. 5:23, 25, 26).

3. In place of the relationship "God-Israel," Paul introduces the relationship "Christ-Church," by applying to Christ all in the Old Testament that refers to Yahweh (*Adonai-Kyrios*). Christ is God, but Paul also applies to Him everything that refers to the Servant of Yahweh in the four canticles (Is. 42:49; 50; 52-53) interpreted in a Messianic sense in the intertestimentary period.

The motif of "Head" and of "Body" is not of biblical derivation, but is probably Hellenistic (Stoic?). In the letter to the Ephesians this theme is utilized in the context of marriage (while in the first letter to the Corinthians the theme of the "Body" serves to demonstrate the order which reigns in society").

From the biblical point of view the introduction of this motif is an absolute novelty.

Analogy of Spousal Love Indicates the Radical Character of Grace

General audience of September 29, 1982.

1. In the letter to the Ephesians (5:22-33) —as in the prophets of the Old Testament (e.g., in Isaiah)—we find the great analogy of marriage or of the spousal love between Christ and the Church.

What function does this analogy fulfill in regard to the mystery revealed in the old and the new covenants? The answer to this question must be gradual. First of all, the analogy of spousal or conjugal love helps to penetrate the very essence of the mystery. It helps to understand it up to a certain point—naturally, in an analogical way. It is obvious that the analogy of earthly human love of the husband for his wife, of human spousal love, cannot provide an adequate and complete understanding of that absolutely transcendent Reality which is the divine mystery, both as hidden for ages in God, and in its "historical" fulfillment in time, when

"Christ so loved the Church and gave himself up for her" (Eph. 5:25). The mystery remains transcendent in regard to this analogy as in regard to any other analogy, whereby we seek to express it in human language. At the same time, however, this analogy offers the possibility of a certain cognoscitive "penetration" into the very essence of the mystery.

REALIZED BY CHRIST

2. The analogy of spousal love permits us to understand in a certain way the mystery which for ages was hidden in God, and which in turn was realized by Christ, as a love proper to a total and irrevocable gift of self on the part of God to man in Christ. It is a question of "man" in the personal and at the same time community dimension (this community dimension is expressed in the book of Isaiah and in the prophets as "Israel," in the letter to the Ephesians as the "Church"; one could say: the People of God of the old and of the new covenant). We may add that in both conceptions, the community dimension is placed, in a certain sense, in the forefront, but not to such an extent as completely to hide the personal dimension, which, on the other hand, pertains simply to the very essence of conjugal love. In both cases we are dealing rather with a significant "reduction of the community to the per-

son"[1]: Israel and the Church are considered as bride-person in relation to the bridegroom-person ("Yahweh" and "Christ"). Every concrete "I" should find itself in that biblical "we."

GOD OF THE COVENANT

3. So then, the analogy of which we are speaking permits us to understand, in a certain degree, the revealed mystery of the living God who is Creator and Redeemer (and as such He is, at the same time, God of the covenant); it permits us to understand this mystery in the manner of a spousal love, just as it allows us to understand it also in the manner of a love of "compassion" (according to the text of the book of Isaiah), or in the manner of a "paternal" love (according to the letter to the Ephesians, especially in the first chapter). The above-mentioned ways of understanding the mystery are also without doubt analogical. The analogy of spousal love contains in itself a characteristic of the mystery, which is not directly emphasized either by the analogy of the love of compassion or by the analogy of paternal love (or by any other analogy used in the Bible to which we would have referred).

RADICAL AND TOTAL GIFT

4. The analogy of spousal love seems to emphasize especially the aspect of the gift of self on the part of God to man, "for ages"

chosen in Christ (literally: to "Israel," to the "Church")—a total (or rather "radical") and irrevocable gift in its essential character, that is, as a gift. This gift is certainly "radical" and therefore "total." We cannot speak of that "totality" in a metaphysical sense. Man, indeed, as a creature is not capable of "receiving" the gift of God in the transcendental fullness of His divinity. Such a "total gift" (uncreated) is shared only by God Himself in the "triune communion of the Persons." On the contrary, the gift of Himself on the part of God to man, of which the analogy of spousal love speaks, can only have the form of a participation in the divine nature (cf. 2 Pt. 1:4), as is made clear by theology with very great precision. Nevertheless, according to this measure, the gift made to man on the part of God in Christ is a "total," that is, "radical" gift, as is indicated precisely by the analogy of spousal love. It is, in a certain sense, "all" that God "could" give of Himself to man, considering the limited faculties of man-creature. In this way, the analogy of spousal love indicates the "radical" character of grace: of the whole order of created grace.

SACRAMENT AND MYSTERY

5. The foregoing seems to be what can be said in reference to the primary function of our great analogy, which has passed from the

writings of the prophets of the Old Testament to the letter to the Ephesians, where, as has already been noted, it underwent a significant transformation. The analogy of marriage, as a human reality, in which spousal love is incarnated, helps to a certain degree and in a certain way to understand the mystery of grace as an eternal reality in God and as an "historical" fruit of mankind's redemption in Christ. However, we said before that this biblical analogy not only "explains" the mystery, but on the other hand the mystery defines and determines the adequate manner of understanding the analogy, and precisely this element, in which the biblical authors see "the image and likeness" of the divine mystery. So then, the comparison of marriage (because of spousal love) to the relationship of "Yahweh-Israel" in the old covenant and of "Christ-Church" in the new covenant decides, at the same time, the manner of understanding marriage itself and determines this manner.

6. This is the second function of our great analogy. In the perspective of this function we approach, in fact, the problem of "sacrament and mystery," that is, in the general and fundamental sense, the problem of the sacramentality of marriage. This seems particularly justified in the light of the analysis of the letter to the Ephesians (5:22-33). Indeed, in presenting the relationship of Christ to the Church, in

the image of the conjugal union of husband and wife, the author of this letter speaks in the most general and at the same time fundamental way, not only of the fulfillment of the eternal divine mystery, but also of the way in which that mystery is expressed in the visible order, of the way in which it has become visible, and therefore has entered into the sphere of sign.

VISIBILITY OF THE MYSTERY

7. By the term "sign" we mean here simply the "visibility of the Invisible." The mystery for ages hidden in God—that is, invisible—has become visible first of all in the very historical event of Christ. The relationship of Christ to the Church, which is defined in the letter to the Ephesians, as "a great mystery," constitutes the fulfillment and the concretization of the visibility of the mystery itself. Moreover, the fact that the author of the letter to the Ephesians compares the indissoluble relationship of Christ to the Church to the relationship between husband and wife, that is, to marriage—referring at the same time to the words of Genesis (2:24), which by God's creative act originally instituted marriage—turns our attention to what was already presented previously —in the context of the very mystery of creation—as the "visibility of the Invisible," to the very "origin" of the theological history of man.

It can be said that the visible sign of marriage "in the beginning," inasmuch as it is linked to the visible sign of Christ and of the Church, to the summit of the salvific economy of God, transfers the eternal plan of love into the "historical" dimension and makes it the foundation of the whole sacramental order. It is a special merit of the author of the letter to the Ephesians that he brought these two signs together, and made of them one great sign—that is, a great sacrament *(sacramentum magnum)*.

NOTE

1. It is not merely a question of the personification of human society which constitutes a fairly common phenomenon in world literature, but of a specific "corporate personality" of the Bible, marked by a continual reciprocal relationship of the individual to the group (cf. H. Wheeler Robinson, "The Hebrew Conception of Corporate Personality," BZAW 66 [1936], pp. 49-62; cf. also J. L. McKenzie, "Aspects of Old Testament Thought," in: "The Jerome Biblical Commentary," vol. 2, London 1970, p. 748).

Marriage, the Central Point of the "Sacrament of Creation"

General audience of October 6, 1982.

1. We continue the analysis of the classical text of the fifth chapter of the letter to the Ephesians, 5:22-23. For this purpose it is necessary to quote some phrases contained in one of the preceding analyses devoted to this theme: "Man appears in the visible world as the highest expression of the divine gift, because he bears within himself the interior dimension of the gift. And with it he brings into the world his particular likeness to God, whereby he transcends and dominates also his 'visibility' in the world, his corporality, his masculinity or femininity, his nakedness. Resulting from this likeness there is also the primordial awareness of the conjugal significance of the body, pervaded by the mystery of original innocence" (*L'amore umano nel piano divino,* Citta del Vaticano 1980, p. 90). These phrases sum up in a few words the result of the analyses devoted

to the first chapters of the book of Genesis, in relation to the words with which Christ, in His conversation with the Pharisees on the subject of marriage and its indissolubility, refers to the "beginning." Other phrases of the same analysis pose the problem of the primordial sacrament: "Thus, in this dimension, there is constituted a primordial sacrament, understood as a sign which effectively transmits in the visible world the invisible mystery hidden from eternity in God. And this is the mystery of truth and love, the mystery of the divine life in which man really shares.... It is the original innocence which initiates this participation..." (*Ibid.*, p. 90).

THE STATE OF MAN
BEFORE ORIGINAL SIN

2. It is necessary to look again at the content of these statements in the light of the Pauline doctrine expressed in the letter to the Ephesians, bearing in mind especially the passage of chapter 5, verses 22-23, situated in the overall context of the entire letter. In any event, the letter authorizes us to do this, because the author himself, in chapter 5, verse 31, refers to the "beginning," and precisely to the words of the institution of marriage in the book of Genesis (Gn. 2:24). In what sense can we see in these words a statement about the

sacrament, about the primordial sacrament? The previous analyses of the biblical "beginning" have led us gradually to this, in consideration of the state of the original endowment of man in existence and in grace, which was the state of innocence and original justice. The letter to the Ephesians leads us to approach this situation—that is, the state of man before original sin—from the point of view of the mystery hidden in God from eternity. In fact, we read in the first phrases of the letter that "God, Father of our Lord Jesus Christ...has blessed us in Christ with every spiritual blessing in the heavenly places. He chose us in him before the foundation of the world, that we should be holy and blameless before him" (Eph. 1:3-4).

GOD'S ETERNAL PLAN

3. The letter to the Ephesians opens up before us the supernatural world of the eternal mystery, of the eternal plans of God the Father concerning man. These plans precede the "creation of the world," and therefore also the creation of man. At the same time those divine plans begin to be put into effect already in the entire reality of creation. If also the state of original innocence of man created, as male and female, in the likeness of God, pertains to the

mystery of creation, this implies that the primordial gift conferred on man by God already includes within itself the fruit of having been chosen, of which we read in the letter to the Ephesians: "He chose us...that we should be holy and blameless before him" (Eph. 1:4). This indeed seems to be indicated by the words of the book of Genesis, when the Creator-Elohim finds in man—male and female—who appeared before him, a good worthy of gratification: "God saw everything that he had made, and behold, it was very good" (Gn. 1:31). Only after sin, after the breaking of the original covenant with the Creator, man feels the need to hide himself "from the Lord God": "I heard the sound of you in the garden, and I was afraid, because I was naked; and I hid myself" (Gn. 3:10).

4. On the contrary, before sin, man bore in his soul the fruit of eternal election in Christ, the eternal Son of the Father. By means of the grace of this election man, male and female, was "holy and blameless" before God. That primordial (or original) holiness and purity were expressed also in the fact that, although both were "naked, they were not ashamed" (Gn. 2:25), as we have already sought to make evident in the previous analyses. Comparing the testimony of the "beginning," found in the first chapters of the book of Genesis, with the testimony of the letter to the Ephesians, one

must deduce that the reality of man's creation, was already imbued by the perennial election of man in Christ: called to sanctity through the grace of the adoption as sons ("he destined us to be his sons through Jesus Christ, according to the purpose of his will, to the praise of his glorious grace which he freely bestowed on us in the Beloved": Eph. 1:5-6).

SUPERNATURAL ENDOWMENT

5. Man, male and female, shared from the "beginning" in this supernatural gift. This bounty was granted in consideration of Him, who from eternity was "beloved" as Son, even though— according to the dimensions of time and history—it had preceded the Incarnation of this "beloved Son" and also the "redemption" which we have in Him "through his blood" (Eph. 1:7). The redemption was to become the source of man's supernatural endowment after sin and, in a certain sense, in spite of sin. This supernatural endowment, which took place before original sin, that is, the grace of justice and original innocence—an endowment which was the fruit of man's election in Christ before the ages—was accomplished precisely in reference to Him, to the beloved One, while anticipating chronologically His coming in the body. In the dimensions of the mystery of creation the election to the dignity of adopted sonship was

proper only to the "first Adam," that is, to the man created in the image and likeness of God, male and female.

THE SUBJECT OF HOLINESS

6. In what way is the reality of the sacrament, of the primordial sacrament, verified in this context? In the analysis of the "beginning," of which we quoted a passage a short time ago, we said that "the sacrament, as a visible sign, is constituted by man inasmuch as he is a 'body,' through his 'visible' masculinity and femininity. The body, in fact, and only it, is capable of making visible what is invisible: the spiritual and the divine. It was created to transfer into the visible reality of the world the mystery hidden from eternity in God, and thus to be its sign" (loc. cit., p. 90).

This sign has besides an efficacy of its own, as I also said: "Original innocence linked to the experience of the conjugal significance of the body" has as its effect "that man feels himself, in his body as male and female, the subject of holiness" (Ibid., p. 91). "He feels" himself such and he is such from the "beginning." That holiness conferred originally on man by the Creator pertains to the reality of the "sacrament of creation." The words of Genesis 2:24, "a man...cleaves to his wife and they become one flesh," spoken in the context of this original reality in a theological sense, constitute marriage as an integral part and, in a certain sense, a central part of the "sacrament of creation." They constitute, or perhaps rather, they simply confirm, the character of its origin. According to these words, marriage is a sacrament inasmuch as it is an integral part and, I would say, the central point of "the sacrament of creation." In this sense it is the primordial sacrament.

7. The institution of marriage, according to the words of Genesis 2:24, expresses not only the beginning of the fundamental human community which through the "procreative" power which is proper to it ("be fruitful and multiply": Gn. 1:28) serves to continue the work of creation, but it expresses at the same time the salvific initiative of the Creator, corresponding to the eternal election of man, of which the letter to the Ephesians speaks. That salvific initiative comes from God-Creator and its supernatural efficacy is identified with the very act of man's creation in the state of original innocence. In this state, already in the act of man's creation, there fructified his eternal election in Christ. In this way one must recognize that the original sacrament of creation draws its efficacy from the "beloved Son" (cf. Eph. 1:6 where it speaks of the "grace which he gave us in his beloved Son"). If then it treats of marriage, one can deduce that—

instituted in the context of the sacrament of creation in its globality, that is, in the state of original innocence—it should serve not only to prolong the work of creation, that is, of procreation, but also to extend to further generations of men the same sacrament of creation, that is, the supernatural fruits of man's eternal election on the part of the Father in the eternal Son: those fruits with which man was endowed by God in the very act of creation.

The letter to the Ephesians seems to authorize us to interpret in this way the book of Genesis and the truth about the "beginning" of man and of marriage contained therein.

Loss of Original Sacrament Restored with Redemption in the Marriage-Sacrament

General audience of October 13, 1982.

1. In our previous consideration we have tried to study in depth—in the light of the letter to the Ephesians—the sacramental "beginning" of man and marriage in the state of original justice (or innocence).

We know, however, that the heritage of grace was driven out of the human heart at the time of the breaking of the first covenant with the Creator. The perspective of procreation, *instead of being illuminated by the heritage of original grace,* given by God as soon as He infused a rational soul, became dimmed by the *heritage of original sin.* We can say that marriage, as a primordial sacrament, was deprived of that supernatural efficacy which at the moment of its institution belonged to the sacrament of creation in its totality. Nonetheless, even in this state, that is, in the state of man's hereditary sinfulness, *marriage never ceased being the figure of that sacrament* we read about in the letter to the Ephesians (Eph. 5:22-33) and which the author of that letter does not hesitate to call a "great mystery." Can we not perhaps deduce that marriage has remained the platform for the actuation of God's eternal designs, according to which the sacrament of creation had drawn near to men and had prepared them for the sacrament of redemption, introducing them into the dimension of the work of salvation? The analysis of the letter to the Ephesians, particularly the "classic" text of chapter 5, verses 22 to 33, seems to lean toward such a conclusion.

REDEMPTIVE GIFT
OF HIMSELF
FOR THE CHURCH

2. When in verse 31 the author refers to the words of the institution of marriage contained in Genesis (2:24: "For this reason man will leave his father and mother and will cling to his wife, and the two shall become one body"), and then immediately states: "This is a great mystery; I mean that it refers to Christ and the Church" (Eph. 5:32), he seems to indicate not only the identity of the mystery hidden in God from all eternity, but also that continuity of its actuation, which exists between

the primordial sacrament connected with the supernatural gracing of man in creation itself and the new gracing, which occurred when "Christ loved the Church and gave himself up for her to make her holy..." (Eph. 5:25-26)— *gracing that can be defined in its entirety as the sacrament of redemption*. In this redemptive gift of Himself "for" the Church, there is also contained—according to Pauline thought— Christ's gift of Himself to the Church, in the image of the nuptial relationship that unites husband and wife in marriage. In this way, the sacrament of redemption again takes on, in a certain sense, the figure and form of the primordial sacrament. To the marriage of the first husband and wife, as a sign of the supernatural gracing of man in the sacrament of creation, there corresponds the marriage, or rather the analogy of the marriage, of Christ with the Church as the fundamental "great" sign of the supernatural gracing of man in the sacrament of redemption—of the gracing in which there is renewed in a definitive way the covenant of the grace of election, which was broken in the "beginning" by sin.

SUPERNATURAL GRACING

3. The image contained in the quoted passage from the letter to the Ephesians seems to speak above all of the sacrament of redemp-

tion as that *definitive fulfillment of the mystery hidden from eternity in God*. In this *mysterium magnum* (great mystery) there is actuated precisely everything that the same letter to the Ephesians had treated in the first chapter. In fact, as we recall, it says not only "In him (that is, in Christ) God chose us before the world began, to be holy and blameless in his sight..." (Eph. 1:4), but also "in whom (Christ) we have redemption through his blood, the remission of sins, so immeasurably generous is God's favor to us..." (Eph. 1:7-8). The new supernatural gracing of man in the "sacrament of redemption" is also a new actuation of the mystery hidden in God from all eternity—new in relation to the sacrament of creation. At this moment, gracing is in a certain sense a "new creation." However, it differs from the sacrament of creation insofar as the original gracing, united to man's creation, constituted that man "in the beginning," through grace, in the state of original innocence and justice. The new gracing of man in the sacrament of redemption, instead, gives him above all the "remission of sins." Yet even here grace can "abound even more," as St. Paul expresses elsewhere: "Where sin increased, grace has abounded even more" (Rom. 5:20).

4. The sacrament of redemption—the fruit of Christ's redemptive love—becomes, *on the basis of His spousal love* for the Church, *a*

permanent dimension of the life of the Church
herself, a fundamental and life-giving dimension. It is the *mysterium magnum* (great mystery) of Christ and the Church: the eternal
mystery actuated by Christ, who "gave himself
up for her"? (Eph. 5:25); the mystery that is
continually actuated in the Church, because
Christ "loved the Church" (Eph. 5:25), uniting
Himself with her in an indissoluble love, just as
spouses, husband and wife, unite themselves in
marriage. In this way the Church lives on the
sacrament of redemption, and in her turn
completes this sacrament as the wife, in virtue
of spousal love, completes her husband, which
in a certain way had already been pointed out
"in the beginning" when the first man found in
the first woman "a helper fit for him" (Gn.
2:20). Although the analogy in the letter to the
Ephesians does not state it precisely, nevertheless we can add also that the Church united
to Christ, as the wife to her husband, draws
from the sacrament of redemption all her
fruitfulness and spiritual motherhood. Testify-
ing to this in some way are the words of the
letter of St. Peter, when he writes that we have
been "reborn not from a corruptible, but from
an incorruptible seed, through the living and
enduring word of God" (1 Pt. 1:23). So the
mystery hidden in God from all eternity—the
mystery that "in the beginning," in the sacrament of creation, became *a visible reality*

through the union of the first man and woman in the perspective of marriage—becomes in the sacrament of redemption *a visible reality of the indissoluble union of Christ with the Church,* which the author of the letter to the Ephesians presents as the nuptial union of spouses, husband and wife.

NEW ACTUATION OF MYSTERY

5. The *sacramentum magnum* (the Greek text reads: *tò mystérion toûto méga estín)* of the letter to the Ephesians speaks of the new actuation of the mystery hidden in God from all eternity; the definitive actuation from the point of view of the earthly history of salvation. It speaks besides of "making the mystery visible": the visibility of the Invisible. This visibility is not had unless the mystery ceases to be a mystery. This referred to the marriage constituted in the "beginning," in the state of original innocence, in the context of the sacrament of creation. It refers also to the union of Christ with the Church, as the "great mystery" of the sacrament of redemption. The visibility of the Invisible does not mean—if it can be said this way—a total clearing of the mystery. The mystery, as an object of faith, remains veiled even through what is precisely expressed and fulfilled. The visibility of the Invisible therefore belongs to the order of signs, and the

"sign" indicates only the reality of the mystery, but not the "unveiling." As the "first Adam"— man, male and female—created in the state of original innocence and called in this state to conjugal union (in this sense we are speaking of the sacrament of creation) was a sign of the eternal mystery, so the "second Adam," Christ, united with the Church through the sacrament of redemption by an indissoluble bond, analogous to the indissoluble covenant of spouses, is a definitive sign of the same eternal mystery. *Therefore, in speaking about the eternal mystery being actuated,* we are speaking *also about the fact that it becomes visible with the visibility of the sign.* And therefore we are speaking also about the *sacramentality* of the whole heritage of the sacrament of redemption, in reference to the entire work of creation and redemption, and more so in reference to marriage instituted within the context of the sacrament of creation, as also in reference to the Church as the spouse of Christ, endowed by a quasi-conjugal covenant with Him.

Marriage—An Integral Part of the New Sacramental Economy

General audience of October 20, 1982.

1. Last Wednesday we spoke of the integral heritage of the covenant with God, and of the grace originally united to the divine work of creation. Marriage also was a part of this integral heritage—as can be deduced from the text of the letter to the Ephesians 5:22-23—marriage, that is, as a primordial sacrament instituted from the "beginning" and linked with the sacrament of creation in its globality. The sacramentality of marriage is not merely a *model and figure* of the sacrament of the Church (of Christ and of the Church), but constitutes also an *essential part* of the new heritage: that of the sacrament of redemption, with which the Church is endowed in Christ.

Here it is necessary yet again to refer back to Christ's words in Matthew 19:3-9 (cf. also Mk. 10:5-9), in which Christ, in replying to the question of the Pharisees concerning marriage, *refers only and exclusively to its original institution* on the part of the Creator at the "beginning." Reflecting on the significance of this reply in the light of the letter to the Ephesians, and in particular of Ephesians 5:22-23, we end up with a relationship—in a certain sense twofold—of marriage with the whole sacramental order which, in the new covenant, emerges from the same sacrament of redemption.

MARRIAGE—THE PRIMORDIAL SACRAMENT

2. Marriage as a primordial sacrament constitutes, on the one hand, the *figure* (and so: the likeness, the analogy), according to which there is constructed the basic main structure of the new economy of salvation and of the sacramental order which draws its origin from the spousal gracing which the Church received from Christ, together with all the benefits of redemption (one could say, using the opening words of the letter to the Ephesians: "with every spiritual blessing": 1:3). In this way marriage, as a primordial sacrament, is assumed and inserted into the integral structure of the new sacramental economy, arising from redemption *in the form, I would say, of a "prototype"*: it is assumed and inserted as it

were from its very bases. Christ Himself, in conversation with the Pharisees (Mt. 19:3-9), reconfirmed first of all its existence. Reflecting deeply on this dimension, one would have to conclude that all the sacraments of the new covenant find in a certain sense their prototype in marriage as the primordial sacrament. This seems to be indicated in the classical passage quoted from the letter to the Ephesians, as we shall say again soon.

3. However, the relationship of marriage with the whole sacramental order, deriving from the endowment of the Church with the benefits of the redemption, is not limited merely to the dimension of model. Christ in His conversation with the Pharisees (Mt. 19), not only confirms the existence of marriage instituted from the "beginning" by the Creator, but He declares it *also an integral part of the new sacramental economy,* of the new order of salvific "signs" which derives its origin from the sacrament of redemption, just as the original economy emerged from the sacrament of creation; and, in fact, Christ limited Himself to the unique sacrament which was marriage instituted in the state of innocence and of original justice of man, created male and female "in the image and likeness of God."

4. The new sacramental economy which is constituted on the basis of the sacrament of redemption, deriving from the spousal gracing

of the Church on the part of Christ, *differs from the original economy*. Indeed, it is directed not to the man of justice and original innocence, but to the man burdened with the heritage of original sin and with the state of sinfulness *(status naturae lapsae)*. It is directed *to the man of the threefold concupiscence*, according to the classical words of the first letter of John (2:16), to the man in whom "the desires of the flesh are against the Spirit, and the desires of the Spirit are against the flesh" (Gal. 5:17), according to the Pauline theology (and anthropology), to which we have devoted much space in our previous reflections.

SACRAMENT
OF THE NEW COVENANT

5. These considerations, following upon a deeper analysis of the significance of Christ's statement in the Sermon on the Mount concerning "the lustful look" as "adultery of the heart," prepare for an understanding of marriage as an integral part of the new sacramental order which has its origin in the sacrament of redemption, that is to say, in that "great mystery" which, as the mystery of Christ and of the Church, determines the sacramentality of the Church itself. These considerations, besides, prepare for an understanding of *marriage as a sacrament of the new covenant,* whose salvific

work is organically linked with the *ensemble* of that ethos which was defined in the previous analyses as the *ethos of redemption*. The letter to the Ephesians expresses the same truth in its own way: it speaks in fact of marriage as a "great" sacrament in a wide paranaetic context, that is, in the context of the exhortations of a moral nature, concerning precisely the ethos which should characterize the life of Christians, that is, of people aware of the election which is realized in Christ and in the Church.

6. Against this vast background of the reflections which emerge from a reading of the letter to the Ephesians (particularly 5:22-33), one can and should eventually touch again the problem of the sacraments of the Church. The text cited from Ephesians speaks of it in an indirect and, I would say, secondary way, though sufficient to bring this problem within the scope of our considerations. However, it is fitting to clarify here, at least briefly, *the sense in which we use the term "sacrament,"* which is significant for our considerations.

7. Until now, indeed, we have used the term "sacrament" (in conformity with the whole of bibilical-patristic tradition)[1] in a sense wider than that proper to traditional and contemporary theological terminology, which means by the word "sacrament" the signs instituted by Christ and administered by the Church, which signify and confer divine grace on the person

who receives the relative sacrament. In this sense each of the seven sacraments of the Church is characterized by a determinate liturgical action, made up of words (the form) and the specific sacramental "matter"—according to the widespread hylomorphic theory deriving from Thomas Aquinas and the whole scholastic tradition.

8. In relationship to this rather restricted meaning, we have used in our considerations *a wider and perhaps also more ancient and fundamental meaning of the term "sacrament."*[2] The letter to the Ephesians, and especially 5:22-23, seems in a particular way to authorize us to do so. Here sacrament signifies the very mystery of God, which is hidden from eternity, however, not in an eternal concealment, but above all, in its very revelation and actuation (furthermore: in its revelation through its actuation). In this sense we spoke also of the sacrament of creation and of the sacrament of redemption. On the basis of the sacrament of creation, one must understand the original sacramentality of marriage (the primordial sacrament). Following upon this, on the basis of the sacrament of redemption one can understand the sacramentality of the Church, or rather the sacramentality of the union of Christ with the Church which the author of the letter to the Ephesians presents under the simile of marriage, of the conjugal union of husband and

wife. A careful analysis of the text shows that in this case, it is not merely a comparison in a metaphorical sense, but of a real *renewal* (or of a "re-creation," that is, of a new creation) of *that which constituted the salvific content* (in a certain sense, the "salvific substance") of the primordial sacrament. This observation has an essential significance both for the clarification of the sacramentality of the Church (and to this are referred the very significant words of the first chapter of the Constitution *Lumen gentium),* and also for the understanding of the sacramentality of marriage understood precisely as one of the sacraments of the Church.

NOTES

1. Cf. Leo XIII, Acta, vol. II, 1881, p. 22.
2. In this regard, cf. discourse at the general audience of September 8, 1982, note 1 *(L'Osservatore Romano,* English edition: September 13, 1982, p. 2).

Indissolubility of the Sacrament of Marriage in the Mystery of "Redemption of the Body"

General audience of October 27, 1982.

1. The text of the letter to the Ephesians (5:22-33) speaks of the sacraments of the Church—and in particular of Baptism and the Eucharist—but only in an indirect and, in a certain sense, allusive manner, developing the analogy of marriage in reference to Christ and the Church. And so we read at first that Christ who "loved the Church and gave himself up for her" (5:25), did so "that he might sanctify her, having cleansed her by the washing of water with the word" (5:26). This treats doubtlessly of the sacrament of Baptism, which by Christ's institution was from the beginning conferred on those who were converted. The words quoted show very graphically in what way Baptism draws its essential significance and its sac-

ramental power from that spousal love of the Redeemer by means of which there is constituted above all the sacramentality of the Church itself *(sacramentum magnum.)* The same can also be said perhaps of the Eucharist which would seem to be indicated by the following words about the nourishing of one's own body, which indeed every man nourishes and cherishes "as Christ does the Church, because we are members of his body" (5:29-30). In fact Christ nourishes the Church with His body precisely in the Eucharist.

2. One sees, however, that neither in the first nor second case can we speak of a well-developed sacramental theology. One cannot speak about it even when treating of the *sacrament of marriage as one of the sacraments of the Church.* The letter to the Ephesians, expressing the spousal relationship of Christ to the Church, lets it be understood that on the basis of this relationship the Church itself is the "great sacrament," the new sign of the covenant and of grace, which draws its roots from the depths of the sacrament of redemption, just as from the depths of the sacrament of creation there has emerged marriage, a primordial sign of the covenant and of grace. The author of the letter to the Ephesians proclaims that that primordial sacrament is realized in a new way in the "sacrament" of

Christ and of the Church. For this reason also the Apostle, in the same "classical" text of Ephesians 5:21-33, urges spouses to be "subject to one another out of reverence for Christ" (5:21) and model their conjugal life by basing it on the sacrament instituted at the beginning by the Creator: a sacrament which found its definitive greatness and holiness in the spousal covenant of grace between Christ and the Church.

"REDEMPTION OF THE BODY"

3. Even though the letter to the Ephesians does not speak directly and immediately of marriage as one of the sacraments of the Church, nevertheless the sacramentality of marriage is particularly confirmed and closely examined in it. In "the great sacrament" of Christ and of the Church Christian spouses are called upon to model their life and their vocation on the sacramental foundation.

4. After the analysis of the classical text of Ephesians 5:21-33, addressed to Christian spouses in which Paul announces to them the "great mystery" (sacramentum magnum) of the spousal love of Christ and of the Church, it is opportune to return to those significant words

of the Gospel which we have already analyzed previously, seeing in them the key statements for the theology of the body. Christ speaks these words, one might say, from the divine depth of the "redemption of the body" (Rom. 8:23). All these words have a fundamental significance for man inasmuch as he is a body— inasmuch as he is male or female. They have a significance for marriage in which man and woman unite so that the two become "one flesh," according to the expression of the book of Genesis (2:24), even though, at the same time, Christ's words also indicate the vocation to continence "for the sake of the kingdom of heaven" (Mt. 19:12).

5. In each of these ways "the redemption of the body" is not only a great expectation of those who possess "the first fruits of the spirit" (Rom. 8:23), but also a permanent source of hope that creation will be "set free from its bondage to decay and obtain the glorious liberty of the children of God" (ibid., 8:21). Christ's words, spoken from the divine depth of the mystery of redemption, and of the "redemption of the body," bear within them the leaven of this hope; they open to it a perspective both in the eschatological dimension and also in the dimension of daily life. In fact, the words addressed to the immediate hearers are simultaneously addressed to "historical" man of various times and places. That man

indeed who possesses "the first fruits of the spirit...groans...waiting for the redemption...of the body" *(ibid.,* 8:23). In him there is concentrated also the "cosmic" hope of the whole of creation, which in him, in man, "waits with eager longing for the revealing of the sons of God" *(ibid.,* 8:19).

THE PRIMORDIAL SACRAMENT

6. Christ speaks with the Pharisees, who ask Him: "Is it lawful to divorce one's wife for any cause?" (Mt. 19:3) They question Him in this way precisely because the law attributed to Moses permitted the so-called "bill of divorce" (Dt. 24:1). Christ's reply was as follows: "Have you not read that he who made them from the beginning made them male and female, and said, 'for this reason a man shall leave his father and mother and be joined to his wife, and the two shall become one'? So they are no longer two but one. What therefore God has joined together, let no man put asunder" (Mt. 19:2-6). They then went on to speak about the "bill of divorce" and Christ said to them: "For your hardness of heart Moses allowed you to divorce your wives, but from the beginning it was not so. And I say to you: Whoever divorces his wife, except for unchastity, and marries another, commits adultery" *(ibid.,* 19:8-9). "He

who marries a woman divorced from her husband, commits adultery" (Lk. 16:18).

7. The horizon of the "redemption of the body" is opened up with these words which constitute the reply to a concrete question of a juridical-moral nature; it is opened up, especially, by the fact that Christ takes His stand on the plane of that primordial sacrament which His questioners inherit in a singular manner, given that they also inherit the revelation of the mystery of creation, contained in the first chapters of the book of Genesis.

These words contain at the same time a universal reply addressed to "historical" man of all times and places, since they are decisive for marriage and for its indissolubility; in fact they refer to that which man is, male and female, such as he has become in an irreversible way by the fact of having been created "in the image and likeness of God." Man does not cease to be such even after original sin, even though this has deprived him of original innocence and justice. Christ who, in replying to the query of the Pharisees, refers to the "beginning," seems in this way to stress particularly the fact that He is speaking from the depth of the mystery of redemption, and of the redemption of the body. In fact *redemption* signifies, as it were, a *"new creation"*—it signifies the *assuming of all that is created:* to express in creation the fullness of justice, of equity and of sanctity designated by God, and to express that fullness especially in man, created as male and female "in the image of God."

In the perspective of Christ's words to the Pharisees on that which marriage was "from the beginning," we reread also the classical text of the letter to the Ephesians (5:22-33) as a testimony of the sacramentality of marriage based on the "great mystery" of Christ and of the Church.

Christ Opened Marriage to the Saving Action of God

General audience of November 24, 1982.

1. We have analyzed the letter to the Ephesians, and especially the passage of chapter 5, verses 22-23, from the point of view of the sacramentality of marriage. Now we shall examine the same text in the perspective of the words of the Gospel.

Christ's words to the Pharisees (cf. Mt. 19) refer to marriage as a sacrament, that is, to the primordial revelation of God's salvific will and deed "at the beginning" in the very mystery of creation. In virtue of that salvific will and deed of God, man and woman, joining together in such a way as to become "one flesh" (Gn. 2:24), were at the same time destined to be united "in truth and love" as children of God (cf. GS 24), adopted children in the only-begotten Son, beloved from all eternity. It is to this unity and towards this communion of persons, in the likeness of the union of the divine persons (cf. GS 24), that the words of Christ are directed which refer to marriage as the primordial sacrament and at the same time confirm that sacrament on the basis of the mystery of redemption. In fact, the original "unity in the body" of man and woman does not cease to mold the history of man on earth, even though it has lost the clarity of the sacrament, of the sign of salvation, which it possessed "at the beginning."

SALVIFIC REDEMPTION

2. If Christ in the presence of those with whom He was conversing, in the Gospels of Matthew and Mark (cf. Mt. 19; Mk. 10), confirms marriage as a sacrament instituted by the Creator "at the beginning"—if in conformity with this He insists on its indissolubility—He thereby opens marriage to the salvific action of God, to the forces which flow "from the redemption of the body" and which help to overcome the consequences of sin and to constitute the unity of man and woman according to the eternal plan of the Creator. The salvific action which derives from the mystery of redemption assumes in itself the original sanctifying action of God in the very mystery of creation.

3. The words of the Gospel of Matthew (cf. Mt. 19:3-9; Mk. 10:2-12), have at the

same time a very expressive ethical eloquence. These words confirm—on the basis of the mystery of redemption—the primordial sacrament and, at the same time, they establish an adequate ethos which in our previous reflections we have called "the ethos of redemption." The evangelical and Christian ethos, in its theological essence, is the ethos of redemption. Certainly, for that ethos we can find a rational interpretation, a philosophical interpretation of a personalistic character; however, in its theological essence, it is an ethos of redemption, rather, an *ethos of the redemption of the body*. Redemption becomes at the same time the basis for understanding the particular dignity of the human body, rooted in the personal dignity of the man and the woman. The reason of this dignity lies at the very root of the indissolubility of the conjugal covenant.

MORALITY CORRESPONDING TO GOD'S ACTION

4. Christ refers to the indissoluble character of marriage as a primordial sacrament, and, confirming this sacrament on the basis of the mystery of redemption, He simultaneously draws conclusions of an ethical nature: "Whoever divorces his wife and marries another commits adultery against her; and if she di-

vorces her husband and marries another, she commits adultery" (Mk. 10:11-12; cf. Mt. 19:9). It can be said that in this way redemption is given to man as a grace of the new covenant with God in Christ—and at the same time it is assigned to him as an ethos: as the form of the morality corresponding to God's action in the mystery of redemption. If marriage as a sacrament is an effective sign of God's salvific action "from the beginning," at the same time—in the light of Christ's words which are here under consideration—this sacrament constitutes also an exhortation addressed to man, male and female, so that they may participate consciously in the redemption of the body.

5. The ethical dimension of the redemption of the body is delineated in a particularly profound way when we meditate on Christ's words in the Sermon on the Mount in regard to the commandment "You shall not commit adultery." "You have heard that it was said, 'You shall not commit adultery.' But I say to you that everyone who looks at a woman lustfully has already committed adultery with her in his heart" (Mt. 5:27-28). We have previously given an ample commentary on this statement of Christ in the conviction that it has a fundamental significance for the whole theology of the body especially in the dimension of "historical" man. And even though these words do not refer directly and immediately to mar-

riage as a sacrament, nevertheless it is impossible to separate them from the whole sacramental substratum in which, as far as concerns the conjugal pact, there is placed the existence of man as male and female: both in the original context of the mystery of creation and then, later, in the context of the mystery of redemption. This sacramental substratum always regards individual persons, it penetrates into that which man and woman are (or rather, into *who* man and woman are) in their original dignity of image and likeness of God by reason of creation, and at the same time, in the same dignity inherited in spite of sin and again continually "assigned" to man as a duty through the reality of the redemption.

A NEW ETHOS

6. Christ, in the Sermon on the Mount, gives His own interpretation of the commandment: "You shall not commit adultery"—an interpretation which constitutes a new ethos—with the same lapidary words He assigns as a duty to every man the dignity of every woman; and simultaneously (even though this can be deduced from the text only in an indirect way), He also assigns to every woman the dignity of every man.[1] Finally He assigns to every one—both to man and woman—their own dignity: in a certain sense, the *"sacrum"* of the person, and

this in consideration of their femininity or masculinity, in consideration of the "body." It is not difficult to see that the words of Christ in the Sermon on the Mount regard the ethos. At the same time, it is not difficult to affirm, after deeper reflection, that these words flow from the very profundity of the redemption of the body. Even though they do not refer directly to marriage as a sacrament, it is not difficult to observe that they achieve their proper and full significance in relationship with the sacrament: whether that primordial sacrament which is united with the mystery of creation, or that in which "historical" man, after sin and because of his hereditary sinfulness, should find again the dignity and holiness of the conjugal union "in the body," on the basis of the mystery of redemption.

7. In the Sermon on the Mount—as also in the conversation with the Pharisees on the indissolubility of marriage—Christ speaks from the depths of that divine mystery. And at the same time He enters into the very depths of the human mystery. For that reason He makes mention of the "heart," of that "intimate place" in which there struggle in man good and evil, sin and justice, concupiscence and holiness. Speaking of concupiscence (of the lustful look: cf. Mt. 5:28), Christ makes His hearers aware that everyone bears within himself, together with the mystery of sin, the interior dimension

"of the man of concupiscence" (which is three-fold: "the concupiscence of the flesh, the concupiscence of the eyes and the pride of life," 1 Jn. 2:16).

It is precisely to this man of concupiscence that there is given in marriage the sacrament of redemption as a grace and a sign of the covenant with God—and it is assigned to him as an ethos. Simultaneously, in regard to marriage as a sacrament, it is assigned as an ethos to every man, male and female; it is assigned to his "heart," to his conscience, to his looks, and to his behavior. Marriage, according to Christ's words (cf. Mt. 19:4), is a sacrament from the very "beginning" and at the same time, on the basis of man's "historic" sinfulness, it is a sacrament arising from the mystery of the "redemption of the body."

NOTE

1. The text of St. Mark which speaks of the indissolubility of marriage clearly states that the woman also becomes a subject of adultery when she divorces her husband and marries another (cf. Mk. 10:12).

Marriage Sacrament Is an Effective Sign of God's Saving Power

General audience of December 1, 1982.

1. We have made an analysis of the letter to the Ephesians, and in particular of the passage of chapter 5:22-33, in the perspective of the sacramentality of marriage. Now we shall seek once again to consider the same text in the light of the words of the Gospel and of St. Paul's letters to the Corinthians and the Romans.

Marriage—as a sacrament born of the mystery of the redemption and reborn, in a certain sense, in the spousal love of Christ and of the Church—is an efficacious expression of the saving power of God who accomplishes His eternal plan even after sin and in spite of the threefold concupiscence hidden in the heart of every man, male and female. As a sacramental expression of that saving power, marriage is also an exhortation to dominate concupiscence (as Christ speaks of it in the Sermon on the Mount). The unity and indissolubility of marriage are the fruit of this dominion, as is also a deepened sense of the dignity of woman in the heart of a man (and also the dignity of man in the heart of woman), both in conjugal life together, and in every other circle of mutual relations.

MARRIAGE
IN THE TEACHING
OF ST. PAUL

2. The truth, according to which marriage as a sacrament of redemption is given to the "man of concupiscence" as a grace and at the same time as an ethos, has also found particular expression in the teaching of St. Paul, especially in the seventh chapter of the first letter to the Corinthians. The Apostle, comparing marriage with virginity (or with "celibacy for the sake of the kingdom of heaven") and deciding for the "superiority" of virginity, observes at the same time that "each has his own special gift from God, one of one kind and one of another" (1 Cor. 7:7). On the basis of the mystery of redemption, there corresponds to marriage a special "gift," that is, a grace. In the same text the Apostle, giving advice to those to whom he is writing, recommends marriage

"because of the temptation to immorality" (*ibid.,* 7:2), and later he recommends to the married couple that "the husband should give to his wife her conjugal rights, and likewise the wife to her husband" (*ibid.,* 7:3). And he continues thus: "It is better to marry than to be aflame with passion" (*ibid.,* 7:9).

3. These statements of St. Paul have given rise to the opinion that marriage constitutes a specific remedy for concupiscence. However, St. Paul—who, as we have already observed, teaches explicitly that marriage has a corresponding special "gift," and that in the mystery of redemption marriage is given to a man and a woman as a grace—expresses in his striking and at the same time paradoxical words, simply the thought that marriage is assigned to the spouses as an ethos. In the Pauline words, "it is better to marry than to be aflame with passion," the verb *ardere* signifies a disorder of the passions, deriving from the concupiscence of the flesh (concupiscence is presented in a similar way in the Old Testament by Sirach: cf. Sir. 23:17). "Marriage," however, signifies the ethical order, which is consciously introduced in this context. It can be said that marriage is the meeting place of eros with ethos and of their mutual compenetration in the "heart" of man and of woman, as also in all their mutual relationships.

A SACRAMENT DERIVED FROM THE MYSTERY OF REDEMPTION

4. This truth—namely, that marriage as a sacrament derived from the mystery of redemption is given to "historical" man as a grace and at the same time as an ethos—determines moreover the character of marriage as one of the sacraments of the Church. As a sacrament of the Church, marriage has the nature of indissolubility. As a sacrament of the Church, it is also a word of the Spirit which exhorts man and woman to model their whole life together by drawing power from the mystery of the "redemption of the body." In this way they are called to chastity as to a state of life "according to the Spirit" which is proper to them (cf. Rom. 8:4-5; Gal. 5:25). The redemption of the body also signifies in this case that "hope" which, in the dimension of marriage, can be defined as the hope of daily life, the hope of temporal life. On the basis of such a hope there is dominated the concupiscence of the flesh as the source of the tendency towards an egoistic gratification, and the same "flesh," in the sacramental alliance of masculinity and femininity, becomes the specific "substratum" of an enduring and indissoluble communion of the persons (*communio personarum*) in a manner worthy of the persons.

LIFE "ACCORDING
TO THE SPIRIT"

5. Those who, as spouses, according to the eternal divine plan, join together so as to become in a certain sense "one flesh," are also in their turn called, through the sacrament, to a life "according to the Spirit," such as corresponds to the "gift" received in the sacrament. In virtue of that "gift," the spouses, by leading a life "according to the Spirit," are capable of rediscovering the particular gratification of which they have become sharers. As much as "concupiscence" darkens the horizon of the inward vision and deprives the heart of the clarity of desires and aspirations, so much does "life according to the Spirit" (that is, the grace of the sacrament of marriage) permit man and woman to find again the true liberty of the gift, united to the awareness of the spousal meaning of the body in its masculinity and femininity.

6. The life "according to the Spirit" is also expressed in the mutual "union" (cf. Gn. 4:1), whereby the spouses, becoming "one flesh," submit their femininity and masculinity to the blessing of procreation: "Adam knew Eve his wife, and she conceived and gave birth...saying: 'I have gotten a man with the help of the Lord'" (Gn. 4:1).

The life "according to the Spirit" is also expressed here in the consciousness of the gratification, to which there corresponds the dignity of the spouses themselves as parents, that is to say, it is expressed in the profound awareness of the sanctity of the life *(sacrum)*, to which the two give origin, participating—as progenitors—in the forces of the mystery of creation. In the light of that hope, which is connected with the mystery of the redemption of the body (cf. Rom. 8:19-23), this new human. life, a new man conceived and born of the conjugal union of his father and mother, opens to "the first fruits of the Spirit" *(ibid., 8:23)* "to enter into the liberty of the glory of the children of God" *(ibid., 8:21).* And if "the whole creation has been groaning in travail together until now" *(ibid., 8:22),* a particular hope accompanies the pains of the mother in labor, that is, the hope of the "revelation of the sons of God" *(ibid., 8:22),* a hope of which every newborn babe that comes into the world bears within himself a spark.

7. This hope which is "in the world," penetrating—as St. Paul teaches—the whole of creation, is not at the same time "from the world." Still further: it must struggle in the human heart with that which is "from the world," with that which is "in the world." "Because everything that is in the world, the

lust of the flesh and the lust of the eyes and the pride of life, is not of the Father, but is of the world" (1 Jn. 2:16). Marriage, as the primordial sacrament, and at the same time as the sacrament born in the mystery of the redemption of the body from the spousal love of Christ and of the Church, "comes from the Father." It is not "from the world" but "from the Father." Consequently, marriage also as a sacrament constitutes the basis of hope for the person, that is, for man and woman, for parents and children, for the human generations. On the one hand, indeed, "the world passes away and the lust thereof," while on the other, "he who does the will of God abides forever" *(ibid., 2:17)*. With marriage, as a sacrament, is united the origin of man in the world, and in it there is also inscribed its future, and this not merely in the historical dimensions, but also in the eschatological.

THE RESURRECTION OF THE BODY

8. It is to this that Christ's words refer when He speaks of the resurrection of the body—words reported by the three synoptics (cf. Mt. 22:23-32; Mk. 12:18-27; Lk. 20:34-39). "In the resurrection they neither marry nor are given in marriage, but are like angels in

heaven": thus states Matthew, and in like manner Mark. In Luke we read: "The sons of this age marry and are given in marriage; but those who are accounted worthy to attain to that age and to the resurrection of the dead neither marry nor are given in marriage, for they cannot die any more, because they are equal to angels and are sons of God" (Luke 20:34-36). These texts were previously subjected to a detailed analysis.

9. Christ states that marriage—the sacrament of the origin of man in the temporal visible world—does not pertain to the eschatological reality of the "future world." However, man, called to participate in this eschatological future by means of the resurrection of the body, is the same man, male and female, whose origin in the temporal visible world is linked with marriage as the primordial sacrament of the very mystery of creation. Rather, every man, called to share in the reality of the future resurrection, brings into the world this vocation by the fact that in the temporal visible world he has his origin by means of the marriage of his parents. Thus, then, Christ's words which exclude marriage from the reality of the "future world," reveal indirectly at the same time the significance of this sacrament for the participation of men, sons and daughters, in the future resurrection.

10. Marriage, which is the primordial sacrament—reborn in a certain sense in the spousal love of Christ and of the Church—does not pertain to the "redemption of the body" in the dimension of the eschatological hope (cf. Rom. 8:23). The same marriage given to man as a grace, as a "gift" destined by God precisely for the spouses, and at the same time assigned to them by Christ's words as an ethos—that sacramental marriage is accomplished and realized in the perspective of the eschatological hope. It has an essential significance for the "redemption of the body" in the dimension of this hope. It comes indeed from the Father and to Him it owes its origin in the world. And if this "world passes," and if with it there pass also the lust of the flesh, the lust of the eyes and the pride of life which come "from the world," marriage as a sacrament immutably ensures that man, male and female, by dominating concupiscence, does the will of the Father. And he "who does the will of God remains forever" (1 Jn. 2:17).

11. In this sense marriage as a sacrament also bears within itself the germ of man's eschatological future, that is, the perspective of the "redemption of the body" in the dimension of the eschatological hope to which correspond Christ's words about the resurrection: "In the resurrection they neither marry nor are given in marriage" (Mt. 22:30). However, also those

who, "being sons of the resurrection...are equal to angels and are sons of God" (Lk. 20:36), owe their origin in the temporal visible world to the marriage and procreation of man and woman. Marriage, as the sacrament of the human "beginning," as the sacrament of the temporality of the historical man, fulfills in this way an irreplaceable service in regard to his extra-temporal future, in regard to the mystery of the "redemption of the body" in the dimension of the eschatological hope.

The Redemptive and Spousal Dimension of Love

General audience of December 15, 1982.

1. The author of the letter to the Ephesians, as we have already seen, speaks of a "great mystery," linked to the primordial sacrament through the continuity of God's saving plan. He also refers to the "beginning," as Christ did in His conversation with the Pharisees (cf. Mt. 19:8), quoting the same words: "Therefore a man leaves his father and his mother and cleaves to his wife, and they become one flesh" (Gn. 2:24). This "great mystery" is above all the mystery of the union of Christ with the Church which the Apostle presents under the similitude of the unity of the spouses: "I mean it in reference to Christ and the Church" (Eph. 5:32). We find ourselves in the domain of the great analogy in which marriage as a sacrament on the one hand is presupposed, and on the other hand, rediscovered. It is presupposed as the sacrament of the "beginning" of mankind united to the

mystery of the creation. It is, however, redis-covered as the fruit of the spousal love of Christ and of the Church linked with the mystery of the redemption.

ADDRESS TO SPOUSES

2. The author of the letter to the Ephe-sians, addressing spouses directly, exhorts them to mold their reciprocal relationship on the model of the spousal union of Christ and the Church. It can be said that—presupposing the sacramentality of marriage in its primordial significance—he orders them to learn anew this sacrament of the spousal unity of Christ and the Church: "Husbands, love your wives, as Christ loved the Church and gave himself up for her, that he might sanctify her..." (cf. Eph. 5:25-26). This invitation addressed to Christian spouses by the Apostle is fully motivated by the fact that they, through marriage as a sacrament, participate in Christ's saving love which is expressed at the same time as His spousal love for the Church. In the light of the letter to the Ephesians—precisely through par-ticipation in this saving love of Christ—mar-riage as a sacrament of the human "beginning" is confirmed and at the same time renewed, that is, the sacrament in which man and woman, called to become "one flesh," partici-pate in God's own creative love. And they

participate in it both by the fact that, created in the image of God, they are called by reason of this image to a particular union *(communio personarum)*, and because this same union has from the beginning been blessed with the blessing of fruitfulness (cf. Gn. 1:28).

DRAWING FROM
NEW DEPTHS OF LOVE

3. All this original and stable structure of marriage as a sacrament of the mystery of creation—according to the "classic" text of the letter to the Ephesians (Eph. 5:21-33)—is renewed in the mystery of the redemption, when that mystery assumes the aspect of the spousal love of the Church on the part of Christ. That original and stable form of marriage is renewed when the spouses receive it as a sacrament of the Church, drawing from the new depths of the love for man on the part of God, which is revealed and opened with the mystery of the redemption, "when Christ loved the Church and gave himself up for her to make her holy..." (Eph. 5:25-26). That original and stable image of marriage as a sacrament is renewed when Christian spouses—conscious of the authentic profundity of the "redemption of the body"—are united "out of reverence for Christ" (Eph. 5:21).

FUSING THE DIMENSIONS

4. The Pauline image of marriage, inscribed in the "great mystery" of Christ and of the Church, brings together the redemptive dimension and the spousal dimension of love. In a certain sense it fuses these two dimensions into one. Christ has become the spouse of the Church, He has married the Church as a bride, because "he has given himself up for her" (Eph. 5:25). Through marriage as a sacrament (as one of the sacraments of the Church) both these dimensions of love, the spousal and the redemptive, together with the grace of the sacrament, permeate the life of the spouses. The spousal significance of the body in its masculinity and femininity, which was manifested for the first time in the mystery of creation against the background of man's original innocence, is linked in the image of the letter to the Ephesians with the redemptive significance and in this way it is confirmed and in a certain sense, "newly created."

UNDERSTANDING THE LINK

5. This is important in regard to marriage and to the Christian vocation of husbands and wives. The text of the letter to the Ephesians (5:21-33) is directly addressed to them and speaks especially to them. However, that link-

ing of the spousal significance of the body with its "redemptive" significance is equally essential and valid for the understanding of man in general: for the fundamental problem of understanding him and for the self-comprehension of his being in the world. It is obvious that we cannot exclude from this problem the question on the meaning of being a body, on the sense of being, as a body, man and woman. These questions were posed for the first time in relation to the analysis of the human "beginning," in the context of the book of Genesis. It was that very context, in a certain sense, that demanded that they should be posed. It is equally demanded by the "classic" text of the letter to the Ephesians. And if the "great mystery" of the union of Christ to the Church obliges us to link the spousal significance of the body with its redemptive significance, in this link the spouses find the answer to the question concerning the meaning of "being a body," and not only they, although this text of the Apostle's letter is addressed especially to them.

EXPLANATION BY ANALOGY

6. The Pauline image of the "great mystery" of Christ and of the Church also speaks indirectly of "celibacy for the sake of the

kingdom of heaven," in which both dimensions of love, the spousal and redemptive, are reciprocally united in a way different from that of marriage, according to diverse proportions. Is not perhaps that spousal love wherewith Christ "loved the church"—His bride—"and gave himself up for her," at the same time the fullest incarnation of the ideal of "celibacy for the kingdom of heaven" (cf. Mt. 19:12)? Is not support found precisely in this by all those— men and women—who, choosing the same ideal, desire to link the spousal dimension of love with the redemptive dimension according to the model of Christ Himself? They wish to confirm with their life that the spousal significance of the body—of its masculinity and femininity—profoundly inscribed in the essential structure of the human person, has been opened in a new way on the part of Christ and with the example of His life, to the hope united to the redemption of the body. Thus, then, the grace of the mystery of the redemption bears fruit also—rather bears fruit in a special way— with the vocation to celibacy "for the kingdom of heaven."

7. The text of the letter to the Ephesians (5:22-33) does not speak of it explicitly. It is addressed to spouses and constructed according to the image of marriage, which by analogy explains the union of Christ with the Church: a union in both redemptive and spousal love

together. Is it not perhaps precisely this love which, as the living and vivifying expression of the mystery of the redemption, goes beyond the circle of the recipients of the letter circumscribed by the analogy of marriage? Does it not embrace every man and, in a certain sense, the whole of creation as indicated by the Pauline text on the "redemption of the body" in the letter to the Romans (cf. Rom. 8:23)? The "great sacrament" in this sense is in fact a new sacrament of man in Christ and in the Church: the sacrament "of man and of the world," just as the creation of man, male and female, in the image of God, was the original sacrament of man and of the world. In this new sacrament of redemption marriage is organically inscribed, just as it was inscribed in the original sacrament of creation.

FULFILLMENT
OF THE KINGDOM

8. Man, who "from the beginning" is male and female, should seek the meaning of his existence and the meaning of his humanity by reaching out to the mystery of creation through the reality of redemption. There one finds also the essential answer to the question on the significance of the human body, and the significance of the masculinity and femininity of the

human person. The union of Christ with the Church permits us to understand in what way the spousal significance of the body is completed with the redemptive significance, and this in the diverse ways of life and in diverse situations: not only in marriage or in "continency" (that is, virginity and celibacy), but also, for example, in the many forms of human suffering, indeed, in the very birth and death of man. By means of the "great mystery" of which the letter to the Ephesians treats, by means of the new covenant of Christ with the Church, marriage is again inscribed in that "sacrament of man" which embraces the universe, in the sacrament of man and of the world which, thanks to the forces of the "redemption of the body" is modelled on the spousal love of Christ for the Church, to the measure of the definitive fulfillment of the kingdom of the Father.

Marriage as a sacrament remains a living and vivifying part of this saving process.

"Language of the Body"— the Substratum and Content of the Sacramental Sign of Spousal Communion

General audience of January 5, 1983.

1. "I take you as my wife"; "I take you as my husband"—these words are at the center of the liturgy of marriage as a sacrament of the Church. These words spoken by the engaged couple are inserted in the following formula of consent: "...I promise to be faithful to you always, in joy and in sorrow, in sickness and in health, and to love and honor you all the days of my life." With these words the engaged couple enter the marriage contract and at the same time receive the sacrament of which both are the ministers. Both of them, the man and the woman, administer the sacrament. They do it before witnesses. The priest is a qualified witness, and at the same time he blesses the marriage and presides over the whole sacramental liturgy. Moreover, all those participat-

ing in the marriage rite are in a certain sense witnesses, and some of them (usually two) are called specifically to act as witnesses in an "official" way. They must testify that the marriage was contracted before God and confirmed by the Church. In the ordinary course of events sacramental marriage is a public act by means of which two persons, a man and a woman, become husband and wife before the ecclesial society, that is, they become the actual subject of the marriage vocation and life.

CONSUMMATION
OF MARRIAGE

2. Marriage is a sacrament which is contracted by means of the word which is a sacramental sign by reason of its content: "I take you as my wife—as my husband—and I promise to be always faithful to you, in joy and sorrow, in sickness and in health, and to love you and honor you all the days of my life." However, this sacramental word is, *per se,* merely the sign of the coming into being of marriage. And the coming into being of marriage is distinguished from its consummation to the extent that without this consummation the marriage is not yet constituted in its full reality. The fact that a marriage is juridically contracted but not consummated (*ratum—no*

consummatum) corresponds to the fact that it has not been fully constituted as a marriage. Indeed the very words "I take you as my wife—my husband" refer not only to a determinate reality, but they can be fulfilled only by means of conjugal intercourse. This reality (conjugal intercourse) has moreover been determined from the very beginning by institution of the Creator: "Therefore a man leaves his father and his mother and cleaves to his wife, and they become one flesh" (cf. Gn. 2:24).

3. Thus then, from the words whereby the man and the woman express their willingness to become "one flesh" according to the eternal truth established in the mystery of creation, we pass to the reality which corresponds to these words. Both the one and the other element are important in regard to the structure of the sacramental sign to which it is fitting to devote the remainder of the present reflections. Granted that the sacrament is a sign which expresses and at the same time effects the saving reality of grace and of the covenant, one must now consider it under the aspect of sign, whereas the previous reflections were dedicated to the reality of grace and of the covenant.

Marriage, as a sacrament of the Church, is contracted by means of the words of the ministers, that is, of the newlyweds: words which signify and indicate, in the order of intention, that which (or rather: who) both have decided to be from now on, the one for the other and the one with the other. The words of the newlyweds form a part of the integral structure of the sacramental sign, not merely *for what* they signify but also, in a certain sense, *with what* they signify and determine. The sacramental sign is constituted in the order of intention insofar as it is simultaneously constituted in the real order.

THE SACRAMENTAL SIGN OF MARRIAGE

4. Consequently, the sacramental sign of marriage is constituted by the words of the newlyweds inasmuch as the "reality" which they themselves constitute corresponds to those words. Both of them, as man and woman, being the ministers of the sacrament in the moment of contracting marriage, constitute at the same time the full and real visible sign of the sacrament itself. The words spoken by them would not *per se* constitute the sacramental sign of marriage unless there corresponded to them the human subjectivity of the engaged couple and at the same time the awareness of the body, linked to the masculinity and femininity of the husband and wife. Here it is necessary to recall to mind the whole series of

our previous analyses in regard to the book of Genesis (cf. Gn. 1:2). The structure of the sacramental sign remains in fact essentially the same as "in the beginning." It is determined, in a certain sense, by "the language of the body," inasmuch as the man and the woman, who through marriage should become one flesh, express in this sign the reciprocal gift of masculinity and femininity as the basis of the conjugal union of the persons.

5. The sacramental sign of marriage is constituted by the fact that the words spoken by the newlyweds use again the same "language of the body" as at the "beginning," and in any case they give to it a concrete and unique expression. They give it an intentional expression on the level of intellect and will, of consciousness and of the heart. The words "I take you as my wife/as my husband" imply precisely that perennial, unique and unrepeatable "language of the body," and at the same time they situate it in the context of the communion of the persons: "I promise to be always faithful to you, in joy and in sadness, in sickness and in health, and to love you and honor you all the days of my life." In this way the enduring and ever new "language of the body" is not only the "substratum" but, in a certain sense, the constitutive element of the communion of the persons. The persons—man and woman—become for each other a mutual

gift. They become that gift in their masculinity and femininity, discovering the spousal significance of the body and referring it reciprocally to themselves in an irreversible manner: in a life-long dimension.

SIGN OF THE COVENANT

6. Thus the sacrament of marriage as a sign enables us to understand the words of the newlyweds, words which confer a new aspect on their life in a dimension strictly personal (and interpersonal: *communio personarum*), on the basis of the "language of the body." The administration of the sacrament consists in this: that in the moment of contracting marriage the man and the woman, by means of suitable words and recalling the perennial "language of the body," form a sign, an unrepeatable sign, which has also a significance for the future: "all the days of my life," that is to say, until death. This is a visible and efficacious sign of the covenant with God in Christ, that is, of grace which in this sign should become a part of them as "their own special gift" (according to the expression of the first letter to the Corinthians 7:7).

7. Expressing this matter in socio-juridical terms one can say that between the newlyweds there is a stipulated, a well-defined conjugal

pact. It can also be said that following upon this pact, they have become spouses in a manner socially recognized, and that in this way there is also constituted in germ the family as the fundamental social cell. This manner of understanding it is obviously in agreement with the human reality of marriage, indeed, it is also fundamental in the religious and religious-moral sense. However, from the point of view of the theology of the sacrament, the key for the understanding of marriage is always the reality of the sign whereby marriage is constituted on the basis of the covenant of man with God in Christ and in the Church: it is constituted in the supernatural order of the sacred bond requiring grace. In this order marriage is a visible and efficacious sign. Having its origin in the mystery of creation, it derives its new origin from the mystery of redemption at the service of the "union of the sons of God in truth and in love" (GS 24). The liturgy of the sacrament of marriage gives a form to that sign: directly, during the sacramental rite, on the basis of the *ensemble* of its eloquent expressions; indirectly, throughout the whole of life. The man and woman, as spouses, bear this sign throughout the whole of their lives and they remain as that sign until death.

The "Language of the Body" in the Structure of Marriage

General audience of January 12, 1983.

1. We now analyze the sacramentality of marriage under the aspect of sign.

When we say that the "language of the body" also enters essentially into the structure of marriage as a sacramental sign, we refer to a long biblical tradition. This has its origin in the book of Genesis (especially 2:23 to 25) and it finds its definitive culmination in the letter to the Ephesians (cf. Eph. 5:21-33). The prophets of the Old Testament had an essential role in forming this tradition. Analyzing the texts of Hosea, Ezekiel, Deutero-Isaiah, and of the other prophets, we find ourselves face to face with the great analogy whose final expression is the proclamation of the New Covenant under the form of a marriage between Christ and the Church (cf. *ibid.*). On the basis of this long tradition it is possible to speak of a specific "prophetism of the body," both because of the fact that we find this analogy especially in the prophets, and also in regard to its very content. Here, the "prophetism of the body" signifies precisely the "language of the body."

THE COVENANT BETWEEN GOD AND ISRAEL

2. The analogy seems to have two levels. On the first and fundamental level the prophets present the Covenant between God and Israel as a marriage (which also permits us to understand marriage itself as a covenant between husband and wife) (cf. Prv. 2:17; Mal. 2:14). In this case the Covenant derives from the initiative of God, the Lord of Israel. The fact that He, as Creator and Lord, makes a Covenant first of all with Abraham and then with Moses, already bears witness to a special choice. And therefore the prophets, presupposing the entire juridical-moral content of the Covenant, go much deeper and reveal a dimension incomparably more profound than that of a mere "pact." God, in choosing Israel, is united with His people through love and grace. He is bound with a special bond, profoundly personal, and therefore Israel, even though a people, is

presented in this prophetic vision of the Covenant as a "spouse" or "wife," and therefore, in a certain sense, as a person:

> "For your Maker is your husband,
>   the Lord of Hosts is his name;
>   and the Holy One of Israel is your
>   Redeemer,
> the God of the whole earth he is called.
> ...says your God.
> ...But my steadfast love shall not depart
>   from you
> and my covenant of peace shall not be
>   removed" (Is. 54:5, 6, 10).

3. Yahweh is the Lord of Israel, but He also becomes her Spouse. The books of the Old Testament bear witness to the absolute original character of the "dominion" of Yahweh over His people. To the other aspects of the dominion of Yahweh, Lord of the Covenant and Father of Israel, there is added a new aspect revealed by the prophets, that is to say, the stupendous dimension of this "dominion," which is the spousal dimension. In this way, the absolute of dominion is the absolute of love. In regard to this absolute, the breach of the Covenant signifies not only an infraction of the "pact" linked with the authority of the supreme Legislator, but also infidelity and betrayal: it is a blow which even pierces His heart as Father, as Spouse and as Lord.

4. If, in the analogy employed by the prophets, one can speak of levels, this is in a certain sense the first and fundamental level. Given that the Covenant of Yahweh with Israel has the character of a spousal bond like to the conjugal pact, that first level of the analogy reveals a second which is precisely the "language of the body." Here we have in mind, in the first place, the language in an objective sense. The prophets compare the Covenant to marriage, they refer to the primordial sacrament spoken of by Genesis 2, verse 24, in which the man and the woman, by free choice, become "one flesh." However, it is characteristic of the prophets' manner of expressing themselves that, presupposing the "language of the body" in the objective sense, they pass at the same time to its subjective meaning: that is to say, after a manner of speaking, they allow the body itself to speak. In the prophetic texts of the Covenant, on the basis of the analogy of the spousal union of the married couple, it is the body itself which "speaks"; it speaks by means of its masculinity and femininity, it speaks in the mysterious language of the personal gift, it speaks ultimately—and this happens more frequently—both in the language of fidelity, that is, of love, and also in the language of conjugal infidelity, that is, of "adultery."

HOSEA AND EZEKIEL

5. It is well known that the different sins of the Chosen People—and especially their frequent infidelities in regard to the worship of the one God, that is, various forms of idolatry—offered the prophets the occasion to denounce the aforesaid sins. The prophet of the "adultery" of Israel was, in a special way, Hosea, who condemned it, not only in words, but also, in a certain sense, in actions of a symbolical significance: "Go, take to yourself a wife of harlotry and have children of harlotry, for the land commits great harlotry by forsaking the Lord" (Hos. 1:2). Hosea sets out in relief all the splendor of the Covenant—of that marriage in which Yahweh manifests Himself as a sensitive, affectionate Spouse disposed to forgiveness, and at the same time, exigent and severe. The "adultery" and the "harlotry" of Israel are in evident contrast with the marriage bond on which is based the Covenant, as likewise, analogically, the marriage of man and woman.

6. In a similar way, Ezekiel condemned idolatry, making use of the symbol of the adultery of Jerusalem (cf. Ez. 16) and, in another passage, of Jerusalem and of Samaria (cf. Ez. 23): "When I passed by you again and looked upon you, behold, you were at the age for love.... I plighted my troth to you and entered into a covenant with you, says the Lord

God, and you became mine" (Ez. 16:8). "But
you trusted in your beauty and played the
harlot because of your renown, and lavished
your harlotry on any passer-by" (Ez. 16:15).

"LANGUAGE OF THE BODY"

7. In the texts of the prophets the human
body speaks a "language" of which it is not the
author. Its author is man as male or female, as
husband or wife—man with his everlasting
vocation to the communion of persons. Man,
however, cannot, in a certain sense, express this
singular language of his personal existence and
of his vocation without the body. He has
already been constituted in such a way from
the "beginning," in such wise that the most
profound words of the spirit—words of love, of
giving, of fidelity—demand an adequate "language of the body." And without that they
cannot be fully expressed. We know from the
Gospel that this refers both to marriage and
also to celibacy "for the sake of the kingdom."

8. The prophets, as the inspired mouth-
pieces of the Covenant of Yahweh with Israel,
seek precisely through this "language of the
body" to express both the spousal profundity of
the aforesaid Covenant and all that is opposed
to it. They praise fidelity, they condemn infidelity as "adultery"—they speak therefore

according to ethical categories, setting in mutual opposition moral good and evil. The opposition between good and evil is essential for morality. The texts of the prophets have an essential significance in this sphere, as we have already shown in our previous reflections. It seems, however, that the "language of the body" according to the prophets is not merely a language of morality, a praise of fidelity and of purity, and a condemnation of "adultery" and of "harlotry." In fact, for every language as an expression of knowledge, the categories of truth and of non-truth (that is, of falsity) are essential. In the writings of the prophets, who catch a fleeting glimpse of the analogy of the Covenant of Yahweh with Israel in marriage, the body speaks the truth through fidelity and conjugal love, and when it commits "adultery" it speaks lies, it is guilty of falsity.

9. It is not a case of substituting ethical with logical differentiations. If the texts of the prophets indicate conjugal fidelity and chastity as "truth," and adultery or harlotry, on the other hand, as "non-truth," as a falsity of the "language of the body," this happens because in the first case the subject (that is, Israel as a spouse) is in accord with the spousal significance which corresponds to the human body (because of its masculinity or femininity) in the integral structure of the person; in the second

case, however, the same subject contradicts and opposes this significance.

We can then say that the essential element for marriage as a sacrament is the "language of the body" in its aspects of truth. It is precisely by means of that, that the sacramental sign is, in fact, constituted.

The Sacramental Covenant in the Dimension of Sign

General audience of January 19, 1983.

Dear brothers and sisters:

This audience takes place on the second day of the Week of Prayer for Christian Unity among those who believe in Jesus Christ and await salvation from Him. This is a moment of great ecclesial importance: I would like it to be profoundly shared by all the faithful of the Catholic Church and by Christians of the churches and communions still separated from us, to whom I send my affectionate and trustful greetings.

Inspired by the theme proposed to our reflection this year: "Jesus Christ, the life of the world" (cf. 1 Jn. 1:1-4), we pray that He may enliven and unite to an ever greater extent those who believe in Him. By His grace, supported by a persevering effort, composed of humility, charity and good will, we wish to arrive one day at that so much desired goal for which the Lord Himself prayed: "that they may be one" (Jn. 17:11).

1. The texts of the prophets have great importance for understanding marriage as a covenant of persons (in the likeness of the Covenant of Yahweh with Israel) and, in particular, for the understanding of the sacramental covenant of man and woman in the dimension of sign. As already considered beforehand, the "language of the body" enters into the integral structure of the sacramental sign whose principal subject is man, male and female. The words of matrimonial consent *constitute this sign,* because there is found in them the spousal significance of the body in its masculinity and femininity. Such a significance is expressed especially by the words: "I take you as my wife...my husband." Moreover, with these words there is confirmed the essential "truth" of the language of the body and there is also (at least indirectly, *implicitly*) excluded the essential "non-truth," the falsity of the language of the body. The body, in fact, speaks the truth through conjugal love, fidelity and integrity, just as non-truth, that is, falsity, is expressed by all that is the negation of conjugal love, fidelity and integrity. It can then be said that in the moment of pronouncing the words of matrimonial consent, the newlyweds set themselves on the line of the same "prophetism of the body," of which the

ancient prophets were the mouthpiece. The "language of the body," expressed by the ministers of marriage as a sacrament of the Church, institutes the visible sign itself of the Covenant and of grace which, going back to its origin to the mystery of creation, is continually sustained by the power of the "redemption of the body," offered by Christ to the Church.

PERFORM AN ACT
OF PROPHETIC CHARACTER

2. According to the prophetic texts the human body speaks a "language," of which it is not the author. Its author is *man* who, as male and female, husband and wife, correctly re-reads the significance of this "language." He rereads therefore that spousal significance of the body as integrally inscribed in the structure of the masculinity or femininity of the personal subject. A correct rereading "in truth" is an indispensable condition to proclaim this truth, that is, to institute the visible sign of marriage as a sacrament. The spouses proclaim precisely this "language of the body," reread in truth, as the content and principle of their new life in Christ and in the Church. On the basis of the "prophetism of the body" the ministers of the Sacrament of Marriage perform an act of prophetic character. They confirm in this way their participation in the prophetic mission of

the Church received from Christ. A prophet is one who expresses in human words the truth coming from God, one who speaks this truth in the place of God, in His name and in a certain sense with His authority.

MATRIMONIAL CONSENT

3. All this applies to the newlyweds who, as ministers of the Sacrament of Marriage, institute the visible sign by the words of matrimonial consent, proclaiming the "language of the body," reread in truth, as content and principle of their new life in Christ and in the Church. This "prophetic" proclamation has a complex character. The matrimonial consent is at the same time the announcement and the cause of the fact that, from now on, both will be before the Church and society husband and wife. (We understand such an announcement as an "indication" in the ordinary sense of the term.) However, marriage consent has especially the character of a reciprocal profession of the newlyweds made before God. It is enough to examine the text attentively to be convinced that that prophetic proclamation of the language of the body, reread in truth, is immediately and directly addressed to the "I" and the "you": by the man to the woman and by her to him. The central position in the matrimonial consent is held precisely by the words which

indicate the personal subject, the pronouns "I" and "you." The "language of the body," reread in the truth of its spousal significance, constitutes by means of the words of the newlyweds the union-communion of the persons. If the matrimonial consent has a prophetic character, if it is the proclamation of the truth coming from God and, in a certain sense, the statement of this truth in God's name, this is brought about especially in the dimension of the inter-personal communion, and only indirectly "before" others and "for" others.

SACRAMENT'S VISIBLE SIGN

4. Against the background of the words spoken by the ministers of the sacrament of marriage, there stands the enduring "language of the body," which God "originated" by creating man as male and female: a language which has been renewed by Christ. This enduring "language of the body" carries within itself all the richness and depth of the mystery: first of creation and then of redemption. The spouses, bringing into being the visible sign of the sacrament by means of the words of their matrimonial consent, express therein "the language of the body" with all the profundity of the mystery of creation and of redemption (the liturgy of the sacrament of marriage offers a rich context of it). Rereading in this way "the

language of the body," the spouses not only enclose in the words of matrimonial consent the subjective fullness of the profession which is indispensable to bring about the sign proper to the sacrament, but they also arrive in a certain sense at the very sources from which that sign on each occasion draws its prophetic eloquence and its sacramental power. One must not forget that "the language of the body," before being spoken by the lips of the spouses, the ministers of marriage as a sacrament of the Church, was spoken by the word of the living God, beginning from the book of Genesis, through the prophets of the Old Covenant, until the author of the letter to the Ephesians.

DECISION AND CHOICE

5. We use over and over again the expression "language of the body," harking back to the prophetic texts. In these texts, as we have already said, the human body speaks a "language" of which it is not the author in the proper sense of the term. The author is man, male and female, who rereads the true sense of that "language," bringing to light the spousal significance of the body as integrally inscribed in the very structure of the masculinity and femininity of the personal subject. This rereading "in truth" of the language of the body already confers *per se* a prophetic character on

the words of marriage consent by means of which man and woman bring into being the visible sign of marriage as a sacrament of the Church. However, these words contain something more than a simple rereading in truth of that language spoken of by the femininity and masculinity of the newlyweds in their reciprocal relationships: "I take you as my wife...as my husband." In the words of matrimonial consent there are contained the intention, the decision and the choice. Both of the spouses decide to act in conformity with the language of the body, reread in truth. If man, male and female, is the author of that language, he is so especially inasmuch as he wishes to confer, and does indeed confer, on this behavior and on his actions a significance in conformity with the reread eloquence of the truth of masculinity and femininity in the mutual conjugal relationship.

HAS LASTING EFFECT

6. In this sphere man is the cause of the actions which have *per se* clear-cut meanings. He is then the cause of the actions and at the same time the author of their significance. The sum total of those meanings constitutes in a certain sense the ensemble of the "language of the body" in which the spouses decide to speak to each other as ministers of the Sacrament of

Marriage. The sign which they constitute by the words of matrimonial consent is not a mere immediate and passing sign, but a sign looking to the future which produces a lasting effect, namely, the marriage bond, one and indissoluble ("all the days of my life," that is, until death). In this perspective they should fulfill that sign of multiple content offered by the conjugal and family communion of the persons and also of that content which, originating from the "language of the body," is continually reread in truth. In this way the essential "truth" of the sign will remain organically linked to the morality of matrimonial conduct. In this truth of the sign and, later, in the morality of matrimonial conduct, there is inserted with a view to the future the procreative significance of the body, that is, paternity and maternity, of which we have previously treated. To the question: "Are you willing to accept responsibly and with love the children that God may give you and to educate them according to the law of Christ and of the Church?"—the man and the woman reply: "Yes."

And now we postpone to later meetings further detailed examinations of the matter.

"Language of the Body" Strengthens Marriage Covenant

General audience of January 26, 1983.

1. The sign of marriage as a sacrament of the Church is constituted each time according to that dimension which is proper to it from the "beginning," and at the same time it is constituted on the foundation of the spousal love of Christ and of the Church as the unique and unrepeatable expression of the covenant between "this" man and "this" woman, who are the ministers of marriage as a sacrament of their vocation and their life. In saying that the sign of marriage as a sacrament of the Church is constituted on the basis of the "language of the body" we are using analogy (the analogy of attribution), which we have sought to clarify previously. It is obvious that the body as such does not "speak," but man speaks rereading that which requires to be expressed precisely

on the basis of the "body," of the masculinity and femininity of the personal subject, indeed, on the basis of what can be expressed by man only by means of the body.

In this sense man—male or female—does not merely speak with the language of the body, but in a certain sense he permits the body to speak "for him" and "on his behalf": I would say, in his name and with his personal authority. In this way even the concept of the "prophetism of the body" seems to be well founded: the "prophet" indeed, is one who speaks "for" and "on behalf of": in the name and with the authority of a person.

"PROPHETISM OF THE BODY"

2. The newlywed spouses are aware of it when in contracting marriage they institute its visible sign. In the perspective of life in common and of the conjugal vocation, that initial sign, the original sign of marriage as a sacrament of the Church, will be continually completed by the "prophetism of the body." The spouses' bodies will speak "for" and "on behalf of" each of them, they will speak in the name of and with the authority of the person, of each of the persons, carrying out the conjugal dialogue proper to their vocation and based on the language of the body, reread in due course opportunely and continually—and it is neces-

sary that it be reread in truth! The spouses are called to form their life and their living together as a "communion of persons" on the basis of that language. Granted that there corresponds to the language a complexus of meaning, the spouses—by means of their conduct and comportment, by means of their actions and gestures ("gestures of tenderness": cf. *Gaudium et spes,* no. 49)—are called to become the authors of such meanings of the "language of the body," of which consequently there are constructed and continually deepened love, fidelity, conjugal uprightness and that union which remains indissoluble until death.

3. The sign of marriage as a sacrament of the Church is formed precisely by those meanings of which the spouses are the authors. All these meanings are initiated and in a certain sense "programmed" in a synthetic manner in the conjugal consent for the purpose of constructing later—in a more analytical way, day by day—the same sign, identifying oneself with it in the dimension of the whole of life. There is an organic bond between rereading in truth the integral significance of the "language of the body" and the consequent *use* of that language in conjugal life. In this last sphere the human being—male and female—is the author of the meanings of the "language of the body." This implies that this language of which he is the

author corresponds to the truth which has been reread. On the basis of biblical tradition we speak here of the "prophetism of the body." If the human being—male and female—in marriage (and indirectly also in all the spheres of mutual life together) confers on his behavior a significance in conformity with the fundamental truth of the language of the body, then he also "is in the truth." In the contrary case he is guilty of a lie and falsifies the language of the body.

CALLED TO BEAR WITNESS

4. If we place ourselves on the perspective line of conjugal consent which, as we have already said, offers the spouses a particular participation in the prophetic mission of the Church handed down from Christ Himself, we can in this regard make use also of the biblical distinction between "true" and "false" prophets. By means of marriage as a sacrament of the Church, man and woman are called explicitly to bear witness—by using correctly the "language of the body"—to spousal and procreative love, a witness worthy of "true prophets." In this consists the true significance and the grandeur of conjugal consent in the sacrament of the Church.

5. The problematic of the sacramental sign of marriage has a highly anthropological

character. We construct it on the basis of theological anthropology and in particular on that which, from the beginning of the present considerations, we have defined as the "theology of the body." Therefore, in continuing these analyses, we should always have before our minds the previous considerations which refer to the analysis of the key words of Christ. (We call them key words because they open up for us, like a key, the individual dimensions of theological anthropology, especially of the theology of the body.) Constructing on this basis the analysis of the sacramental sign of marriage in which the man and woman always participate, even after original sin, that is, man and woman as "historical man," we must constantly bear in mind the fact that that "historical" man, male and female, is at the same time the "man of concupiscence"; as such, every man and every woman enter into the history of salvation and they are involved in it through the sacrament which is the visible sign of the covenant and of grace.

Therefore, in the context of the present reflections, on the sacramental structure of the sign of not only what Christ said on the unity and indissolubility of marriage by referring to the "beginning," but also (and still more) what He said in the Sermon on the Mount when He referred to the "human heart."

Man Called To Overcome Concupiscence

General audience of February 9, 1983.

1. We said previously that in the context of the present reflections on the structure of marriage as a sacramental sign, we should bear in mind not only what Christ said about its unity and indissolubility in reference to the "beginning," but also (and still more) what He said in the Sermon on the Mount when He referred to the "human heart." Referring to the commandment, "You shall not commit adultery," Christ spoke of "adultery in the heart": "Everyone who looks at a woman lustfully has already committed adultery with her in his heart" (Mt. 5:28).

So then, in stating that the sacramental sign of marriage—the sign of the conjugal covenant of a man and a woman—is formed on the basis of the "language of the body" reread in truth (and continuously reread), we realize that he who rereads this "language" and then expresses it, not according to the requirements proper to marriage as a pact and a sacrament, is naturally and morally the man of concupiscence: male and female, both of them understood as the "man of concupiscence." The prophets of the Old Testament have certainly this man before their eyes when, making use of an analogy, they condemn the "adultery of Israel and Judah." The analysis of the words spoken by Christ in the Sermon on the Mount, lead us to understand more deeply "adultery" itself. And at the same time it leads us to the conviction that the human "heart" is not so much "accused and condemned" by Christ because of concupiscence (*concupiscentia carnalis*), as first of all "called." Here there is a decisive difference between the anthropology (or the anthropological hermeneutics) of the Gospel and some influential representatives of the contemporary hermeneutics of man (the so-called masters of suspicion).

THE MAN WHO IS "CALLED"

2. Continuing our present analysis we can observe that even though man, notwithstanding the sacramental sign of marriage, notwithstanding conjugal consent and its actuation, remains naturally the "man of concupiscence"; however, he is at the same time *the man who*

has been "called." He is "called" through the mystery of the redemption of the body, a divine mystery, which at the same time is—in Christ and through Christ in every man—a human reality. That mystery, besides, implies a determinate ethos which is essentially "human," and which we have previously called the ethos of the redemption.

3. In the light of the words spoken by Christ in the Sermon on the Mount, in the light of the whole Gospel and of the New Covenant, the threefold *concupiscence* (and in particular the concupiscence of the flesh) does not destroy the capacity to reread in truth the "language of the body"—and to reread it continually in an ever more mature and fuller way—whereby the sacramental sign is constituted both in its first liturgical moment, and also later in the dimension of the whole of life. In this light one must note that, if concupiscence *per se* causes many "errors" in rereading the "language of the body" and together with this gives rise also to "sin"—moral evil, contrary to the virtue of chastity (whether conjugal or extra-conjugal)—nevertheless in the sphere of the ethos of redemption there always remains the possibility of passing from "error" to the "truth," as also the possibility of returning, that is, of conversion, from sin to chastity, as an expression of a life according to the Spirit (cf. Gal. 5:16).

SACRAMENTAL SIGN OF LOVE

4. In this way, in the evangelical and Christian perspective of the problem, "historical" man (after original sin), on the basis of the "language of the body" reread in truth, is able—as male and female—to constitute the sacramental sign of love, of conjugal fidelity and integrity, and this as an *enduring sign:* "To be faithful to you always in joy and in sorrow, in sickness and in health, and to love and honor you all the days of my life." This signifies that man, in a real way, is the author of the meanings whereby, after having reread in truth the "language of the body," is also capable of forming in truth that language in the conjugal and family communion of the persons. He is capable of it also as "the man of concupiscence," being at the same time "called" by the reality of the redemption of Christ *(simul lapsus et redemptus).*

HERMENEUTICS OF THE SACRAMENT

5. By means of the dimension of the sign proper to marriage as a sacrament there is confirmed the specific theological anthropology, the specific hermeneutics of man, which in this case could also be called "the hermeneutics of the sacrament," because it

permits us to understand man on the basis of the analysis of the sacramental sign. Man —male and female—as the minister of the sacrament, the author (co-author) of the sacramental sign, is a conscious and capable subject of self-determination. Only on this basis can he be the author of the "language of the body," the author (co-author) of marriage as a sign: a sign of the divine creation and "redemption of the body." The fact that man (male and female) is the man of concupiscence does not prejudice his capacity to reread the language of the body in truth. He is "the man of concupiscence," but at the same time he is capable of discerning truth from falsity in the language of the body and he can be the author of the meanings, true or false, of that language.

CALLED, NOT ACCUSED

6. He is the man of concupiscence, but he is not completely determined by *"libido"* (in the sense in which this term is often used). Such a determination would imply that the ensemble of man's behavior, even, for example, the choice of continence for religious motives, would be explained only by means of the specific transformations of this *"libido."* In such a case—in the sphere of the language of the body—man would, in a certain sense, be condemned to essential falsifications: he would

merely be one who expresses a specific determination on the part of the *"libido,"* but he would not express the truth or falsity of spousal love and of the communion of the persons, even though he might think to manifest it. Consequently, he would then be condemned to suspect himself and others in regard to the truth of the language of the body. Because of the concupiscence of the flesh he could only be "accused," but he could not be really "called."

The "hermeneutics of the sacrament" permits us to draw the conclusion that man is always essentially "called" and not merely "accused," and this precisely inasmuch as he is the "man of concupiscence."

Beginning of the Reflections of Human Love on the Song of Songs

General audience of May 23, 1984.

1.   During the Holy Year I postponed the treatment of the theme of human love in the divine plan. I would now like to conclude that topic with some considerations especially about the teaching of *Humanae Vitae*, premising some reflections on the Song of Songs and the book of Tobit. It seems to me, indeed, that what I intend to explain in the coming weeks constitutes as it were the crowning of what I have illustrated.

The theme of marital love, which unites man and woman, in a certain sense connects this part of the Bible with the whole tradition of the "great analogy" which, through the writings of the prophets, flows into the New Testament and especially into the letter to the

Ephesians (cf. Eph 5:21-23), the explanation of which I interrupted at the beginning of the Holy Year.

It has become the object of numerous exegetical studies, commentaries and hypotheses. With regard to its content, apparently "profane," the positions have varied; while on the one hand its reading has often been discouraged, on the other it has been the source from which the greatest mystical writers have drawn, and the verses of the Song of Songs have been inserted into the Church's liturgy.[1]

In fact, although the analysis of the text of this book obliges us to situate its content outside the sphere of the great prophetic analogy, nevertheless it is not possible to detach it from the reality of the original sacrament. It is not possible to reread it except along the lines of what is written in the first chapters of Genesis, as a testimony of the "beginning"—that "beginning" to which Christ referred in His decisive conversation with the Pharisees (cf. Mt. 19:4).[2] The Song of Songs is certainly found in the wake of that sacrament in which, through the "language of the body," there is constituted the visible sign of man and woman's participation in the covenant of grace and love offered by God to man. The Song of Songs demonstrates the richness of this "language," whose first expression is already found in Genesis 2:23-25.

ATMOSPHERE
OF THE SONG OF SONGS

2. Indeed, the first verses of the Song lead us immediately into the atmosphere of the whole "poem," in which the groom and the bride seem to move in the circle traced by the irradiation of love. The words of the spouses, their movements, their gestures, correspond to the interior movement of their hearts. Only through the prism of this movement is it possible to understand the "language of the body," in which there comes to pass that discovery to which the first man gave expression in front of her who had been created as "a helper like himself" (cf. Gen. 2:20 and 23), and who had been taken, as the biblical text reports, from one of his "ribs" ("rib" seems to indicate also the heart).

This discovery—already analyzed on the basis of Genesis 2—in the Song of Songs is invested with all the richness of the language of human love. What was expressed in the second chapter of Genesis (vv. 23-25) in just a few simple and essential words, is developed here in a full dialogue, as it were, or rather in a duet, in which the groom's words are interwoven with the bride's and they complement each other. Man's first words in Genesis, chapter 2, verse 23, on seeing the woman created by God, express wonder and admiration, even more, the sense of fascination. And a similar fascination—which is wonder and admiration—runs in fuller form through the verses of the Song of Songs. It runs in a peaceful and homogeneous wave from the beginning to the end of the poem.

MUTUAL ADMIRATION

3. Even a summary analysis of the text of the Song of Songs allows the "language of the body" to be heard expressing itself in that mutual fascination. The point of departure as well as the point of arrival for this fascination—mutual wonder and admiration—are in fact the bride's femininity and the groom's masculinity in the direct experience of their visibility. The words of love uttered by both of them are therefore concentrated on the "body," not only because in itself it constitutes the source of the mutual fascination, but also, and above all, because it is on the body that there lingers directly and immediately that attraction toward the other person, toward the other "I"—female or male—which in the interior impulse of the heart generates love.

In addition, love unleashes a special experience of the beautiful, which focuses on what is visible, but at the same time involves the entire person. The experience of beauty gives rise to satisfaction, which is mutual.

"O most beautiful among women..." (Sg. 1:8), the groom says, and the bride's words echo back to him: "I am dark—but lovely, O daughters of Jerusalem" (Sg. 1:5). The words of the spellbound man are repeated continually, they return in all five stanzas of the poem. And they are echoed in similar expressions of the bride's.

USE OF METAPHORS

4. It is a question here of metaphors that may surprise us today. Many of them were borrowed from the life of shepherds; others seem to indicate the royal status of the groom.[3] The analysis of that poetic language is left to the experts. The very fact of adopting the metaphor shows how much, in our case, the "language of the body" seeks support and corroboration in the whole visible world. This is without doubt a "language" that is reread at one and the same time with the heart and with the eyes of the groom, in the act of special concentration on the whole female "I" of the bride. This "I" speaks to him through every feminine trait, giving rise to that state of mind that can be defined as fascination, enchantment. This female "I" is expressed almost without words; nevertheless, the "language of

the body" expressed wordlessly, finds a rich echo in the groom's words, in his speaking that is full of poetic transport and metaphors, which attest to the experience of beauty, a love of satisfaction. If the metaphors in the Song seek an analogy for this beauty in the various things of the visible world (in this world which is the groom's "own world"), at the same time they seem to indicate the insufficiency of each of these things in particular. "You are all-beautiful, my beloved, and there is no blemish in you" (Sg. 4:7)—with this saying, the groom ends his song, leaving all the metaphors, in order to address himself to that sole one through which the "language of the body" seems to express what is more proper to femininity and the whole of the person.

We will continue the analysis of the Song of Songs at the next general audience.

NOTES

1. "The Song is therefore to be taken simply for what it manifestly is: a song of human love." This sentence of J. Winandy, O.S.B., expresses the conviction of growing numbers of exegetes (J. Winandy, *Le Cantique des Cantiques,* Poém d'amour mué en écrit de Sagesse, Maredsouse, 1960, p. 26).

M. Dubarle adds: "Catholic exegesis, which sometimes refers to the obvious meaning of biblical texts for passages of great dogmatic importance, should not lightly abandon it when it comes to Songs." Referring to the phrase of G. Gerleman, Dubarle continues: "Songs celebrates the love of man and woman without adding any mythological element, but considering it simply on its own level and in its specific nature. There is implicitly, without didactic insistence, the equivalent of the Jahwist faith (since sexual powers had not been placed under the patronage of foreign divinities and had not been attributed to Jahweh himself who appeared as transcending this sphere.) The poem was therefore in tacit harmony with the fundamental convictions of the faith of Israel.

"The same open, objective, not expressly religious attitude with regard to physical beauty and sensual love is found in some collections of Jahwist documents. These various similarities show that the small book is not so isolated in the sum total of biblical literature as is sometimes stated" (A. M. Dubarle, "Le Cantique des Cantiques dans l'exégèse récente" in: Aux grands carrefours de la Révélation et de l'exégèse de l'Ancien Testament, Recherches Bibliques VIII, Louvain, 1967, pp. 149, 151).

2. This evidently does not exclude the possibility of speaking of a "sensus plenior" in the Song of Songs.

Confer, for example: "Lovers in the ecstasy of love seem to occupy and fill the whole book, as the only protagonists.... Therefore, Paul, in reading the words of Genesis, 'For this reason a man shall leave his father and mother, and shall cling to his wife, and the two shall be made into one' (Eph. 5:31), does not deny the real and immediate meaning of the words that refer to human marriage. However, to this first meaning he adds another deeper one with an indirect reference: 'I mean that it refers to Christ and the Church,' confessing that 'this is a great foreshadowing' (Eph. 5:32)....

"Some readers of the Song of Songs rush to read immediately in its words a disembodied love. They have forgotten the lovers, or have petrified them in fictions, in an intellectual key...they have multiplied the minute allegorical relations in every sentence, word or image....

This is not the right way. Anyone who does not believe in the human love of the spouses, who must seek forgiveness for the body, does not have the right to be elevated.... With the affirmation of human love instead, it is possible to discover in it the revelation of God" (L. Alonso-Schökel, "Cantico dei Cantici—Introduzione": in La Biblia, Parola di Dio scritti per noi. Official text of the Italian Episcopal Conference, vol. II, Torino, 1980, Marietti, pp. 425-427).

3. To explain the inclusion of a love song in the biblical canon, Jewish exegetes already in the first centuries after Christ saw in the Song of Songs an allegory of Yahweh's love for Israel, or an allegory of the history of the Chosen People, in which this love is manifested, and in the Middle Ages the allegory of Divine Wisdom and of man who is in search of it.

Christian exegesis, since the early Fathers, extended such an idea to Christ and the Church (cf. Hippolytus and Origen), or to the individual soul of the Christian (cf. St. Gregory of Nyssa) or to Mary (cf. St. Ambrose) and also to her Immaculate Conception (cf. Richard of St. Victor). St. Bernard saw in the Song of Songs a dialogue of the Word of God with the soul, and this led to St. John of the Cross' concept about mystical marriage.

The only exception in this long tradition was Theodore of Mopsuestia, in the fourth century, who saw in the Song of Songs a poem that celebrated Solomon's human love for Pharaoh's daughter.

Luther, instead, referred the allegory to Solomon and his kingdom. In recent centuries new hypotheses have appeared. Some, for example, consider the Song of Songs as a drama of a bride's fidelity to a shepherd, despite all the temptations, or as a collection of songs used during the popular wedding rites or mythical rituals which reflected the Adonis-Tammuz worship. Finally, there is seen in the Song of Songs the description of a dream, recalling ancient ideas about the significance of dreams and also psycho-analysis.

In the twentieth century there has been a return to the more ancient allegorical traditions (cf. Bea), seeing again in the Song of Songs the history of Israel (cf Jouon, Ricciotte), and a developed midrash (as Robert calls it in his commentary, which constitutes a "summary" of the interpretation of Songs).

Nevertheless, at the same time the book has begun to be read in its most evident significance as a poem exalting natural human love (cf. Rowley, Young, Laurin).

The first to have demonstrated in what way this significance is linked with the biblical context of chapter two of Genesis was Karl Barth. Dubarle begins with the premise that a faithful and happy human love reveals to man the attributes of divine love, and Van den Oudenrijn sees in the Song of Songs the antitype of that typical sense that appears in the letter to the Ephesians, chapter 5, verse 23. Murphy, excluding every allegorical and metaphorical explanation, stresses that human love, created and blessed by God, can be the theme of an inspired biblical book.

D. Lys notes that the content of the Song of Songs is at the same time sensual and sacred. When one prescinds from the second characteristic, the Song comes to be treated as a purely lay erotic composition, and when the first is ignored, one falls into allegorism. Only by putting these two aspects together is it possible to read the book in the right way.

Alongside the works of the above-mentioned authors, and especially with regard to an outline of the history of the exegesis of the Song of Songs, confer H. H. Rowley, "The interpretation of the Song of Songs" in "The Servant of the Lord and other Essays on the Old Testament," London, 1952, Lutterworth, pp. 191-233; A. M. Dubarle, *Le Cantique des Cantiques dans l'exégèse de l'Ancien Testament.*   Recherches Bibliques VIII, Louvain, 1967, Desclée de Brouwer, pp. 139-151; D. Lys, Le plus beau chant de la création—Commentaire de Cantique des Cantiques. Lectio divina 51. Paris 1968, Du Cerf, pp. 31-35; M. H. Pope, "Song of Songs," the Anchor Bible, Garden City, N.Y., 1977, Doubleday, pp. 113-234.

Truth and Freedom— the Foundation of True Love

General audience of May 30, 1984.

In the passage from the Acts of the Apostles, just read, we heard the account of Jesus' ascension into heaven. As is known, tomorrow, according to the calendar of the universal Church, we celebrate the Solemnity of the Ascension.

It is a feast that calls upon us to look up, to think of our destiny beyond this world and to pray with perseverance and consistency that the kingdom of God may come.

Tomorrow afternoon I will ordain seventy-seven new priests. I invite you to pray that, through the Sacrament of Orders, they may become guides to heaven, shepherds of men who generously spend themselves for the glory of God and the service of their brothers and sisters.

1. We resume our analysis of the Song of Songs with the purpose of understanding in a more adequate and exhaustive way the sacramental sign of marriage, which is manifested by the language of the body, a singular language of love originating in the heart.

At a certain point, the groom, expressing a particular experience of values that shines upon everything that relates to the person he loves, says:

"You have ravished my heart, my sister,
    my bride;
you have ravished my heart with one
    glance of your eyes,
with one bead of your necklace.
How sweet are your caresses, my sister,
    my bride..." (Sg. 4:9-10).

From these words emerges what is of essential importance for the theology of the body—and in this case for the theology of the sacramental sign of marriage—to know *who the female "you" is for the male "I"* and vice versa.

The groom in the Song of Songs exclaims: "You are all-beautiful, my beloved" (Sg. 4:7) and calls her "my sister, my bride" (Sg. 4:9). He does not call her by her name, but he uses expressions that say more.

Under a certain aspect, compared with the name "beloved," the name "sister" that is used for the bride seems to be more eloquent and rooted in the sum total of the Song, which illustrates how love reveals the other person.

OPENNESS TOWARD OTHERS

2. The term "beloved" indicates what is always essential for love, which puts the second "I" beside one's own "I." "Friendship—love of friendship (amor amicitiae)"—signifies in the Song a particular approach felt and experienced as an interiorly unifying power. The fact that in this approach that female "I" is revealed for her groom as "sister"—and that precisely as both sister and bride—has a special eloquence. The expression "sister" speaks of the union in mankind and at the same time of her difference and feminine originality with regard not only to sex, but to the very way of "being person," which means both "being subject" and "being in relationship." The term "sister" seems to express, in a more simple way, the subjectivity of the female "I" in personal relationship with the man, that is, in the openness of him toward others, who are understood and perceived as brothers. The "sister" in a certain sense helps man to identify himself and conceive of himself in this way, constituting for him a kind of challenge in this direction.

3. The groom in the Song accepts the challenge and seeks the common past, as though he and his woman were descended from the same family circle, as though from infancy they were united by memories of a common home. And so they mutually feel as close as brother and sister who owe their existence to the same mother. From this there follows a specific sense of common belonging. The fact that they feel like brother and sister allows them to live their mutual closeness in security and to manifest it, finding support in that, and not fearing the unfair judgment of other men.

The groom's words, through the name "sister," tend to reproduce, I would say, the history of the femininity of the person loved. They see her still in the time of girlhood and they embrace her entire "I," soul and body, with a disinterested tenderness. Hence there arises that peace of which the bride speaks. This is the "peace of the body," which in appearance resembles sleep ("Do not arouse, do not stir up love, before its own time"). This is above all the peace of the encounter in mankind as the image of God—and the encounter by means of a reciprocal and disinterested gift ("So am I in your eyes, like one who has found peace": Sg. 8:10).

AWARENESS
OF MUTUAL BELONGING

4. In relation to the preceding plot, which could be called a "fraternal" plot, there emerges in the loving duet of the Song of Songs another plot, we say: another substratum of the content. We can examine it by starting from certain sayings that seem to have a key significance in the poem. This plot never emerges explicitly, but through the whole composition, and is expressly manifested only in a few passages. So the groom says:

"You are an enclosed garden, my sister,
     my bride,
an enclosed garden, a fountain sealed"
     (Sg. 4:12).

The metaphors just read: "enclosed garden, fountain sealed," reveal the presence of another vision of the same female "I," master of her own mystery. We can say that both metaphors express the personal dignity of the woman who as a spiritual subject is in possession and can decide not only on the metaphysical depth, but also on the essential truth and authenticity of the gift of herself, inclined to that union of which the book of Genesis speaks.

The language of metaphors—poetic language—seems to be in this sphere particularly appropriate and precise. The "sister bride" is for the man the master of her own mystery as a "garden enclosed" and a "fountain sealed." The "language of the body" reread in truth keeps pace with the discovery of the interior inviolability of the person. At the same time, this very discovery expresses the authentic depth of the mutual belonging of the spouses who are aware of belonging to each other, of being destined for each other: "My lover belongs to me and I to him" (Sg. 2:16; cf. 6:3).

5. This awareness of mutual belonging resounds especially on the lips of the bride. In a certain sense, with these words she responds to the groom's words with which he acknowledged her as the master of her own mystery. When the bride says, "My lover belongs to me," she means at the same time, "It is he to whom I entrust myself," and therefore, she says, "and I to him" (Sg. 2:16). The words "to me" and "to him" affirm here the whole depth of that entrustment, which corresponds to the interior truth of the person.

It likewise corresponds to the nuptial significance of femininity in relation to the male "I," that is, to the "language of the body" reread in the truth of personal dignity.

This truth was stated by the groom with the metaphors of the "garden enclosed" and the "fountain sealed." The bride answers him with the words of the gift, that is, the entrustment of herself. As master of her own choice she says: "I belong to my lover." The Song of Songs subtly reveals the interior truth of this response. The freedom of the gift is the response to the deep awareness of the gift expressed by the groom's words. Through this truth and freedom the love is built up, about which we must affirm that it is authentic love.

Love Is Ever Seeking
and Never Satisfied

General audience of June 6, 1984.

In the passage from the Acts of the Apostles which was just read, we heard the account of that fundamental event in the life of the Church, which was Pentecost. The descent of the Holy Spirit upon Mary and the Apostles, assembled in the Upper Room, signalled the official birth of the Church and its presentation to the world.

In preparing to relive that decisive moment next Sunday, let us pray to the Holy Spirit to dispose the hearts of the faithful to welcome joyfully a new outpouring of His gifts. Strengthened by the fire of His love, may they make themselves courageous witnesses of the Gospel, bringing also to this generation of ours the announcement of Christ the Redeemer.

We will now resume the subject of the audiences of past Wednesdays.

SACRAMENTAL SIGN
OF MARRIAGE

1. Again today we will reflect on the Song of Songs with the aim of better understanding the sacramental sign of marriage.

The truth about love, proclaimed by the Song of Songs, cannot be separated from the "language of the body." The truth about love enables the same "language of the body" to be reread in truth. This is also the truth about the progressive approach of the spouses which increases through love: and the nearness means also the initiation into the mystery of the person, without, however, implying its violation (cf. Sg. 1:13-14, 16).

The truth about the increasing nearness of the spouses through love is developed in the subjective dimension "of the heart," of affection and sentiment, and this dimension allows one to discover in itself the other as a gift and, in a certain sense, to "taste it" in itself (cf. Sg. 2:3-6).

Through this nearness the groom more fully lives the experience of that gift which on the part of the female "I" is united with the spousal expression and meaning of the body. The man's words (cf. Sg. 7:1-8) do not only contain a poetic description of his beloved, of her feminine beauty, on which his senses dwell, but they speak of the gift and the self-giving of the person.

The bride knows that the groom's "longing" is for her and she goes to meet him with the quickness of the gift of herself (cf. Sg. 7:9-13) because the love that unites them is at one and the same time of a spiritual and a sensual nature. And it is also on the basis of this love that there comes to pass the rereading of the significance of the body in the truth, since the man and woman must together constitute that sign of the mutual gift of self, which puts the seal on their whole life.

A CONTINUAL SEARCH

2. In the Song of Songs the "language of the body" becomes a part of the single process of the mutual attraction of the man and woman, which is expressed in the frequent refrains that speak of the search that is full of nostalgia, of affectionate solicitude (cf. Sg. 2:7) and of the spouses' mutual rediscovery (cf. Sg. 5:2). This brings them joy and calm, and seems to lead them to a continual search. One has the impression that in meeting each other, in reaching each other, in experiencing one's nearness, they ceaselessly continued to tend toward something: they yield to the call of something that dominates the content of the moment and surpasses the limits of the eros, limits that are reread in the words of the mu-

tual "language of the body" (cf. Sg. 1:7-8; 2:17). This search has its interior dimension: "the heart is awake" even in sleep. This aspiration, born of love on the basis of the "language of the body," is a search for integral beauty, for purity that is free of all stain: it is a search for perfection that contains, I would say, the synthesis of human beauty, beauty of soul and body.

In the Song of Songs the human eros reveals the countenance of love ever in search and, as it were, never satisfied. The echo of this restlessness runs through the strophes of the poem:

"I opened to my lover—but my lover had departed, gone.
I sought him but I did not find him;
I called to him but he did not answer me" (Sg. 5:6).

"I adjure you, daughters of Jerusalem, if you find my lover—
What shall you tell him?
that I am faint with love" (Sg. 5:9).

3. So then some strophes of the Song of Songs present the eros as the form of human love in which the energies of desire are at work. And it is in them that there is rooted the awareness or the subjective certainty of the mutual, faithful and exclusive belonging. At the same time, however, many other strophes

of the poem lead us to reflect on the cause of the search and the restlessness that accompanies the awareness of belonging to each other. Is this restlessness also part of the nature of the eros? If it were, this restlessness would indicate also the need for self-control. The truth about love is expressed in the awareness of mutual belonging, the fruit of the aspiration and search for each other, and in the need for the aspiration and the search, the outcome of mutual belonging.

In this interior necessity, in this dynamic of love, there is indirectly revealed the near impossibility of one person's being appropriated and mastered by the other. The person is someone who surpasses all measures of appropriation and domination, of possession and gratification, which emerge from the same "language of the body." If the groom and the bride reread this "language" in the full truth about the person and about love, they arrive at the ever deeper conviction that the fullness of their belonging constitutes that mutual gift in which love is revealed as "stern as death," that is, it goes to the furthest limits of the "language of the body" in order to exceed them. The truth about interior love and the truth about the mutual gift, in a certain sense continually call the groom and the bride—through the means of expressing the mutual belonging, and even by breaking away from those means—to arrive at what constitutes the very nucleus of the gift from person to person.

THE TRUTH ABOUT LOVE

4. Following the paths of the words marked out by the strophes of the Song of Songs, it seems that we are therefore approaching the dimension in which the "eros" seeks to be integrated, through still another truth about love. Centuries later—in the light of the death and resurrection of Christ—Paul of Tarsus will proclaim this truth in the words of his letter to the Corinthians:

"Love is patient; love is kind.

Love is not jealous, it does not put on airs, it is not snobbish.

Love is never rude, it is not self-seeking, it is not prone to anger; neither does it brood over injuries.

Love does not rejoice in what is wrong but rejoices with the truth.

There is no limit to love's forbearance, to its trust, its hope, its power to endure.

Love never fails" (1 Cor. 13:4-8).

Is the truth about love, expressed in the strophes of the Song of Songs, confirmed in the light of these words of Paul? In the Song we read, as an example of love, that its "jealousy" is "relentless as the nether world" (Sg.

8:6), and in the Pauline letter we read that "love is not jealous." What relationship do both of these expressions about love have? What relationship has the love that is "stern as death," according to the Song of Songs, with the love that "never fails," according to the Pauline letter? We will not multiply these questions, we will not open the comparative analysis. Nevertheless, it seems that love opens up before us here in two perspectives: as though that in which the human "eros" closes its horizon is still opened, through Paul's words, to another horizon of love that speaks another language; the love that seems to emerge from another dimension of the person, and which calls, invites, to another communion. This love has been called "agape" and agape brings the eros to completion by purifying it.

And so we have concluded these brief meditations on the Song of Songs, intended to further examine the theme of the "language of the body." In this framework, the Song of Songs has a totally singular meaning.

Love Is Victorious
in the Struggle
Between Good and Evil

General audience of June 27, 1984.

1. During these past weeks, in commenting on the Song of Songs, I emphasized how the sacramental sign of matrimony is constituted on the basis of the "language of the body," which man and woman express in the truth that is proper to it. Under this aspect, today I intend to analyze some passages from the book of Tobit.

In the account of the wedding of Tobiah with Sarah, besides the expression "sister"— through which there seems to be a fraternal character rooted in spousal love—there is found also another expression likewise analogous to those in Songs.

As you will recall, in the spouses' duet, the love which they declare to each other is "stern as death" (Sg. 8:6). In the book of Tobit we find a phrase which, in saying that he fell deeply in love with Sarah and "his heart became set on her" (Tb. 6:19), presents a situation confirming the truth of the words about love "stern as death."

THE TEST
OF LIFE AND DEATH

2. For a better understanding, we must go back to some details that are explained against the background of the specific nature of the book of Tobit. We read there that Sarah, daughter of Raguel, had "already been married seven times" (Tb. 6:14), but all her husbands had died before having intercourse with her. This had happened through the work of a demon, and young Tobiah too had reason to fear a similar death.

So from the very first moment Tobiah's love had to face the test of life and death. The words about love "stern as death," spoken by the spouses in the Song of Songs in the transport of the heart, assume here the nature of a real test. If love is demonstrated as stern as death, this happens above all in the sense that Tobiah and, together with him, Sarah, unhesitatingly face this test. But in this test of life and death, life wins because, during the test on the wedding night, love, supported by prayer, is revealed as more stern than death.

3. This test of life and death has also another significance that enables us to understand the love and the marriage of the newlyweds. They, in fact, becoming one as husband

and wife, find themselves in the situation in which the powers of good and evil fight and compete against each other. The spouses' duet in the Song of Songs seems not to perceive completely this dimension of reality. The spouses of the Song live and express themselves in an ideal or "abstract" world in which it is as though the struggle of the objective forces between good and evil did not exist. Is it not precisely the power and the interior truth of love that subdues the struggle that goes on in man and around him?

The fullness of this truth and this power proper to love seems nevertheless to be different and seems to tend rather to where the experience in the book of Tobit leads us. The truth and the power of love are shown in the ability to place oneself between the forces of good and evil which are fighting in man and around him, because love is confident in the victory of good and is ready to do everything so that good may conquer. As a result, the love of the spouses in the book of Tobit is not confirmed by the words expressed by the language of loving transport as in the Song of Songs, but by the choices and the actions that take on all the weight of human existence in the union of the two. The "language of the body" here seems to use the words of the choices and the acts stemming from the love that is victorious because it prays.

THE PRAYER
OF TOBIAH AND SARAH

4. Tobiah's prayer (Tb. 8:5-8), which is above all a prayer of praise and thanksgiving, then one of supplication, situates the "language of the body" on the level of the essential terms of the theology of the body. It is an "objectivized" language, pervaded not so much by the emotive power of the experience as by the depth and gravity of the very truth of the experience.

The spouses profess this truth together, in unison before the God of the Covenant: "God of our fathers." We can say that under this aspect the "language of the body" becomes the language of the ministers of the sacrament, aware that in the conjugal pact there is expressed and realized the mystery that has its origin in God Himself. Their conjugal pact is, in fact, the image—and the original sacrament of the Covenant of God with man, with the human race—of that covenant which takes its origin from eternal Love.

Tobiah and Sarah end their prayer with the following words: "Call down your mercy on me and on her, and allow us to live together to a happy old age" (Tb. 8:7).

We can admit (on the basis of the context) that they have before their eyes the prospect of persevering in their union to the end of their days—a prospect that opens up before them with the trial of life and death, already during their wedding night. At the same time, they see with the glance of faith the sanctity of this vocation in which—through the unity of the two, built upon the mutual truth of the "language of the body"—they must respond to the call of God Himself which is contained in the mystery of the Beginning. And this is why they ask: "Call down your mercy on me and on her."

5. The spouses in the Song of Songs, with ardent words, declare to each other their human love. The newlyweds in the book of Tobit ask God that they be able to respond to love. Both the one and the other find their place in what constitutes the sacramental sign of marriage. Both the one and the other share in forming this sign.

We can say that through the one and the other the "language of the body," reread in the subjective dimension of the truth of human hearts and in the "objective" dimension of the truth of living in union, becomes the language of the liturgy.

The prayer of the newlyweds in the book of Tobit certainly seems to confirm this differently from the Song of Songs, and even in a way that is undoubtedly more deeply moving.

"Language of the Body" Actions and Duties Forming the Spirituality of Marriage

General audience of July 4, 1984.

1. Today let us return to the classical text of the fifth chapter of the letter to the Ephesians, which reveals the eternal sources of the Covenant of the Father's love and at the same time the new and definitive institution of that Covenant in Jesus Christ.

This text brings us to such a dimension of the "language of the body" that could be called "mystical." It speaks of marriage, in fact, as a "great mystery" ("This is a great mystery": Eph. 5:32). And although this mystery is fulfilled in the spousal union of Christ the Redeemer with the Church, and of the Church-Spouse with Christ ("I mean that it refers to Christ and the Church": Eph. 5:22), although it is definitively carried out in eschatological dimensions, nevertheless the author of the letter to the Ephesians does not hesitate to extend the analogy of Christ's union with the

Church in spousal love, outlined in such an "absolute" and "eschatological" way, to the sacramental sign of the matrimonial pact between man and woman, who "defer to one another out of reverence for Christ" (Eph. 5:11). He does not hesitate to extend that mystical analogy to the "language of the body," reread in the truth of the spousal love and the conjugal union of the two.

2. We must recognize the logic of this marvelous text which radically frees our way of thinking from elements of Manichaeism or from a non-personalistic consideration of the body, and at the same time brings the "language of the body," contained in the sacramental sign of matrimony, nearer to the dimension of real sanctity.

The sacraments inject sanctity into the plan of man's humanity: they penetrate the soul and body, the femininity and the masculinity of the personal subject, with the power of sanctity. All of this is expressed in the language of the liturgy: it is expressed there and brought about there.

The liturgy, liturgical language, elevates the conjugal pact of man and woman, based on the "language of the body" reread in truth, to the dimensions of "mystery," and at the same time enables that pact to be fulfilled in these dimensions through the "language of the body."

It is precisely the sign of the sacrament of marriage that speaks of this, and in liturgical language this sign expresses an interpersonal event, laden with intense personal content, assigned to the two "until death." The sacramental sign signifies not only the *fieri* (the "becoming")—the birth of the marriage—but builds its whole *esse* (its "being"), its duration: both the one and the other as a sacred and sacramental reality, rooted in the dimension of the Covenant and grace—in the dimension of creation and redemption. In this way, the liturgical language assigns to both, to the man and to the woman, love, fidelity and conjugal honesty through the "language of the body." It assigns them the unity and the indissolubility of marriage in the "language of the body." It assigns them as a duty all the *sacrum* (holy) of the person and of the communion of persons, and likewise their femininity and masculinity—precisely in this language.

PROFOUND EXPERIENCE OF THE HOLY

3. In this sense we affirm that liturgical language becomes the "language of the body." This signifies a series of acts and duties which form the "spirituality" of marriage, its "ethos." In the daily life of the spouses these acts become duties, and the duties become acts.

These acts—as also the commitments—are of a spiritual nature. Nevertheless, they are expressed at the same time with the "language of the body."

The author of the letter to the Ephesians writes in this regard: "...Husbands should love their wives as they do their own bodies..." (Eph. 5:28) ("as he loves himself": Eph. 5:33), and "the wife for her part showing respect for her husband" (Eph. 5:33). Both, for that matter, are to "defer to one another out of reverence for Christ" (Eph. 5:21).

The "language of the body," as an uninterrupted continuity of liturgical language, is expressed not only as the attraction and mutual pleasure of the Song of Songs, but also as a profound experience of the *sacrum* (the holy), which seems to be infused in the very masculinity and femininity through the dimension of the *mysterium* (mystery): the *mysterium magnum* of the letter to the Ephesians, which sinks its roots precisely in the "beginning," that is, in the mystery of the creation of man: male and female in the image of God, called from "the beginning" to be the visible sign of God's creative love.

4. So therefore that "reverence for Christ" and "respect" of which the author of the letter to the Ephesians speaks, is none other than a spiritually mature form of that mutual attrac-

tion: man's attraction to femininity and woman's attraction to masculinity, which is revealed for the first time in the book of Genesis (Gn. 2:23-25). Consequently, the same attraction seems to flow like a wide stream through the verses of the Song of Songs to find, under entirely different circumstances, its concise and concentrated expression in the book of Tobit.

The spiritual maturity of this attraction is none other than the blossoming of the gift of fear—one of the seven gifts of the Holy Spirit, of which St. Paul speaks in his first letter to the Thessalonians (1 Thes. 4:4-7).

On the other hand, Paul's doctrine on chastity as "life according to the Spirit" (cf. Rom. 8:5) allows us (especially on the basis of the first letter to the Corinthians, chapter 6) to interpret that "respect" in a charismatic sense, that is, as a gift of the Holy Spirit.

A VIRTUE AND A GIFT

5. The letter to the Ephesians, in exhorting spouses to defer to each other "out of reverence for Christ" (Eph. 5:21) and in urging them, consequently, to "respect" in their conjugal relationship, seems to point out—in keeping with Pauline tradition—chastity as a virtue and as a gift.

In this way, through the virtue and still more through the gift ("life according to the

Spirit") the mutual attraction of masculinity and femininity spiritually matures. Both the man and woman, getting away from concupiscence, find the proper dimension of the freedom of the gift, united to femininity and masculinity in the true spousal significance of the body.

Thus liturgical language, that is, the language of the sacrament and of the *mysterium,* becomes in their life and in their living together the "language of the body" in a depth, simplicity and beauty hitherto altogether unknown.

CONJUGAL LIFE BECOMES LITURGICAL

6. This seems to be the integral significance of the sacramental sign of marriage. In that sign—through the "language of the body"—man and woman encounter the great "mystery" in order to transfer the light of that mystery—the light of truth and beauty, expressed in liturgical language—to the "language of the body," that is, to the language of the practice of love, of fidelity, of conjugal honesty, that is, to the ethos rooted in the "redemption of the body" (cf. Rom. 8:23). In this way, conjugal life becomes in a certain sense liturgical.

INDEX

Daughters of St. Paul

MASSACHUSETTS
50 St. Paul's Ave, Jamaica Plain, Boston, MA 02130; 617-522-8811
172 Tremont Street, Boston, MA 02111; 617-426-5464

NEW YORK
78 Fort Place, Staten Island, NY 10301; 718-447-5071; 718-761-0085
59 East 43rd Street, New York, NY 10017; 212-986-7580
625 East 187th Street, Bronx, NY 10458; 212-458-5840
525 Main Street, Buffalo, NY 14203; 716-847-6044

NEW JERSEY
Hudson Mall Route 440 and Communipaw Ave, Jersey City, NJ 07304; 201-433-7740

CONNECTICUT
202 Fairfield Ave, Bridgeport, CT 06604; 203-335-9913

OHIO
2105 Ontario Street (at Prospect Ave), Cleveland, OH 44115; 216-621-9427
616 Walnut Street, Cincinnati, OH 45202; 513-421-5733

PENNSYLVANIA
1719 Chestnut Street, Philadelphia, PA 19103; 215-568-2638; 215-464-8901

VIRGINIA
1025 King Street, Alexandria, VA 22314; 703-549-3806

SOUTH CAROLINA
243 King Street, Charleston, SC 29401; 803-577-0175

FLORIDA
2700 Biscayne Blvd, Miami, FL 33137; 305-573-1618

LOUISIANA
4403 Veterans Memorial Blvd, Metairie, LA 70006; 504-887-7631
423 Main Street, Baton Rouge, LA 70802; 504-343-4057

MISSOURI
1001 Pine Street (at N. 10th), St. Louis, MO 63101; 314-621-0346

ILLINOIS
172 North Michigan Ave, Chicago, IL 60601; 312-346-4228; 312-346-3240

TEXAS
114 Main Plaza, San Antonio, TX 78205; 512-224-8101

CALIFORNIA
1570 Fifth Ave, San Diego, CA 92101; 619-232-1442
46 Geary Street, San Francisco, CA 94108; 415-781-5180

WASHINGTON
2301 Second Ave, Seattle, WA 98121; 206-441-5740

HAWAII
1143 Bishop Street, Honolulu, HI 96813; 808-521-2731

ALASKA
750 West 5th Ave, Anchorage, AK 99501; 907-272-8183

CANADA
3022 Dufferin Street, Toronto, Ontario, Canada

Daughters of St. Paul

MASSACHUSETTS
50 St. Paul's Ave., Jamaica Plain Boston, MA 02130 **617-522-8911.**
172 Tremont Street, Boston, MA 02111 **617-426-5464; 617-426-4230.**

NEW YORK
78 Fort Place, Staten Island, NY 10301 **718-447-5071; 718-447-5086.**
59 East 43rd Street, New York, NY 10017 **212-986-7580.**
625 East 187th Street, Bronx, NY 10458 **212-584-0440.**
525 Main Street, Buffalo, NY 14203 **716-847-6044.**

NEW JERSEY
Hudson Mall Route 440 and Communipaw Ave., Jersey City, NJ 07304 **201-433-7740.**

CONNECTICUT
202 Fairfield Ave., Bridgeport, CT 06604 **203-335-9913.**

OHIO
2105 Ontario Street (at Prospect Ave.), Cleveland, OH 44115 **216-621-9427.**
616 Walnut Street, Cincinnati, OH 45202 **513-421-5733.**

PENNSYLVANIA
1719 Chestnut Street, Philadelphia, PA 19103 **215-568-2638; 215-864-0991.**

VIRGINIA
1025 King Street, Alexandria, VA 22314 **703-549-3806.**

SOUTH CAROLINA
243 King Street, Charleston, SC 29401 **803-577-0175.**

FLORIDA
2700 Biscayne Blvd. Miami, FL 33137 **305-573-1618.**

LOUISIANA
4403 Veterans Memorial Blvd. Metairie, LA 70006 **504-887-7631; 504-887-0113.**
423 Main Street, Baton Rouge, LA 70802 **504-343-4057 504-381-9485.**

MISSOURI
1001 Pine Street (at North 10th), St. Louis, MO 63101 **314-621-0346.**

ILLINOIS
172 North Michigan Ave., Chicago, IL 60601 **312-346-4228; 312-346-3240.**

TEXAS
114 Main Plaza San Antonio, TX 78205 **512-224-8101.**

CALIFORNIA
1570 Fifth Ave. (at Cedar Street), San Diego, CA 92101 **619-232-1442.**
46 Geary Street, San Francisco, CA 94108 **415-781-5180.**

WASHINGTON
2301 Second Ave., Seattle, WA 98121 **206-441-3300.**

HAWAII
1143 Bishop Street, Honolulu, HI 96813 **808-521-2731.**

ALASKA
750 West 5th Ave., Anchorage, AK 99501 **907-272-8183.**

CANADA
3022 Dufferin Street, Toronto 395, Ontario, Canada.